TOOLS FOR THE TRADE

STUDENT DISCIPLINE RESOURCE BINDER

A Comprehensive Guide for K-12 Schools

DORA DOME, Esq.

Cover Design by Ryan Brockmeier for Two Seven Eight Media

Layout Design by Taisha Rucker, Esq.

ISBN-13: 979-8633201673

Contents

◆ ◆ ◆

Dedication

As I reflect on my 23 years of practicing Education Law, I am humbled by the dedication and perseverance of the educators who have dedicated their "life's work" to caring for and educating our young people. Their work gets more and more challenging as the years go by, yet they remain steadfast in their commitment to make a difference in the lives of the children they serve.

This book is dedicated to all the educators who show up day after day, with a smile or kind word, who convey to the children, through their expectations and caring, that they are seen, that they are valued, and that they can succeed. I believe that my contribution to their work is through the provision of resources that support their best practice, build capacity and, hopefully, help make schools a more equitable place.

I would be remiss if I did not acknowledge Laura Chism, Assistant Superintendent for Student Services and Angela Lawyer, Positive Behavioral Intervention Support Coordinator, with the Beverly Hills Unified School District for their encouragement and occasional kick in the pants to finish this book. I appreciate their confidence and faith in my ability to create a useful resource tool for their administrators. Thank you!

Dora J. Dome

2020

About the Author

Dora J. Dome, Esq. has practiced Education Law for over 23 years, primarily in the areas of student issues and special education. She graduated from University of Hawaii, Richardson School of Law (J.D.) and from University of California, Los Angeles (B.A.).

In 2016, she published her first book, ***Student Discipline, Special Education Discipline, Anti-Bullying and Other Relevant Student Issues: A Guide For Practitioners***, which has been described as a "**must-have**" for anyone seeking to understand student discipline and bullying. In 2017, Ms. Dome published her second book, ***Understanding Student Discipline in California Schools: A Parent's Guide to General and Special Education Discipline***, to assist parents in navigating the school discipline process. This book has also been translated into Spanish! In 2020, Ms. Dome published her fourth and fifth books, respectively, ***Student Discipline Resource Binder: A Comprehensive Guide for K-12 Schools,*** and ***Improving Student Achievement Through The Creation of Relationships: A Critical Race Theory Counter-Story.*** Both books are part of her new series called ***Tools For The Trade.***

Ms. Dome currently provides legal representation to school districts on student issues and develops and conducts professional development trainings for district staff that focus on Bullying and Legal Compliance, viewed through an Equity Lens, in a proactive effort to build staff capacity to address the changing needs of their students.

Admitted to the Hawaii State Bar in 1996, Ms. Dome served as a special education consultant and trainer for the Hawaii State Department of Education and Hawaii State Department of Health for five years. Ms. Dome was admitted to the California Bar in 2003. She worked with the education law firm of Dannis Woliver Kelley, (fka Miller Brown and Dannis) for eight years.

Ms. Dome has studied in the areas of Race and Ethnicity, Critical Legal Studies and Critical Race Theory and has been certified as a Cultural Diversity Trainer by the National Coalition Building Institute (aka NCBI). She has developed and conducted trainings for numerous school districts and school boards in the areas of student diversity and equity, student and special education discipline, harassment/discrimination, bullying, special education, trauma sensitive schools, alternative assessments for African American students, Section 504, and student records.

Ms. Dome also regularly presents at association conferences such as ACSA, CSBA and CASCWA. She participated on the Gay & Lesbian Athletics Foundations (aka GLAF) Keynote Panel on "Race and Racism in LGBT Athletics" and presented at the NCAA Black Coaches

Association Annual Conference on "Homophobia in Sports."

Ms. Dome is a Lecturer at the University of California at Berkeley, teaching Education Law and Policy in Principal Leadership Institute (PLI) Program. She was also an Adjunct Professor at Mills College teaching in the administrative credential program for soon to be administrators.

CHAPTER 1

Student Suspensions

Principal's Designee

A "principal's designee" is one or more administrators at the schoolsite specifically designated by the principal, in writing, to assist with disciplinary procedures.

In the event that there is not an administrator in addition to the principal at the schoolsite, a certificated person at the schoolsite may be specifically designated by the principal, in writing, as a "principal's designee," to assist with disciplinary procedures. The principal may designate only one person at a time as the principal's primary designee for the school year.

An additional certificated person may be designated by the principal, in writing, to act when both the principal and the principal's primary designee are absent from the schoolsite. The name of the person, and the names of any person or persons designated as "principal's designee," shall be on file in the principal's office. (CA Ed. Code 48911(h)) (See 1.1 - Sample Principal's Designee Form at the end of this chapter)

Alternatives to Student Suspension

The law **encourages** schools to provide alternatives to suspension or expulsion that are age appropriate and designed to address and correct the student's specific misbehavior. (CA Ed. Code 48900(v)) Effective January 1, 2020, the legislature further clarified its intent that alternatives to suspension or expulsion be utilized by providing the following examples of alternatives: "the Multi-Tiered System of Supports (MTSS), which includes restorative justice practices, trauma-informed practices, social and emotional learning, and schoolwide positive behavior interventions and support, may be used to help pupils gain critical social and emotional skills, receive support to help transform trauma-related responses, understand the impact of their actions, and develop meaningful methods for repairing harm to the school community." (CA Ed. Code 48900(w)(2)) The law also **requires** that schools first utilize other means of correction prior to suspending a student, in most situations. (CA Ed. Code 48900.5)

Other Means of Correction

When Other Means of Correction Are Required

In an effort to reduce the overuse of exclusionary discipline for all students, and in particular students of color and other marginalized groups who experience disproportionate levels of exclusionary discipline, **CA Ed. Code 48900.5 requires that there must be evidence documented by the school that "other means of correction" have failed to bring about proper conduct** prior to suspending a student, including when the student is suspended from class by the teacher and/or suspended but attending school in supervised suspension classroom.

Exclusionary discipline should rarely be the first recourse. Teachers and administrators are encouraged to consider how the proposed disciplinary consequences are designed to change the misbehavior or help the student make better choices. If the teacher or administrator is unable to articulate how the proposed consequence will help change the student's behavior or help the student make better choices, it should be considered whether the proposed consequence is appropriate or whether something else should be done in addition to the proposed consequence. Punishment, by itself, does not improve student behavior or conduct and should rarely be administered in isolation.

Below is a non-exhaustive list of "other means of correction" described in the law:

(1) A conference between school personnel, the pupil's parent or guardian, and the pupil.

(2) Referrals to the school counselor, psychologist, social worker, child welfare attendance personnel, or other school support service personnel for case management and counseling.

(3) Study teams, guidance teams, resource panel teams, or other intervention-related teams that assess the behavior, and develop and implement individualized plans to address the behavior in partnership with the pupil and his or her parents.

(4) Referral for a comprehensive psychosocial or psychoeducational assessment, including for

purposes of creating an individualized education program, or a plan adopted pursuant to Section 504 of the federal Rehabilitation Act of 1973 (29 U.S.C. Sec. 794(a)).

(5) Enrollment in a program for teaching prosocial behavior or anger management.

(6) Participation in a restorative justice program.

(7) A positive behavior support approach with tiered interventions that occur during the schoolday on campus.

(8) After-school programs that address specific behavioral issues or expose pupils to positive activities and behaviors, including, but not limited to, those operated in collaboration with local parent and community groups.

(9) Any of the alternatives described in CA Ed. Code 48900.6.

An examination of the list makes it clear that the legislature did not intend that "other means of correction" include progressive discipline that is punitive in nature.

Sample Interventions

Below are additional examples of Tier 1 and Tier 2 interventions that a school may consider incorporating into its MTSS or PBIS structure.

Sample Tier 1 Interventions

Break, moving position in class

Have student take frequent breaks or activity

Send student on errand

Snack break

Avoid power struggles

Call parent or positive note home

Card Flip

Clear, consistent, and predictable consequences

Do unfinished work during recess or unstructured time

Have student say a nice thing to the student they called a name

Office referral for intervention

Reflection sheet

Speak in calm and neutral tone

Take away privileges, with explanation and clear parameters

Take away unstructured or free time, with explanation and clear parameters

The Praise Game

Acknowledging positive behavior

Praise student frequently

Praise when cooperative and well behaved

Praise when good attitude and involvement occur

Praise when on task

Rewards

Rewards, Simple Reward Systems, & Incentives

Alternate Seating In Own Space

Alternative modes of completing assignments

Peace Corner

Assign a buddy or partner

Assign a classroom job

Break down assignment

Break down directions

Call on student frequently

Clear and concise directions

Color coded folders

Count to 10

Daily planner

Deep breathing

Draw a picture or write in a journal

Encourage interaction with a more self-confident student

Engage student

Explain assignment

Explain directions

Frequent eye contact

Frequent home contact

Give choices

Have student repeat directions back

Headphones

Helping Students With Home Work

Help student start assignment

Individual work space

Listen to music

Model appropriate language

More structured routine

Move to new location in the classroom

Non-verbal cues

Organize materials daily

Pause before giving a direction

Provide a container for the student's belongings

Proximity to students

Reassurance

Redirection

Reduce assignment

Reflective listening

Review PBIS expectations and rules

Speak with student in hallway

Stand while working

Start Commands

Stop, Walk, Talk

Stress ball or fidget

Talk one on one with student

Talk Ticket

Teach conflict resolution skills

Teach coping skills

Teach organizational skills

Teach relationship skills

Teach relaxation techniques

Teach social skills

Teach substitute words

Touch base with student

Touch student on shoulder

Turn desk around

Use seating disk

Use timer

VELCRO® brand hook and loop fasteners on/under the desk

Visual schedule

Sample Tier 2 Interventions

Alternatives To Suspension

Behavior Contract

Behavior Intervention Plan (BIP)

Check In Check Out (CICO)

Classroom Management Support

Counselor Referral

Daily Behavior Form

Forced Choice Reinforcement Survey

Functional Behavior Assessment (FBA)

Individual & Visual Schedules

Mentoring

Non-Verbal Cues & Signals

Organizational Tools

Peer Tutoring

Response To Intervention (RTI)

Reward System

Self-Monitoring

Sensory Tools

Social Stories

Structured Breaks

Teach Conflict Resolution Skills

Teach Coping Skills

Teach Relationship Skills

Teach Relaxation Techniques

Teach Social Skills

The Praise Game

When Other Means of Correction Are Not Required

CA Ed. Code 48900.5 allows administrators to exercise their discretion and consider suspension upon a first offence (no requirement of other means of correction) when specific conditions are met. However, just because the school can suspend on a first offense for some conduct violations, does not always mean it should. It is important for administrators to always consider whether exclusionary discipline is necessary for safety reasons or whether it will change the student's behavior. If exclusionary discipline is not necessary for safety reasons, then it would be appropriate for the administrator to consider alternatives to excluding the student.

A student, including an individual with exceptional needs, as defined in Section 56026, may be suspended, subject to certain procedural protections, for any of the reasons listed in Section CA Ed. Code 48900 upon a first offense, if the principal or superintendent of schools determines that the pupil violated any of the following subdivisions **OR** determines that the student's presence causes a danger to other persons:

(a) (1) Caused, attempted to cause, or threatened to cause physical injury to another person.

(a) (2) Willfully used force or violence upon the person of another, except in self-defense.

(b) Possessed, sold, or otherwise furnished a firearm, knife, explosive, or other dangerous object, unless, in the case of possession of an object of this type, the pupil had obtained written permission to possess the item from a certificated school employee, which is concurred in by the principal or the designee of the principal.

(c) Unlawfully possessed, used, sold, or otherwise furnished, or been under the influence of, a controlled substance listed in Chapter 2 (commencing with Section 11053) of Division 10 of the Health and Safety Code, an alcoholic beverage, or an intoxicant of any kind.

(d) Unlawfully offered, arranged, or negotiated to sell a controlled substance listed in Chapter 2 (commencing with Section 11053) of Division 10 of the Health and Safety Code, an alcoholic beverage, or an intoxicant of any kind, and either sold, delivered, or otherwise furnished to a person another liquid, substance, or material and represented the liquid, substance, or material as a controlled substance, alcoholic beverage, or intoxicant.

(e) Committed or attempted to commit robbery or extortion.

When a student engages in a minor rule violation, and redirection is not effective, a referral to the school administrator or counselor to discuss the misbehavior and appropriate alternative responses or conduct may be appropriate. Once they have completed their discussion, the student **must** be allowed to return to the class. The reason for the referral and the intervention must be documented in the school's student information system, either in the student's disciplinary or intervention tracker. This record is maintained throughout a student's K-12 education and is accessible to the parent as part of the child's student record.

When the misconduct involves more serious rule violations, below are some examples of other consequences the school may consider imposing as other means of correction:

- Parent conference and/or attendance in class

- Write an age appropriate paper about the impact of the conduct

- Develop a behavior contract

- Detention – which includes an opportunity to reflect on their behavior and discuss alternative choices

- Counseling – social-emotional, anger management, substance abuse, etc.

- Restorative Process – meeting/circle

- Corrective instruction/education relevant to the offense

- Student leadership opportunities

- Mentoring program

- Peer counseling

- Home visitation

- Referral to Student Study Team (SST)

- Referral to School Attendance Review Board (SARB)

- Community service

As part of, or instead of disciplinary action, the student may be required to perform community service on school grounds or, with written permission of the parent or guardian, off school grounds during the student's non-school hours. (CA Ed. Code 48900.6)

Teacher Referrals

A teacher referral is when a teacher sends a student out of class for an intervention, with the expectation that the student will be allowed to return to class once the intervention has been completed. A student can receive a referral for any reason and at any time. A teacher referral is different than a teacher suspension, which can only occur for CA Ed. Code 48900 et. Seq. violations and must be documented on a Teacher Suspension form. (See 1.2 - Sample Teacher Classroom Referral Form at the end of this chapter; See also, Teacher Classroom Suspension section below)

When addressing students who are truant, tardy, or otherwise absent from school activities, it is the intent of the Legislature that alternatives to suspension or expulsion be imposed. (CA Ed. Code 48900(w)) Therefore, **the school will not suspend students as a consequence for missing school** and are encouraged to work with parents to understand the underlying reasons for the lack of attendance, or the barriers that inhibit attendance, and create a plan designed to improve the student's attendance. In an effort to help transform trauma-related responses, understand the impact of their actions, and develop meaningful methods for repairing harm to the school community, the Legislature intends that the Multi-Tiered System of Supports, which includes restorative justice practices, trauma-informed practices, social and emotional learning, and schoolwide positive behavior interventions and support, may be used to help pupils gain critical social and emotional skills, and receive support. (CA Ed. Code 48900(w)(2))

Suspension Generally

<u>Suspension Definition - What it is…</u>

CA Ed. Code 48925(d) defines suspension as removal of a pupil from ongoing instruction for adjustment purposes.

- No student may be suspended from school for more than <u>five consecutive days for any single act of misconduct.</u>

- A student's suspension may be extended beyond five days **only** pending a recommendation for expulsion.

- A student may not be suspended from school for more than twenty (20) cumulative days in the school year. **Days on extended suspension pending expulsion DO NOT count toward to twenty cumulative days.**

- A student may be suspended for an additional ten (10) days for reassignment or adjustment purposes. When a student transfers mid-year into a new school district, it is up to the new district whether or not to begin counting days of suspension from the number of days suspended in the previous district or to start over.

<u>Suspension Definition - What it isn't…</u>

"Suspension" **does not mean** any of the following:

(1) Reassignment to another education program or class at the same school where the pupil will receive continuing instruction for the length of day prescribed by the governing board for pupils of the same grade level.

A pupil who is reassigned to another class, at the same grade level, and continues to receive instruction is not suspended.

(2) Referral to a certificated employee designated by the principal to advise pupils.

A pupil who is referred to an administrator or counselor, etc., for the purpose of discussing the appropriateness of the pupil's behavior, **who is allowed to return to the class from which the referral came following the discussion**, is not suspended.

(3) Removal from the class, but without reassignment to another class or program, for the remainder of the class period without sending the pupil to the principal or the principal's designee as provided in Section 48910. Removal from a particular class shall not occur more than once every five schooldays.

A pupil who is referred to a "buddy classroom" for the remainder of the class period as a timeout or other intervention, is not suspended. However, this type of removal can only occur once every five schooldays. To the extent this strategy is utilized more frequently than once every five days, it would be considered a suspension and, potentially, a violation of the pupil's civil rights.

Teacher Class Suspensions

Teachers may suspend a student from their class for any act listed in CA Ed. Code 48900, subject to the requirement of establishing that other means of correction have failed to bring about proper conduct, as stated in CA Ed. Code 48900.5, for the remainder of the class day and the next day. (See 1.3 - Sample Teacher Suspension Form at the end of this chapter) When a teacher suspends a student from her/his class, there are certain steps that must be taken:

1. The teacher **must** immediately report the suspension to the principal and send the student to the principal or designee for appropriate action.
2. As soon as possible, the teacher **must** ask the parent to attend a parent-teacher conference regarding the suspension.
3. If practicable, a school counselor or school psychologist **may** attend.
4. A school administrator **must** attend the conference if the teacher or parent so requests.
5. The student shall not be returned to the class from which s/he was suspended, during the period of suspension, without the agreement of the teacher of the class and the Principal.
6. A student suspended from a class cannot be placed in another regular class during the period of suspension. However, if the student has more than one class per day, the student will attend her/his other classes.
7. The teacher may refer the student to the Principal for consideration of a suspension

from the school.

(CA Ed. Code 48910)

School Suspensions

Similar to teacher suspensions from class, the principal or designee may suspend a student from school for any of the reasons listed in CA Ed. Code 48900, subject to the limitations stated in CA Ed. Code 48900.5, for no more than five consecutive school days. (CA Ed. Code 48911(a))

Suspension - Due Process

Prior to suspending a student from school, the principal or designee must provide the student with due process. The principal or designee must hold an informal conference with the student and cover the following:

> Informed the student of the reason for the disciplinary action, **including the other means of correction that were attempted before the suspension as required under Section 48900.5**;

> Inform the student of the evidence against her/him; and

> Give the student the opportunity to present her/his version and evidence in her/his defense. (CA Ed. Code 48911(b)).

The administrator is not required to contact or notify the parent prior to holding this meeting with the student. The administrator may suspend the student without the informal conference if an "emergency situation" exists. The informal conference must be held within two days following the emergency situation, unless the student waives her/his right to the conference or is physically unable to attend for any reason, including incarceration or hospitalization. (CA Ed. Code 48911(c)).

At the time of suspension, a school employee shall make a reasonable effort to contact the student's parent or guardian in person or by telephone. If a student is suspended from school, the parent or guardian shall be notified in writing of the suspension. (CA Ed. Code 48911(d)) Print out the written notice of suspension and place a hard copy of the Notice in the students CUM file. A hard copy should be mailed or emailed to the parent/guardian. DO NOT rely on the student to take the written notice home to the parent/guardian. (See 1.4 - Sample Notice of Suspension Form at the end of this chapter)

Parents are required to respond without delay to a request from school officials to attend a conference regarding her/his child's behavior. (CA Ed. Code 48911(f)). (See 1.5 - Sample Request For Parent To Attend Class Form at the end of this chapter)

Legal Standard to Suspend

If a student has engaged in conduct that has lead to a suspension from school, the "burden of proof" required before suspending a student from school is a "preponderance of the evidence," which is interpreted to mean the student "more likely than not" engaged in the conduct for which s/he is being charged.

There is no specific mention of burden of proof in the Education Code or underlying legal authority. The best practice for an administrator charged with deciding whether to suspend a pupil is to be convinced by a preponderance of the available evidence that suspension is justified and appropriate after meeting with the student, presenting the student with the evidence against her/him, and soliciting the student's version of the facts. The "preponderance" standard does NOT require that there be corroborating evidence or that there is more evidence on one side than the other. The determination for the administrator when assessing conflicting versions of an incident is "who do you believe," "which is the more plausible story," and/or "which version is more likely than not."

Jurisdiction to Suspend - 48900(s)

In order for a school to suspend a student, it must have jurisdiction over the student at the time s/he committed the offense. The act must be related to a school activity or school attendance occurring within a school under the jurisdiction of the superintendent of the school district or principal, or occurring within any other school district. The student may be suspended or expelled for acts that are enumerated in 48900 et seq. and **related to a school activity or school attendance that occur at any time**, including, but not limited to, any of the following:

> (1) While on school grounds.
>
> (2) While going to or coming from school.
>
> (3) During the lunch period whether on or off the campus.
>
> (4) During, or while going to or coming from, a school-sponsored activity.

Note that the jurisdictional statement described above does NOT apply to expulsion recommendations based on CA Ed. Code 48915. (See Chapter 3 - Expulsion Recommendations, for the applicable jurisdictional statement; See also, 1.6 – Sample Student Suspension Checklist Form at the end of this chapter)

Teacher Notification of Student Suspensions

A school district must inform the teacher of each pupil who has engaged in, or is reasonably suspected to have engaged in, any act described in Section 48900 (except Tobacco) or in Section 48900.2, 48900.3, 48900.4, or 48900.7. The district shall provide the information to the teacher based upon any records that the district maintains in its ordinary course of business, or receives from a law enforcement agency, regarding a pupil described in this section. The information provided shall be from the previous three school years. (See 1.7 – Sample Teacher Notice of Previous Suspension/Expulsion Form at the end of this chapter)

Any information received by a teacher pursuant to this section shall be received in confidence for the limited purpose for which it was provided and shall not be further disseminated by the teacher. (CA Ed Code 49079)

Protocol For Notification of Teachers of Student Suspensions

Each school administrator must ensure that teachers receive the required notice at the beginning of the school year and at any point a new student is added to their class during the school year. The following protocol will assist administrators with compliance.

1. Inform all teachers prior to the first day of school of the following:

    a. Students who have engaged in, or are reasonably suspected to have engaged in conduct for which they are entitled to notice, are identified by an asterisk (*) printed next to their name on the teacher's roster.

    b. The teacher may come to the office and be informed of the infraction committed by the student assigned to their class.

    c. Administrators may ask that teachers make an appointment to review the infraction information about their student.

2. Inform teachers that any information received by a teacher pursuant to this section shall be received in confidence for the limited purpose for which it was provided and shall not be further disseminated by the teacher.

3. Inform teachers that this information will also be available for infractions that occur during the school year and for students that enter their classroom mid-year.

Mandatory Reporting to Law Enforcement of Attack, Assault, or Physical Threat Toward and Employee

Whenever any employee of a school district or of the office of a county superintendent of schools is attacked, assaulted, or physically threatened by any pupil, it shall be the duty of the employee, and the duty of any person under whose direction or supervision the employee is employed in the public school system who has knowledge of the incident, to promptly report the incident to the appropriate law enforcement authorities of the county or city in which the incident occurred. Failure to make the report shall be an infraction punishable by a fine of not more than one thousand dollars ($1,000). (CA Ed Code 44014) (See 1.8 – Sample Report Regarding Attack, Assault or Physical Threat to School District Employee Form at the end of this chapter)

While the law requires this report be made, it should be noted that the law does not require a particular response by law enforcement. There are many instances when a student has hit or threatened a staff member and the staff member does not want the student to be arrested or criminalized. In those instances, the report is still required, but the law enforcement agency can also be informed that the employee does not desire any adverse action be taken against the student.

Mandatory Law Enforcement Notifications

Over the past ten years the "school-to-prison pipeline" has become an issue championed by groups across the political spectrum. The concern arises because, over the past ten to twenty years, schools across the country have increasingly involved law enforcement in incidents involving pupils which, in earlier years, would have been managed internally within the school through its own disciplinary system. Various causes of this increased criminalization of student behavior have been identified, but much of it has resulted from "zero tolerance" policies following tragic and extreme incidents such as the Columbine High School shooting. These "zero tolerance" policies have resulted in severe discipline, and even arrests, for innocent behaviors as districts abandoned the ability to apply common sense and to view incidents in their proper contexts.

Although there is no *legal* mandate or directive that California schools report, or not report, crimes not covered by CA Ed. Code 48902, schools are encouraged to adopt policies that balance the need to evaluate individual incidents to determine whether there is a need to involve law enforcement, with the danger that such discretion can result, intentionally or not, in disparate negative impact on certain racial and socio-economic groups. Failure to assure equitable application of policies theoretically could result in litigation alleging discrimination, lack of equal protection and/or due process violations

CA Ed. Code section 48902 sets out which crimes a school district *must* report to law enforcement. These include assaults with deadly weapons, assaults with sufficient force likely to cause severe bodily injury, incidents involving the use, sale, possession, and distribution of illegal substances, alcohol, or imitation substances, and incidents involving a firearm or possession of explosives. Failure to report these crimes is an infraction and, conversely, reports made in good faith cannot result in civil liability. (See 1.9 – Sample Law Enforcement Notification Form at the end of this chapter)

Required Notice From Courts to School Districts – Welfare & Institutions Code Section 827(b)(2)(A)

The law requires that the court provide written notice that a minor enrolled in a public school, kindergarten to 12, has been found by a court of competent jurisdiction to have committed a felony or misdemeanor involving curfew, gambling, alcohol, drugs, tobacco products, carrying of weapons, a sex offense listed in Section 290 of the Penal Code, assault or battery, larceny, vandalism, or graffiti, to the superintendent of the school district of attendance. Unfortunately, this requirement is typically unknown by the courts and rarely complied with. However, if a school administrator has reason to believe that a student has been convicted as described above, the administrator is encouraged to contact the school district's Director of Student Services and request assistance in obtaining the information in the interest of school safety. The law goes on to require the following:

> Written notice shall include only the offense found to have been committed by the minor and the disposition of the minor's case. This notice shall be expeditiously transmitted by the district superintendent to the principal at the school of attendance. The principal shall expeditiously disseminate the information to those counselors directly supervising or reporting on the behavior or progress of the minor. In addition, the principal shall disseminate the information to any teacher or administrator directly supervising or reporting on the behavior or progress of the minor whom the principal

believes needs the information to work with the pupil in an appropriate fashion to avoid being needlessly vulnerable or to protect other persons from needless vulnerability.

Any information received by a teacher, counselor, or administrator pursuant to this requirement shall be received in confidence for the limited purpose of rehabilitating the minor and protecting students and staff, and shall not be further disseminated by the teacher, counselor, or administrator, except insofar as communication with the juvenile, the juvenile's parents or guardians, law enforcement personnel, and the juvenile's probation officer is necessary to effectuate the juvenile's rehabilitation or to protect students and staff.

If a minor is removed from public school as a result of the court's finding, the superintendent shall maintain the information in a confidential file and shall defer transmittal of the information received from the court until the minor is returned to public school. If the minor is returned to a school district other than the one from which the minor came, the parole or probation officer having jurisdiction over the minor shall so notify the superintendent of the last district of attendance, who shall transmit the notice received from the court to the superintendent of the new district of attendance.

Each notice sent by the court pursuant to this requirement, shall be stamped with the instruction: "Unlawful Dissemination Of This Information Is A Misdemeanor." Any information received from the court shall be kept in a separate confidential file at the school of attendance and shall be transferred to the minor's subsequent schools of attendance and maintained until the minor graduates from high school, is released from juvenile court jurisdiction, or reaches 18 years of age, whichever occurs first. After that time the confidential record shall be destroyed. At any time after the date by which a record required to be destroyed by this section should have been destroyed, the minor or the minor's parent or guardian shall have the right to make a written request to the principal of the school that the minor's school records be reviewed to ensure that the record has been destroyed. Upon completion of the requested review and no later than 30 days after the request for the review was received, the principal or a designee shall respond in writing to the written request and either shall confirm that the record has been destroyed or, if the record has not been destroyed, shall explain why destruction has not yet occurred.

Special Consideration

Below are situations that can be challenging if the administrator does not fully understand the implications of the law.

Self-Defense

The issue of self-defense comes up often when students are involved in physical altercations. Many administrators take the position that if a student throws a punch, they can be disciplined, regardless of whether the student acted in self-defense. This position is wrong. CA Ed. Code 48900(a)(2) explicitly allows a student to use force in self-defense. As a matter of fact, CA Ed. Code 48915(a)(1)(A) allows a student to cause serious bodily injury when acting in self-defense. As a result, it is essential that the administrator understand the legal analysis to determine whether the student appropriately acted in self-defense.

When two students get into a fight, where both are throwing punches, and one of the students alleges that s/he was acting in self-defense, the administrator has an affirmative obligation to investigate the self-defense claim and determine if it is valid. If the administrator determines that the student had a right to act in self-defense, and that the amount of force that was used was reasonable under the circumstances, the student cannot be disciplined for the use of force.

The California Jury Instructions provides guidance into the analysis for determining whether the student's actions were in self-defense.

1. The student reasonably believed that s/he was in imminent danger of suffering bodily injury;
2. The student reasonably believed that the immediate use of force was necessary to defend against that danger; AND
3. S/he used no more force than was reasonably necessary to defend against that danger.

In addition to the considerations listed above, there are a few more factors that the administrator should keep in mind as s/he analyzes the facts.

1. The student's belief in future harm is not sufficient to support a self-defense claim.
2. If the student's beliefs are reasonable, the danger does not need to have actually existed.

3. The student's belief that is based on false information is sufficient, if the student actually and reasonably believed the information was true.

4. If there was a past threat or harm, the student is justified in acting more quickly or taking greater measures.

5. The student is not required to retreat. Entitled to stand ground and defend her/his self. This is so even if safety could have been achieved by retreating.

Defiance/Disruption

In many school districts, the underlying legal basis for a large percentage of the exclusionary discipline students face is conduct that is considered disruptive or defiant. The problem with this is that disruption and defiance are very subjective terms, which allow for multiple different interpretations of identical conduct by different people. Left unchecked, the subjective nature of the offense can lead to the perpetuation of implicit (and/or explicit) biases, to the detriment of students who are members of marginalized groups.

In an effort to curtail the exclusion of students from school for conduct that is considered disruptive of defiant, in 2019 the California State Legislature amended the CA Ed. Code to provide additional limits to the use of disruption and defiance as a basis for exclusion from school. CA Ed. Code 48900 (k) (1) allows and administrator to suspend a student from school when that student's conduct has "disrupted school activities or otherwise willfully defied the valid authority of supervisors, teachers, administrators, school officials, or other school personnel engaged in the performance of their duties." However, this authority is limited as follows:

1. Teachers can **suspend from class** for disruption or defiance as described above. (Ed. Code 48900(k)(2))

2. Students grades K to 3, **shall not be suspended from school** for disruption or defiance. This becomes inoperative July 1, 2020.

3. Effective July 1, 2020, students grades K to 5, **shall not be suspended from school** for disruption or defiance.

4. Effective July 1, 2020, students grades K to 8, **shall not be suspended from school** for disruption or defiance. This becomes inoperative July 1, 2025.

5. Students grades K to 12, inclusive, **shall not be recommended for expulsion** for disruption or defiance.

Effective July 1, 2020, these limitations expand the ban on out of school suspension for disruption or defiance to 8th grade. Therefore, effective the 2020 -2021 school year, no student in grades K-8 can be suspended from school for disruption or defiance. This ban will stay in effect through July 1, 2025, at which point the ban will be modified to grades K-5, unless new legislation is passed.

Bullying

Bullying is a term that is widely used, with individuals attributing many different meanings to the word. It is used to refer to the conduct of a first grade boy who pulls the hair of a female classmate, to the conduct of a high school student who calls another student a derogatory name every time she sees that student, and everything in between. Many of the nationally available anti-bullying programs often describe bullying conduct as being "repeated over time," and involving an "imbalance of power."

While these are often characteristics of bullying, it is important for administrators, school staff, students, and parents to understand that California has a legal definition of bullying that does not require the conduct be "repeated over time," or involve an "imbalance of power." Therefore, it is imperative that administrators understand the elements of California's "bullying" definition and the conduct that violates it.

CA Ed. Code Section 48900(r) defines bullying as:

- **Severe** or **pervasive physical** or **verbal** act or conduct, including communications made in writing or by means of an electronic act, and including one or more of the following:

    o   Sex Harassment (48900.2)

    o   Hate Violence (48900.3)

    o   Threats, harassment, intimidation (48900.4)

- Has or is reasonably predicted to have one or more of the following:

    o   Reasonable pupil in fear of harm to person or property

    o   Reasonable pupil to experience substantially detrimental effect to physical or mental health

- o Reasonable pupil to experience substantial interference with academic performance

- o Reasonable pupil to experience substantial interference with ability to participate in or benefit from services, activities, or privileges provided by the school

Breaking this definition down into its three main sections will help you better understand its elements.

First Section

Severe or **pervasive physical** or **verbal** act or conduct, including communications made in writing or by means of an electronic act

The first section of the bullying definition describes the severity and nature of the bullying conduct. The use of the word "severe" suggests that the bullying conduct only needs to happen once, and if the conduct is severe enough, it would be sufficient to constitute bullying as defined in law. The bullying conduct can be physical, verbal, written or electronic. So, the first step in determining whether a student's conduct amounts to bullying, is to understand the severity and nature of the conduct.

Second Section

… including one or more of the following:

- o Sex Harassment (48900.2)

- o Hate Violence (48900.3)

- o Threats, harassment, intimidation (48900.4)

The second section of the bullying definition requires that the bullying conduct violate one of these three existing sections in the CA Ed. Code. Specifically, it means that in California, for the underlying conduct to be considered bullying, it must be in the form of "Sexual Harassment," "Hate Violence," or "Threats, Harassment or Intimidation."

CA Ed. Code defines each of the above sections as follows:

§48900.2 – Sexual Harassment

Unwelcome sexual advances, requests for sexual favors, and other verbal, visual, or physical conduct of a sexual nature, made by someone from or in the work or educational setting that is:

1.   Considered by a reasonable person of the same gender as the victim;

2.   To be sufficiently severe or pervasive;

3.   Has a negative impact upon the individual's academic performance; **or**

4.   Creates an intimidating, hostile, or offensive educational environment.

§48900.3 – Hate Violence

Caused, attempted to cause, threatened to cause, or participated in an act of hate violence. Hate violence is violence directed toward an individual based on that person's membership to protected class. (i.e. disability, gender, gender identity, gender expression, nationality, race or ethnicity, religion, sexual orientation, or association with a person or group with one or more of these actual or perceived characteristics.) Hate violence is conduct that:

- Willfully injures, intimidates, interferes with, oppresses, or threatens any other person;

- Defaces, damages, or destroys the real or personal property;

- Based on the targets membership to a protected class.

§48900.4 – Harassment, Threats, Intimidation

The pupil has:

1. **Intentionally** engaged in harassment, threats, or intimidation;

2. Directed against school district personnel or pupils;

3. That is sufficiently severe **or** pervasive;

4. That has the actual **and** reasonably expected effect of:

    a.   Materially disrupting classwork,

    b.   Creating substantial disorder, **and**

    c.   Invading the rights of either school personnel or pupils by creating an intimidating or hostile educational environment.

So, the second step in determining whether the student's conduct amounts to bullying, is to examine the conduct and determine whether it meets the elements of one of the three definitions above. If the student's conduct does not meet all of the elements of one of the three sections above, the conduct is not "bullying" under California Law and the student can't be disciplined for Bullying. However, just because the student's conduct does not meet the bullying definition, does not mean the student can't be disciplined for the misbehavior. It does mean that the administrator would need to identify the appropriate CA Ed. Code section, if applicable, in order to discipline the student.

Be aware that "Sexual Harassment," "Hate Violence," or "Threats, Harassment or Intimidation" are also independent sections of the CA Ed. Code and, simultaneously, subsections of the Bullying definition. As independent sections of the CA Ed. Code, these sections only apply to students in grades 4-12. However, as a subsection of the Bullying definition, the California Department of Education ("CDE") has interpreted these sections to apply to all grades, K-12.

Practically, this means that if the student is a third grader who is being charged with bullying based on conduct that amounts to sexual harassment, the student can be suspended for bullying in violation of CA Ed. Code 48900(r), but the student could not be legally charged with CA Ed. Code 48900.2 - sexual harassment (as a separate section of CA Ed. Code), due to the grade restrictions that apply to sexual harassment.

However, if the student is an eighth grader being charged with bullying based on conduct that amounts to sexual harassment, the student must be charged with both Bullying - 48900(r) and 48900.2 - sexual harassment. This is because any student grade 4-12 who violates the Bullying statute CA Ed. Code 48900(r), is by definition also violating either CA Ed. Code 48900.2 – Sexual Harassment, CA Ed. Code 48900.3 – Hate Violence, or CA Ed. Code 48900.4 – Threats, Harassment, or Intimidation.

Third Section

- Has or is reasonably predicted to have one or more of the following:
    o Reasonable pupil in fear of <u>harm to person or property</u>
    o Reasonable pupil to experience <u>substantially detrimental effect to physical or mental health</u>

o Reasonable pupil to experience <u>substantial interference with academic</u> <u>performance</u>

o Reasonable pupil to experience <u>substantial interference with ability to</u> <u>participate in or benefit from services, activities, or privileges provided by the</u> <u>school</u>

The third and final section of the Bullying definition examines the impact that the bullying conduct had or could have reasonably been predicted to have on a "reasonable person," which often times is the victim.

Therefore, the final step in determining whether the student's conduct amounts to bullying, is to examine the impact of the conduct on a "reasonable person" and determine whether any of the negative impacts listed have occurred or could have reasonably been predicted to occur.

CA Ed. Code 48900(r)(3) defines "reasonable pupil" as a pupil, including, but not limited to, an <u>exceptional needs pupil</u>, who exercises <u>average care</u>, <u>skill</u>, and <u>judgment</u> in conduct for a person of his or her <u>age</u>, or for a person of his or her age with his or her <u>exceptional needs</u>. While it is arguable whether there is really such a thing as a "reasonable pupil," administrators are expected to consider what would be a reasonable response based on the severity and nature of the student's conduct, as well as the characteristics of the victim.

Cyber-Bullying

If the conduct is electronic, then the conduct is considered **cyber-bullying**. Cyber-bullying is the creation **or** transmission **originated on or off the schoolsite**, by means of an electronic device, including, but not limited to, a telephone, wireless telephone, or other wireless communication device, computer, or pager, of a communication, including, but not limited to, a message, text, sound, video, image, or a post on a social network internet web site. Cyber-bullying is bullying by an electronic act and all of the elements of the Bullying definition must be established just as if the bullying had occurred in person.

Once it is established that the cyber-bullying meets all of the elements of the CA Ed. Code 48900(r) bullying definition, the next step is to determine if the conduct has a nexus to school activity or attendance. If the cyber-bullying occurs on campus, using school equipment, or at a school sponsored event, the school absolutely has jurisdiction to discipline the student for the conduct. However, if the cyber-bullying occurs off campus and is unrelated to school, the administrator will need to establish that cyber-bullying has an impact on school activity or attendance.

For example, students have created a Facebook page about another student with inappropriate sexual pictures and comments. The page was created over the weekend and was unrelated to school. Other students at the school have "liked" the posts and have even made additional inappropriate sexual comments in the comment section. On Monday, students at school are making fun of and teasing the target of the posts, reiterating some of the inappropriate comments that were in the original post. Based on the conduct at school by the students, there is a nexus to school activity and attendance and the students at school can be discipline for their harassing behavior at school AND the person who created the posts, anyone who disseminated the post, and students that "liked" the post can also be disciplined for those actions that occurred off campus.

Below are the facts in *Philip Shen v. Albany Unified School District*, 3:17-cv-02478-JD, 2017 WL 5890089, (N.D. Cal. Nov. 29, 2017), which provides excellent guidance on how a court will analyze weather the student's conduct falls under the jurisdiction of the school in a cyber-bullying case.

Judge Donato upheld the discipline of six of the ten Albany High School students who sued the District. Here is a summary of the offenses, the discipline and the judge's ruling as to each.

STUDENT	OFFENSE	DISCIPLINE	RULING
C.E.	Created private Instagram account; Invited nine AHS Students to follow; Made 30 to 40 posts targeting ten AHS African-American students and staff often with pictures of the targeted individuals accompanied with racist and derogatory material; Within a few months, the account's content was disclosed to two of the targeted students by one of C.E.'s account followers and quickly became widely circulated at AHS causing disruption, disturbance, and agitation	Expulsion	Upheld
P.S.	Posted favorable comments to C.E.'S blatantly racist and inflammatory postings	Suspension	Upheld
K.C.	Posted derogatory and obscene racist comments and taunted commentators criticizing the posts	Suspension	Upheld

Doe	Posted "likes" to racist and derogatory Posts and posted laughing emojis material and comments	Suspension	Upheld
R.R.	"Liked" several racist and derogatory posts	Suspension	Upheld
P.P.	"Liked" almost every racist and derogatory post	Suspension	Upheld
N.N.	Had access at C.E.'s request, but claimed not to look at the posts	Suspension	OT
N.K.	Commented on a post of a white male's face with a laughing emoji and the comment, "This account is Racism solely directed at black people."	Suspension	OT
M.B.	Posted "Pls tell me who's the owner of this amazing account	Suspension	OT
J.D.	Posted an ambiguous comment to one post and to another stated "I hope I never end up on this account"	Suspension	OT

The judge concluded that the evidence did not show that these last four students' actions whose suspension were overturned (OT) interfered with the rights of other students and did not create a substantial risk of disruption citing *Tinker v. Des Moines Indep. Cmty Sch. Dist.*,393 U.S. 503, 513 (1969).

The other six had disrupted the school environment and clearly targeted individuals on campus with hateful and derogatory references and interfered with their rights.

*Important Note: Bullying that is based on conduct that amounts to sexual harassment – 48900.2 or hate violence – 48900.3, automatically triggers the districts obligation under federal law to inform the victim (and anyone impacted by the conduct) of their right to file a Uniform Complaint pursuant to Board Policy/Administrative Regulations 1312.3. Additionally, the district is required to investigate allegations of discriminatory harassment and address the hostile educational environment, even if there is not a formal complaint filed. (See Chapter 7 – Discriminatory Harassment)

CHAPTER 1: STUDENT SUSPENSIONS

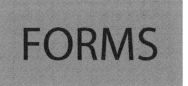

INSERT NAME OF DISTRICT AND/OR LOGO

Principal's Designee

_____   _____
Name of Primary Designee   **Title**

_____   _____
Name of Primary Designee   **Title**

_____   _____
Name of Primary Designee   **Title**

Is hereby designated by_____

Principal of_____**as my primary designees for the 2020-2021 school
year, for any purpose authorized by Education Code Section 48900 through 48925, inclusive, and as my
hereafter by amended.**

_____   _____
(Signature)   **(Date)**

Education Code Section 48911

*(h) For the purposes of this section, a "principal's designee" is any one or more administrators at the school site
specifically designated by the principal in writing, to assist with disciplinary procedures.*

*In the event that there is not an administrator in addition to the principal at school site, a certificated person at
the school site may be specifically designated by the principal, in writing, as a "principal's designee," to assist
with disciplinary procedures. The principal may designate only one such person at a time as the principal's
primary designee for the school year.*

*An additional person meeting the requirements of this subdivision may be designated by the principal, in
writing, to act for the purposes of this article when both the principal and the principal's primary designee are
absent from the school site. The name of the person, and the names of any person or persons designated as
"principal's designee," shall be on file in the principal's office.*

This section is not an exception to, nor does it place any limitation on Section 48903.

Teacher Classroom Referral Form 1.2

INSERT DISTRICT LETTERHEAD AND/OR LOGO

TEACHER CLASSROOM REFERRAL FORM

A CLASSROOM REFERRAL IS NOT A SUSPENSION. AFTER ADMINISTRATIVE INTERVENTION, THE STUDENT HAS A RIGHT TO RETURN TO CLASS.

Name: _____   **Location of Incident:** _____

Teacher:_____

Grade:_____

Problem Behavior	Possible Motivation
• Inappropriate language • Abusive language • Weapon • Not following directions • Harassment/bullying • Physical contact • Fighting/ Physical aggression • Property misuse • Homework • Cheating • Tardy • Other _____	• Obtain peer attention • Obtain adult attention • Obtain items/activities • Avoid Peer(s) • Avoid Adult • Avoid task or activity • Obtain item • Don't know • Other _____

Others involved in incident:
☐ None_____ ☐ Peers_____ ☐ Staff_____ ☐ Teacher _____
☐ Substitute_____   ☐ Unknown _____   ☐ Other_____

Comments: _____

Administrative Action:_____

Principal Signature: _____   **Date:** _____

Sent to Parent on _____ **(Date)**

Notification of Teacher Suspension from Class | **1.3**

INSERT DISTRICT LETTERHEAD AND/OR LOGO
Notification of Teacher Suspension from Class

Date		School	Student's Phone Number		
Student's Name:	Last First		Grade	Student ID	Birthdate
Suspension From:	Day	Time	Date / /	Section 504 ☐ Yes ☐ No	Special Ed Student ☐ Yes ☐ No
Return:	Day	Time	Date / /	Police Report ☐ N/A ☐ Pending ☐ Filed #	Expulsion Review ☐ N/A ☐ Recommended ☐ Pending

EDUCATION CODE SECTION 48900

☐ a.1. Caused, attempted to cause, or threatened to cause physical injury.

☐ a.2. Willfully used force or violence on another person, except in self-defense.

☐ b. Possessed, sold or otherwise furnished any firearm, knife, explosive, or other dangerous object. ++

☐ c. Possessed, used, sold, furnished, or been under the influence of any controlled substance, alcohol, or intoxicant. ++

☐ d. Offered, arranged, or negotiated to sell a controlled substance, alcohol or intoxicant and then provided a replica substance. ++

☐ e. Attempted or committed robbery or extortion.

☐ f. Attempted or caused damage to school or private property.

☐ g. Attempted or stole school or private property.

☐ h. Possessed, or used a tobacco product.

☐ i. Committed an obscene act or engaged in habitual profanity or vulgarity.

☐ j. Possessed, offered, arranged, or negotiated to sell drug paraphernalia.

☐ k. Disrupted school activities or defied school personnel.

☐ l. Knowingly received stolen school or private property.

☐ m. Possessed an imitation firearm.++ - if fires metallic projectile

☐ n. Attempted or committed sexual assault or committed a sexual battery. ++

☐ o. Harassed, threatened, or intimidated a student complainant or witness in a school disciplinary matter.

☐ p. Unlawfully offered, arranged to sell, negotiated to sell, or sold the prescription drug Soma. ++

☐ q. Engaged in, or attempted to engage in, hazing.

☐ r. Engaged in an act of bullying, including electronic means EC 48900.2 ☐, 48900.3 ☐, 48900.4 ☐

☐ t. A pupil who aids or abets in the attempted or infliction of physical injury to another.

☐ .2 Committed sexual harassment. (Gr.4-12)

☐ .3 Attempted, threatened, caused, or participated in hate violence. (Grades 4-12)

☐ .4 Harassment, Threats, or Intimidation that created an intimidating or hostile educational environment. (Gr.4-12)

☐ .7 Made terroristic threats against school officials or property.
++Indicates law enforcement MUST be notified.

MANDATORY RECOMMENDATION FOR EXPULSION
(Education Code 48915(c)):

☐ c. 1. Sale, possession or furnishing a firearm. ++

☐ c. 2. Brandishing a knife at another person. ++

☐ c. 3. Selling a controlled substance. ++

☐ c. 4. Sexual assault or sexual battery. ++

☐ c. 5. Possession of an explosive. ++

DISCRETIONARY MANDATORY RECOMMENDATION FOR EXPULSION
(Education Code 48915 (a)(1):

☐ 1.A Causing serious injury to another person, except in self-defense.++

☐ 1.B Possession of a knife, or other dangerous object of no reasonable use to the pupil.++

☐ 1.C Unlawful possession of any controlled substance except for the first offense for the possession of not more than one avoirdupois ounce of marijuana, other than centrated cannabis, over the counter medications, or prescribed medication.++

☐ 1.D Robbery or extortion.

☐ 1.E Assault or battery on any school employee.++

Parent Conference ☐ Held ☐ Requested ☐ Via Phone

Date:_____ Time:_____

Contact Name:_____

Student Conference ☐ Held ☐ Postponed until _____

Date: _____ Time:_____

Total classes Suspended in the School Year: _____

Total classes Suspended for this incident: _____

Factual explanation of incident(s):

Date:_____ Time: _____
Location: On Campus ____ School activity off school grounds _____

Dear Parents/Guardians:

This suspension is in compliance with Education Code Section 48900 and 48910. A teacher may suspend your student from class, for violations of the Ed Code sections above, for the day of the suspension and the day following. The teacher shall immediately report the suspension to the principal of the school and send the student to the principal or the designee for appropriate action. As soon as possible, the teacher shall ask the parent or guardian of the pupil to attend a parent-teacher conference regarding the suspension. If practicable, a school counselor or a school psychologist may attend the conference. A school administrator shall attend the conference if the teacher or the parent or guardian so requests. Under state law, you are required to respond to this request without delay. If you wish, you and your student may review his/her record as provided in Education Code 49069. Make-up work and/or test may be provided for your student, if requested, for the period of suspensions.

By_____
      Teacher   Teacher Signature

© 2020 Dora Dome Law

********* School District
(School address)

Notification of Administrative Suspension from School

Date	School	Student's Phone Number		
Student's Name: Last First		Grade	Student ID	Birthdate

Suspension From:	Day	Time	Date / /	Suspension Code:	Special Ed Student ☐Yes ☐No
Return:	Day	Time	Date / /	Police Report ☐N/A ☐Pending ☐Filed #	Expulsion Review ☐N/A ☐Recommended ☐Pending

EDUCATION CODE SECTION 48900

☐ a.1. Caused, attempted to cause, or threatened to cause physical injury.

☐ a.2. Willfully used force or violence on another person, except in self defense.

☐ b. Possessed, sold or otherwise furnished any firearm, knife, explosive, or other dangerous object. ++

☐ c. Possessed, used, sold, furnished, or been under the influence of any controlled substance, alcohol, or intoxicant. ++

☐ d. Offered, arranged, or negotiated to sell a controlled substance, alcohol or intoxicant and then provided a replica substance. ++

☐ e. Attempted or committed robbery or extortion.

☐ f. Attempted or caused damage to school or private property.

☐ g. Attempted or stole school or private property.

☐ h. Possessed, or used a tobacco product.

☐ i. Committed an obscene act or engaged in habitual profanity or vulgarity.

☐ j. Possessed, offered, arranged, or negotiated to sell drug paraphernalia.

☐ k. Disrupted school activities or defied school personnel.

☐ l. Knowingly received stolen school or private property.

☐ m. Possessed an imitation firearm.++ - **if fires metallic projectile**

☐ n. Attempted or committed sexual assault or committed a sexual battery. ++

☐ o. Harassed, threatened, or intimidated a student complainant or witness in a school disciplinary matter.

☐ p. Unlawfully offered, arranged to sell, negotiated to sell, or sold the prescription drug Soma. ++

☐ q. Engaged in, or attempted to engage in, hazing.

☐ r. Engaged in an act of bullying, including electronic means
☐ 48900.2 ☐ 48900.3 ☐ 48900.4 (indicate which was violated)

☐ t. A pupil who aids or abets in the attempted or infliction of physical injury to another.

☐ .2 Committed sexual harassment. (Gr.4-12)

☐ .3 Attempted, threatened, caused, or participated in hate violence. (Grades 4-12)

☐ .4 Harassment, Threats, or intimidating. (Gr.4-12)

☐ .7 Made terroristic threats against school officials or property.

++ Indicates law enforcement MUST be notified

MANDATORY RECOMMENDATION FOR EXPULSION
(Education Code 48915(c)):

☐ c. 1. Sale, possession or furnishing a firearm. ++

☐ c. 2. Brandishing a knife at another person. ++

☐ c. 3. Selling a controlled substance. ++

☐ c. 4. Sexual assault or sexual battery. ++

☐ c. 5. Possession of an explosive. ++

DISCRETIONARY MANDATORY RECOMMENDATION FOR EXPULSION
(Education Code 48915 (a)(1):

☐ (A) Causing serious physical injury to another person, except in self-defense.++

☐ (B) Possession of a knife, or other dangerous object of no reasonable use to the pupil.++

☐ (C) Unlawful possession of any controlled substance except for the first offense for the possession of not more than one avoirdupois ounce of marijuana, other than concentrated cannabis, over the counter medications, or prescribed medication.++

☐ (D) Robbery or extortion.

☐ (E) Assault or battery on any school employee.++

Parent Conference   ☐ Held ☐ Requested ☐ Via Phone
Date:_____   Time:_____
Contact Name:_____

Student Conference ☐ Held ☐ Postponed until _____
Date: _____   Time:_____

Total Days Suspended in the School Year: _____

Factual explanation of incident(s): Date:_____ Time:_____

Location: ☐ On Campus ☐ Off Campus ☐ School activity off school grounds ☐ Attendance related

_____

Dear Parents/Guardians:

This suspension is in compliance with Education Code Section 48900 and 48915 et seq. The suspension has been discussed with your student and he/she has been informed of the reasons for the disciplinary action, including the other means of correction that were attempted before the suspension, and the evidence against him/her, and given an opportunity to explain his/her side of the incident. * If a conference has been requested, please make every effort to attend. Under state law, you are required to respond to this request without delay. If you wish, you and your student may review his/her record as provided in Education Code 49069. Make-up work and/or tests may be provided for your student, if requested, for the period of suspension.

If you feel the suspension is inappropriate and have discussed your concerns with the school principal, you may appeal the suspension to (Name of appropriate person), Assistant Superintendent. Call the Educational Services Department, (***-****) for an appointment.

PLEASE NOTE: During the school day, your student must not be on or near any school campus. Supervision is the responsibility of the parent/guardian during the suspension.

By:_____
Principal/Designee

*The principal or designee may suspend a student without a conference if an emergency situation exists.

State laws allow the principal to recommend suspension for violations of Education Code section 48900 subdivisions (a), (b), (c), (d), (e), and other subdivisions upon a first offense, if the pupil's presence is deemed to be a danger to persons.

Request for Parent to Attend Class   1.5

INSERT DISTRICT LETTERHEARD AND/OR LOGO

REQUEST FOR PARENT TO ATTEND CLASS

Dear_____,
            Parent's Name

_____ is requesting you to attend a portion of

_____class for the following reason(s):

_____.

The date and time for your classroom visit is on_____at_____.
                                                        Date   Time

Your attendance is required by law. (Education Code, Section 48900.1(c))

If for some reason, you are unable to attend on the date indicated, please contact the school to schedule a new date.

Section 48900.1 of the Education Code, authorizes a teacher to require a parent or guardian to attend a portion of the school day when a student has violated the following CA Ed. Code sections:

> (i) Committed an obscene act or engaged in habitual profanity or vulgarity.
> (k) (1) Disrupted school activities or otherwise willfully defied the valid authority of supervisors, teachers, administrators, school officials, or other school personnel engaged in the performance of their duties.

Attached is a copy of the Teacher Suspension Form, along with a brief explanation of the policy and the Education Code sections dealing with this issue.

I am also requesting a conference with you upon completion of your visit to the classroom. This will provide us with an opportunity to discuss your child's discipline issues and create a plan for your child's success. Please contact my office as soon as possible to confirm the date for your visitation to the class.

Sincerely,

_____
Principal/Designee
Attachments: Copy of Teacher Suspension

Site Administrator Student Suspension Checklist

Dear Administrator:

Before you decide to suspend a student and complete a suspension form for a student at your school site, be sure that you have sufficiently answered each question below. It is recommended that you keep this checklist in a visible area of your office to ensure proper compliance due process for every student that is suspended from school.

Ed. Code 48900 series violation_____

(Write the actual Ed. Code of 48900)

YES	NO	
		1. Special Ed.? If yes, how many days has the student been suspended this school year counting this proposed suspension? If more than10 school days, is a manifestation determination required?
		2. 504? If yes, how many days has the student been suspended this school year counting this proposed suspension? If more than10 school days, is a manifestation determination required?
		3. Is the violation a first offense?
		4. Other means of correction attempted prior to suspending for this offense? Note: You may not suspend a student from school for 48900 (k) violations for grades k-8.
		5. Is the student a continuing danger for this offense? Note: You may not suspend a student from school for 48900 (k) violations for grades k-8.
		6. Police contacted? Why?_____Report#_____
		7. Physical evidence collected? If so, where is the evidence being stored?
		8. Previous parent contacts? If so when? _____
		9. Student provided with informal conference prior to suspension?
		10. Student informed of the other means of correction that have been tried during the suspension conference?
		11. Community Service offered? If so, specify type of community service_____
		12. Supporting Witness statement available?
		13. Can the offense be considered a 48915 violation? If so, which section of 48915? _____
		14. Parent contacted regarding this violation? When? _____
		15. Date and time of follow up suspension meeting with parent or guardian? Date_____Time_____
		16. Is the student homeless, a foster child, group home student or a ward of the court? (probation) If so, notify the appropriate agency.
		17. Principal's designee who suspended the student is identified in writing and on file in the principal's office.
		18. Has the student been previously suspended for this offense? If so, when? _____

Teacher Notice of Previous Suspension/Expulsion | 1.7

INSERT DISTRICT LETTERHEAD AND/OR LOGO

Date_____

TEACHER NOTICE OF PREVIOUS SUSPENSION/EXPULSION

To: _____
                              Teacher's Name

From: _____
                              Administrator

Re: _____
                              Student

Pursuant to Education Code 49079, this notice is to inform you that the above named student has engaged in, or is reasonably suspected to have engaged in, conduct in violation of Ed. Code Section 48900, except subdivision (h), Section 48900.2, 48900.3, 48900.4, or 48900.7 during the previous three school years.

You have a right to view this information. Please return this notice to my office ASAP. Upon return receipt, you will have the opportunity to view the suspension/expulsion information immediately. Any information received by a teacher pursuant to this section shall be received in confidence for the limited purpose for which it was provided and shall not be further disseminated by the teacher.

Please check one:

_____I wish to view the suspension/expulsion information listed in the student's cumulative file.

_____I do not wish to view the suspension/expulsion information listed in the student's cumulative file.

Signature: _____Date:_____

Report Regarding Attack, Assault or Physical Threat to School District Employee   **1.8**

INSERT DISTRICT LETTERHEAD AND/OR LOGO

REPORT REGARDING ATTACK, ASSAULT, OR PHYSICAL THREAT TO DISTRICT EMPLOYEE

It shall be the duty of the employee, and the duty of any person under whose direction or supervision the employee is employed in the public school system who has knowledge of the incident, to promptly report the incident to the appropriate law enforcement authorities of the county or city in which the incident occurred. (CA Education Code 44014)

Name of Employee: _____

Employee Position: _____

Location of Incident: _____

Time/Date of Incident: _____

Time/Date Supervisor Notified about Incident: _____

Name of Employee who filed Police Report: _____

Police Report # (if available): _____

Briefly describe the attack, assault, or physical threat:

_____

_____

_____

_____

_____

This form was prepared by:

_____
        Name and Title   Date

_____
        Signature

Cc: Risk Management
Cc: Student Services

Mandatory Law Enforcement Notification　1.9

MANDATORY LAW ENFORCEMENT NOTIFICATION

Education Code 48902 requires that the school notify law enforcement when students engage in conduct that violates identified laws. Below is a list of the violations that require law enforcement notification and the required timelines.

- ☐ PC 245: Assault with a deadly weapon, firearm, or by any means of force likely to produce great bodily injury (Report **prior** to suspension)

- ☐ Possession or sale of narcotics or of controlled substance. (No timeframe stated)

- ☐ PC 626.9: possession or discharge of firearm. (No timeframe stated)

- ☐ PC 626.10: bring or possess any of the following dangerous objects/weapons (No timeframe stated):

  - Box cuter
  - Razor blade
  - Dirk
  - Dagger
  - Ice pick
  - Knife having a blade longer than 2.5 inches
  - Folding knife with a blade that locks into place
  - Razor with an unguarded blade
  - Taser or Stun gun
  - Any instrument that expels a metallic projectile such as a BB or pellet, through the force of air pressure, CO_2 pressure or spring action
  - Any spot marker gun

- ☐ EC 48900(c): Unlawfully possessed, used, sold, or otherwise furnished, or been under the influence of, a controlled substance (Report **within one school day** after suspension)
- ☐ EC 48900(d): Unlawfully offered, arranged, or negotiated to sell a controlled substance an alcoholic beverage, or an intoxicant of any kind, and either sold, delivered, or otherwise furnished to a person another liquid, substance, or material and represented the liquid substance, or material as a controlled substance, alcoholic beverage, or intoxicant (Report **within one school day** after suspension)
- ☐ EC 48915(c)(1): Possessing, selling, or otherwise furnishing a firearm. (No timeframe stated)
- ☐ EC 58915(c)(5): Possession of an explosive. (No timeframe stated)

Note: Evidence of law enforcement notification is made via generating a daily report number by law enforcement. The Administrator must ask law enforcement for the daily report number (DR#) upon notification of a call for service.

CHAPTER 2

Disciplinary Investigations

TOOLS FOR THE TRADE

Gathering Evidence

The purpose of a disciplinary investigation is to gather sufficient evidence to determine whether there has been a conduct violation and what would be the appropriate next steps.

Investigative Note-taking

Investigative notes taken at the time of the incident serve as the basis for the written report.

A. Notes must be legible –written in brief, simple statements to provide the writer with factual review of what occurred at the time of the incident.

B. Notes should be easily understood. This is accomplished by using short sentences or facts regarding the incident. Notes should be concise, yet contain sufficient information to cover all the facts of the incident. They will probably result in a series of very short three or four word sentences, which serve to jog the writer's memory at the time of preparing the final written report.

C. Notes must be accurate and show the following information:

   1. Reflect the name of the person being interviewed and the time and date of the interview that the notes are summarizing
   2. Exact time and date of the incident.
   3. Names of persons present or involved to any degree, including the names of all faculty, as well as potential suspects or witnesses.

4. Location of occurrence.

5. Description of the conditions existing at the scene.

6. Accurate descriptions of all persons involved in the incident. Where names are not known, an accurate physical description is a must.

7. Statements of all witnesses to the incident. Where the situation is such that all witnesses cannot be interviewed at that time, it should be done as soon as possible.

8. Opinions and conclusions should not be included in notes taken at the time of the incident. Premature forming of opinions may reflect personal bias or prejudice.

Witness Interviews

Interview the Victim

Once the administrator is informed of a possible conduct violation, the first step in the process is to **interview the victim.** You want to get as much information as possible about what happened--when, where, how, who was involved, and who may have witnessed it. Have the victim write a statement about what happened. (See Statement section below) You will also want to ask the victim whether there are supports or services that the student may need to feel safe at school while the investigation is pending.

Interview the Accused

Once the victim has been interviewed, the **accused needs to be interviewed**, informed of the allegations, given an opportunity to tell her/his side of the story and informed of the "other means of correction" that have been tried. Offer the accused the opportunity to provide a written statement about the incident. Below are some steps to keep in mind when interviewing the accused and asking for a written statement.

1. Inform the accused that he or she has been accused of engaging in misconduct that could lead to suspension and/or expulsion.

2. Inform the accused that he or she is entitled to appropriate due process and that the district will not take any action without conducting a thorough and appropriate investigation.

3. Inform the accused that the investigation shall be confidential, the results of which will be shared only on a need-to-know basis, or during the disciplinary hearing if one

occurs.

4. Describe the specific allegations and give the accused an opportunity to respond to the allegations. You must also inform the accused of the "other means of correction" the school has tried as part of her/his due process.

5. Do not ask leading questions.

6. Determine what relationship, if any, exists or existed between the complaining witness and the accused.

7. Determine whether or not the accused has any documentation of the incident (screenshots of texts, etc.) or names of witnesses s/he believes will corroborate her/his version of the incident.

8. Review the student cumulative file of the accused. (Previous disciplinary action, previous interventions, possible special ed. or 504 issues, etc.)

9. Do not counsel student regarding their role in the alleged act during the interview.

10. Be sure to have the student sign and date their written statement.

11. If the accused refuses to write a statement, the administrator conducting the interview should write a statement indicating the date and time the accused was offered the opportunity to write a statement and that s/he refused. This statement by the administrator should be added to the expulsion packet if the case goes to hearing to demonstrate that the accused was offered due process.

Interview Identified Witnesses

If you are considering an expulsion recommendation based on the alleged conduct, it's critical to interview and obtain statements from witnesses that were identified by the victim and the accused, including any witnesses with firsthand knowledge of the incident. If a staff member was a witness, s/he should be interviewed as well and asked to provide a written statement of the incident.

Statements

School districts are encouraged to have standardized witness statement forms that are used at all levels. The witness completing the form should indicate their name, grade, summary of the incident, date, and signature, and include a declaration under penalty of perjury and the laws of the State of California that their statement is true and correct to the best of their knowledge. Below are some steps to keep in mind when obtaining a written statement. (See

2.1 – Sample Witness Statement Form at the end of this chapter)

Statements of accused, victims and witnesses

1. All statements should be in original handwriting and may be accompanied by a typewritten copy. Please have the witness sign the typewritten copy, if applicable.
2. Statements should include names of other witnesses and be as specific as possible.
3. Statement should be reviewed for clarity, and if necessary, there should be follow-up questions. Any new text added in response to follow-up questions must indicate the date the new text was added, if added on a different day.
4. If possible, obtain statements from all percipient (first-hand) witnesses, including staff members.
5. All statements must include dates and be signed by the witness writing the statement. If the witness is incapable of signing, any mark on the signature line (including printed name) will suffice.
6. Ask all witnesses for the names of any other witnesses.
7. Statements have more weight when they are handwritten by the individual; however, if a person does not want to write a statement or is unable to write a statement, give the option of dictating it. Dictated statements must be read back to the witness verbatim and the witness must sign the dictated statement, acknowledging under penalty of perjury that the statement is true and correct to the best of their knowledge.
8. All names of minors, except the accused, must be redacted from the witness statements once they are included in the expulsion packet or disclosed to the accused pursuant to a pupil record request.

Once the written statement is completed, the administrator should review it with the witness, asking any clarifying questions, and making sure that the witness has signed and dated the document. If any witness, including the accused, writes multiple versions of a witness statement, all versions of the statement should be maintained for possible use in the expulsion hearing, regardless of whether the statements are consistent or inconsistent.

Physical Evidence

During the investigation process, the administrator should be making a list of the documentary and physical evidence needed to establish the conduct violation.

What evidence is needed will be determined by the conduct violations being charged.

Was a weapon involved and has it been recovered? Is there a photo of the weapon if it is not in the possession of the school administrator? Were drugs involved and have they been recovered? Is there a photo of the drugs if they are not in the possession of the school administrator? Are there photos that should be taken of the injuries? Are there screen shots of text messages or social media posts? Was the incident captured on the school's surveillance cameras and has the video footage been preserved? Do you need to obtain medical records or a police report? Have you visited the location where conduct is alleged to have occurred and do you need photos to illustrate the physical environment?

Once the administrator has identified what documentary and physical evidence is needed in the case, the next step is to determine who is in possession of the evidence. Depending on the nature of the evidence, it could be in the possession of the police (i.e. drugs/weapons), IT department (i.e. surveillance tapes), or parents or hospital (medical records). If the case is in fact going forward to an expulsion hearing, it would be important that the administrator begin gathering the necessary evidence early in the process to ensure that the evidence is available for the expulsion hearing.

Searches of Students and Property

When there is an alleged conduct violation, the administrator will have to determine whether there is a need to conduct a search for physical evidence. If so, the administrator needs to be clear what the legal standard is to support a search and the allowable scope of the search.

Legal Standard

The Fourth Amendment to the United States Constitution requires law enforcement to have "probable cause" and obtain a warrant in most cases before conducting a search of persons or property. The law, however, has evolved to recognize the realities of the public school environment with the dual needs to maintain discipline and ensure security. Therefore, the probable cause standard the police must follow does not apply to schools. Administrators need to meet the relatively lower threshold of "reasonable suspicion" before conducting a search of a pupil or a pupil's locker or belongings.

Mandatory Initial Analysis:

Before conducting a search, the administrator must feel comfortable that these two questions are answered in the affirmative:

> 1. Does the administrator have a reasonable suspicion that the student has violated a school rule or the law?
>
> 2. Can the administrator clearly state what rule or law is suspected to have been violated before the search commences and limit the search to those items that are reasonably likely to reveal evidence of the violation?

How do you form a "reasonable suspicion?"

The first point, "reasonable suspicion," does require a judgment call on the administrator's part after becoming aware of some fact or information. Acting on "hunches" or "intuition" is not enough. The information to form a reasonable suspicion needs to be based on recent and credible facts, information, or circumstances that would logically lead to the conclusion that a search of specific places could lead to evidence of a violation of school rules or the law. Information from other students in most circumstances is grounds for forming a reasonable suspicion unless the informant is notoriously unreliable, obviously lying, or the statement grossly unbelievable.

Questions to consider are the relationship between the tipster and the student suspected of violating a rule or the law, the accuracy of prior information from the tipster, and whether the tipster "heard something" ("hearsay") or was an eye witness. Prior experience with the student under suspicion can also be a factor in determining reasonable suspicion.

What violation is the search "reasonably likely" to reveal evidence of?

The second point is to be certain the scope of the search is reasonable in light of what is suspected may be found. If a student tipster tells an administrator that another student brought an automatic rifle to school, searching the other student's locker is clearly allowed. A female student's small purse in this situation would not be reasonable.

The scope and nature of the search also can include factors known to the administrator such age, sex, prior discipline history, nature of the offense relative to particular problems at school, the administrator's experience with the student, the urgency of situation (e.g., the student is said to have a bomb in his backpack), the reliability of the information leading to reasonable suspicion (a surveillance video showing the pupil carrying a weapon into the school).

Examples:

1.   An assistant principal is interviewing a female student who was observed by staff during lunch period smoking in the girls' restroom. The assistant principal can smell tobacco on her breath although she denies that she smokes. These facts create a reasonable suspicion that she could have tobacco products in her purse. A complete search of her purse under these circumstances is legal even if evidence of further violations is uncovered such as marijuana, cigarette papers, and a list of what appear to be customers to whom the student is selling marijuana.

2.   A student walks into class and tosses his backpack onto a metal cabinet and a loud thud follows. A search of the backpack to see if a weapon is inside is reasonable.

3.   An administrator suspects a student is under the influence of alcohol at a school function and takes the student into a private office and asks the student to blow on the administrator's face. This is a reasonable procedure.

Be certain not to impute reasonable suspicion, which may have been present in earlier instances, to be automatically applicable to later events. Each search must be based on specific and recent reasonable suspicion.

Consent Searches

Best practice is to ask the student's permission to search. It is often surprising that students will consent to searches when contraband or weapons may be readily found.   Also, do not be convinced that a refusal of a request to search is an indicator of guilt. If there is an independent basis to form a reasonable suspicion, the search should proceed even with a refusal from the student.

Written consent in advance also will support a universal search of all student property in a specific group, such as bags, purses, and items brought on a field trip, particularly if there is a past issue with drugs or other contraband found on past trips even if the incidents were few and far between.

Searches of Items in Plain View

Reasonable suspicion is only needed as a precursor to a search of items not in sight. If an administrator sees something in plain view, such as a weapon on a car seat in the parking lot, or drugs dropping out of a student's pocket, immediate confiscation is appropriate.

Additionally, it is not improper for an administrator to walk through the school parking lot looking into cars or looking into open lockers while patrolling hallways. If the administrator sees contraband, it may be immediately seized. Reasonable suspicion is not necessary.

Checklist for Searches:

After a reasonable suspicion to search is established by the administrator, best practices for searches include the following:

- All searches, particularly of the person, should be reasonable in scope and consistent with the reasonable suspicion that led to the search in the first place.

- Before a search, the student should be escorted directly to a private place after the student collects all belongings such as jacket, backpack, books, and hats without allowing stops along the way such as to a locker or restroom (an ideal place in some instances to get rid of contraband).

- Have an adult witness present from the beginning of the search until completed. This provides protection to the administrator from adverse claims from the student ("I had a one hundred dollar bill in my purse, and now it is gone").

- Searches should be conducted in private to the greatest extent possible, preferably with only the student, searcher, and witness in the room, to avoid embarrassment to the student.

- Have an administrator and adult witness of the same sex as the student conduct the search, particularly with searches of the person.

- Searches of the person should start with the student's removal of outer garments such as hats, sweaters, and coats and then the student emptying all pockets and laying the objects on a table or shelf.

- The law **does not allow** removal or arranging of a pupil's clothing to permit visual inspection of the pupil's underclothing, breasts, buttocks, or genitalia, or searches of body cavities (Education Code section 49050).

- Search of the person should be from the side of the student's body top to bottom, covering the forearms, thighs, and back, by crushing the fabric of the clothing rather than patting which may miss flat objects. *NOTE: A search of the person by an administrator should be limited to situations where there is a safety concern and law enforcement personnel are not available. If the administrator believes that the student has contraband on her/his person, the administrator should have law enforcement conduct the search.

- Continue through all items to be searched even if contraband is found early in the search.

- Go through items set aside, including those from the pockets, thumb carefully through books and disassemble items in which contraband could conceivably be hidden.

- Locker searches should be, if possible, with the student present but not near the locker, removing items from top to bottom and emptying the locker completely before replacing any items. A staff witness should be stationed to observe both the locker and the student's face because often a student's gaze will go to where the contraband is located. (See 2.2 - Student Searches Checklist Form at the end of this chapter)

- Confiscated items should be photographed (next to a ruler in some instances such as knife blades to show size), placed in an envelope that is then sealed with a label identifying the student, the administrator, the witness, and the date, time, place, and circumstances of the search. The school should have a designated person to be custodian of confiscated items which should be placed in a locked and secure place and kept for disciplinary proceedings or, if appropriate, delivery to law enforcement as soon as possible. (See 2.3 - Sample Evidence Envelope Coversheet at the end of this chapter)

Cell Phone Searches

There is existing California case law recognizing reasonable suspicion searches of cell phones so long as the scope is limited to those items relevant to the particular suspicion. For instance, if a cell phone is confiscated for a use violation, the contents of the phone cannot be searched, as there is no reasonable suspicion to support the search. However, if a teacher reports that she suspects that a student has used a phone to cheat on a test, then there is reasonable suspicion to support a search of the phone's text messages and photos, which are locations where evidence of the cheating may reasonably be found.

However, effective January 1, 2016, through the enactment of SB178, which created Penal Code sections 1546-1546.4, a new law was enacted addressing warrant procedures when searching cell phones in connection with an arrest or traffic stop or seeking of information from electronic device service providers as part of a criminal investigation.

The implications of this new law on the legal standard applicable to searches by school administrators is unclear, as the new law refers to every state "government entity." Penal Code section 1546(i). School districts thus may be subject to the new requirements, because it is well established that school districts are direct political subdivisions of the state.

The question, of course, is what impact the new statutes have on the reasonable suspicion standard with regard to searching electronic devices as part of the disciplinary process. It could be argued that there should not be any change. SB178 focuses on warrants, wire taps, and other criminal law procedure based on a probable cause rationale. Nothing in SB 178 should erode the reasonable suspicion distinction for schools. Neither schools nor reasonable suspicion are mentioned in the act. The emphasis on probable cause and warrants in SB 178 would seem to indicate that if the Legislature wanted to change the established reasonable suspicion rule for schools, it would have expressly stated so. Additionally, the committee analysis of SB 178 does not contain any indication that the legislature intended the bill to apply to warrantless searches conducted in the K-12 public school context. The public policy repeatedly stated in existing case law strongly supports maintaining school discipline especially to combat child pornography, harassment, and bullying. To assume schools are barred from reasonable suspicion searches is such a deviation from long-standing federal and state law, that it would be unreasonable to take that position--especially in the absence of any mention in SB 178.

On March 27, 2017, the Legislative Counsel Bureau issued opinion #1709962 – California Electronic Communications Privacy Act: Kindergarten Through Grade 12 Public Schools, in which they concluded the following:

> While there are strong arguments to the contrary, the provisions of the California Communications Privacy Act likely apply to a student's personal electronic device. … However, it is also our opinion that the California Communications Privacy Act would not require such a teacher or administrator to obtain a warrant before accessing electronic information on a school issued electronic device.

Unfortunately, no matter how compelling an argument may be made that nothing has changed, the reality is that SB 178 creates enough ambiguity about whether school districts must be treated like any other "government entity" that it is likely some attorneys will take a shot and challenge a reasonable suspicion search of a cell phone without express consent of the student.

It is therefore suggested that school districts be aware of this possible legal challenge and consult with the school district's legal counsel regarding their recommendations as to how to respond. Generally, I believe that schools should continue as before with strict limits to cell phone searches within the ambit of reasonable suspicion and the use of ample documentation. There certainly are no guarantees, but the courts should uphold the schools' special status in matters of discipline and school safety.

Breathalyzers, Metal Detectors, Dogs and Other Random Searches

Schools have a broader authority to search and detain students than exists in the general community for law enforcement. So long as there is a "reasonable suspicion" that a violation of law or school rule has occurred, staff may investigate and search. *New Jersey v. T.L.O.,* 469 U.S. 325 (1985). In this context, requiring a student to expel breath into a breathalyzer would be tantamount to a "search."

There legally would be no basis for challenge of any breathalyzer request by District staff of a pupil who reasonably appears to be under the influence of alcohol or other illegal drugs. But how can a random check be legally justified without reasonable suspicion?

Suspicionless searches at school or school-sponsored events under certain circumstances have been upheld as permissible. Examples include the use of metal detectors (75 Ops.Cal.Atty.Gen. 155 (1992)) or drug sniffing dogs (*B.C. v. Plumas,* (9th Cir. 1999) 192 F.3d 1260). The legal rationale is the sound policies against weapons or drugs in the educational environment permits or even demands reasonable preventive steps.

The use of a breathalyzer without reasonable suspicion at a school-sponsored dance can be viewed in the same context. The means is a reasonable one to prevent against the obvious safety risk and potential harm. The United States Supreme Court upheld suspicionless urinalysis of railroad employees based on documented link between drugs and alcohol and train accidents (*Skinner v. Railway Labor Executives' Ass'n,* (1989) 489 U.S. 602, 624) and of student athletes because of a prevalent use of drugs (*Vernonia School Dist. v. Acton,* (1995) 515 U.S. 646, at 652-53, 663).

The case for use of breathalyzers at school dances, beyond the obvious objectives of an alcohol-free event for the health and safety of the participants, will be strengthened if there is a documented history of problems with alcohol at past similar events. If the District has such a history, it would be valuable to make a general, non-specific reference to that in any initial announcement of the policy. Recent issues with alcohol use by students at school-events or in the community along with multiple advance notices will help to gather community support before implementing suspicionless screening.

The District should take steps **prior to beginning a policy of random breathalyzer testing at dances** including:

1. Advance notice that this screening will happen at all school-sponsored events through morning announcements, posters, community postings, and press releases.
2. Notice on tickets and all posters or other publicity relating to each dance.
3. Notice of the District policy in the next annual handbook distributed to parents and students.

Some California districts have adopted a policy of checking every student at the entrance to dances with a breathalyzer following substantial advance notice that this will occur. One out-of-state district requires each student to sign an agreement to submit to a breathalyzer test as a condition of attending the dance. (These options are mentioned for comparison purposes only.)

Whether the checking is for every student or random, a significant point is that dances are voluntary extra-curricular activities which are not mandatory. One anti-breathalyzer argument is that this screening will discourage attendance at school-sponsored dances. But in most instances, generally both parents and students endorse a breathalyzer policy.

The use of breathalyzers, however, is not without the risk of challenges from civil rights groups, and also poses operational challenges. The District should be prepared for civil rights complaints alleging Fourth Amendment infringement or violation of the Right of Privacy in Article 1 of the California State Constitution. Following the steps outlined below, however, will help districts combat such allegations.

Some Practical Considerations Before Implementing a Random Breathalyzer Program

A. Equipment

If breathalyzers are to be used at all, the District should purchase high-quality units and seek law enforcement guidance on acquisition, calibration, use, and maintenance. One of the reasons breathalyzers for alcohol detection have been used more widely in recent years is because these units have come down significantly in price.

There are media reports that breathalyzers have been developed which, in addition to alcohol, can also detect ingestion of marijuana, methamphetamines, and cocaine. These units are in actual use and very likely prohibitively priced. For current data and recommendation of units to purchase, the best source is still local law enforcement.

B. Use and care of the equipment

Most units require regular calibration. The manufacturer's recommendations should be followed and a maintenance and calibration log kept for each unit. Best practices are to keep the units under lock and key and limit access to specified staff who check out the units with a signature log. These steps will combat any argument of tampering or misuse.

To be prepared for challenges, only trained staff or School Resource Officers ("SRO") should use the units. Staff training is best provided by SROs or local law enforcement with training logs kept by the District to minimize potential arguments about the skill of those using the devices. Even law enforcement personnel using the breathalyzers or training for their use should have a record of training on the equipment available if this data is ever needed.

Who actually performs the checks is a question of District policy and culture. There are several practices:

1. Some districts prefer the authority figure of an SRO or other law enforcement personnel doing the screening.
2. Other districts choose trained staff for the assignment as an effort to be less intimidating to students.
3. Some districts use a two-person team, similar to a locker search. One or both may be an SRO or one or both trained staff.

C. Potential Problems with using Breathalyzers

As with any equipment, a breathalyzer is capable of false readings. Obviously, this can happen with a lack of maintenance or calibration. The literature indicates, however, that well maintained breathalyzers by and large are accurate. False positive readings reportedly can also occur if the subject has recently used mouthwash or is on a low carbohydrate diet. Staff should be ready to listen to pupil's explanation and make a judgment call whether there is a false positive. The District should consider having a procedure for handling a positive reading.

Other than immediately barring the student from entrance to the dance or calling parents, one option is to administer a second reading ten minutes later before following disciplinary protocols.

A well planned program of random breathalyzer testing at District-sponsored dances can be legally sustained with ample advance notice, correctly maintained equipment, and trained screeners.

What are the Legal Risks to Administrators?

Conducting searches following reasonable suspicion and along the guidelines suggested above should shield an administrator from any claim of illegal search and seizure. In general, school administrators are charged with being familiar with the legal procedures and limitations discussed above. Good faith exercise of an administrator's duties consistent with these rules is almost always a defense to any legal claim. Legal liability can only result from clear and knowing violation of the law. Personal liability arises if the administrator knew or should have known an action violated a student's rights or if the action was committed maliciously to deprive the student of his or her rights or with reckless disregard of those rights. A prudent administrator who makes a sincere effort to follow the rules in the pursuit of maintaining the discipline and safety of the school should be able to avoid even the appearance of deliberately trying to deprive students' rights.

Special Considerations

Police Questioning

Procedures When Law Enforcement Officers Come to a School Site for Student Interviews

1. Notify site administrator or staff member designated for this purpose.
2. The officer should voluntarily present identification to the administrator or designee who should note the name, badge number, and agency. If not voluntarily produced, ask for identification.
3. The officer will identify the student or students for interviewing.
4. Unless the officer requests a private interview, the administrator or designee should be present for the duration of the interview.
5. Make an effort using all available telephone numbers or email addresses to notify the parents of the police questioning, with consent of the officer. If the officer directs you

not to notify the parent, document that directive on the Police Questioning form. Officers do not need to wait for the parents to arrive to begin the interview. (See 2.4 – Sample Letter to Parent re: Questioning Student Form at the end of this chapter)

6. The school site shall keep a record of law enforcement interviews at school. The record must include the following:

    a. Name and badge number of the officer.

    b. The Officer's agency (police or sheriff department, Highway Patrol, FBI, etc.).

    c. Time when the officer arrived and left.

    d. Whether the administrator or designee was present during the interview.

    e. Telephone numbers or email addresses used to contact the parents, and the success of these efforts, and parent statements or comments.

    f. Any other pertinent information.

7. All questions arising from law enforcement presence at the school site should be directed to the Department of Student Services at the District Office. (See 2.5 – Sample Police Questioning and Release Form at the end of this chapter)

* NOTE - Senate Bill 395, Effective January 1, 2018

Requires a youth 15 years of age and under to consult with legal counsel in person, by telephone or by video conference, prior to custodial interrogation and before waiving any of the above specified rights. The law prohibits a waiver of the consultation.

Note the following:

1. The law applies to police officers only.

2. School officials and school security officers are not affected by this law.

CPS Questioning

Procedures When Representative of CPS arrive at a School Site for Student Interviews

A representative of CPS agency may interview a student who is a suspected victim of child abuse or neglect during school hours and on school premises following up on a report of suspected child abuse or neglect which may have occurred in the student's home, a facility, or in any location that facts indicated abuse or neglect happened. When a CPS representative comes to a school site with the announced intention of interviewing a student, the following are the appropriate procedures:

1. Notify site administrator or staff member designated for this purpose.

2. The CPS representative should voluntarily present identification to the administrator or designee who should note the name, badge number, and agency. If not voluntarily produced, ask for identification. School staff **should not make photocopies of the identification** to prevent the possibility of copies of an official identification card being made.

3. The representative will identify the student or students for interviewing.

4. Before calling a student to the office for interviewing, the administrator or designee must receive from the CPS representative at least one of the items listed below:

   a. A warrant or affidavit, signed by a judge of the superior court, expressly stating that the individual has authority to speak with a specified student

   b. A court order expressly stating that the individual has authority to speak with a specified student. An example is an order placing a minor student on Juvenile Court probation with a condition of submitting to searches and seizures without a warrant, which may include interviews. This may be listed on the order as a waiver of the student's Fourth Amendment rights.

   c. Signed consent by a parent, guardian, or other person with legal custody of the student authorizing the CPS representative to interview the student

   d. A statement of exigent circumstances, which require the CPS representative to speak with the student

   e. A statement from the CPS representative that he or she is not acting for law enforcement purposes and is unaware of any ongoing police investigation of the matter.

5. Once the administrator or designee has received one or more of the five grounds stated in paragraph 4, above, the administrator or designee shall bring the student to the officer. The CPS representative must give the student the choice of an interview in private with the CPS representative or an interview in the presence of any adult member of the school site staff. This adult may be a certificated or classified District employee or a volunteer aide. The role of the school staff person in the interview is to support the student and make him or her as comfortable as possible.

6. The selected staff member shall not participate in the interview nor discuss the facts or circumstances of the case with the student. The selected staff member is under a mandatory duty to maintain the confidentiality of the interview. Before the interview, the

administrator or designee shall notify the selected staff member of this duty as well as the penalty for violating confidentiality for which Penal Code section 11167.5 provides criminal punishment as a consequence for violation. A selected staff member, however, may decline the role in the interview. If the staff member agrees to the interview, it shall be conducted during school hours. Should there be a failure to comply with these rules, the admissibility of information gathered at the interview is not affected in either a criminal or civil proceeding under Penal Code §11174.3(a).

7. The school site shall keep a record of CPS interviews at school. The record shall include the following:

a. Name and badge number (if any) of the CPS representative.

b. The representative's agency and office location.

c. Time when the representative arrived and left.

d. Whether a staff member was present during the interview and, if so, the name of the staff member.

e. Any other pertinent information.

8. All questions arising from CPS presence at the school site should be directed to the Department of Student Services at the District Office.

Procedures For Dealing With Child Pornography

Grounds for Discipline for Possession, Creation, or Distribution of Child Pornography

The following CA Ed. Code sections are to be considered when student conduct involves the possession, creation, or distribution of child Pornography:

48900-A pupil shall not be suspended from school or recommended for expulsion, unless the superintendent of the school district or the principal of the school in which the pupil is enrolled determines that the pupil has committed an act as defined pursuant to any of subdivisions (a) to (r), inclusive:

. . .

(i) Committed an obscene act or engaged in habitual profanity or vulgarity.

. . .

(r) Engaged in an act of bullying. For purposes of this subdivision, the following terms have the following meanings:

(1) "Bullying" means any severe or pervasive physical or verbal act or conduct, including communications made in writing or by means of an electronic act, and including one or more acts committed by a pupil or group of pupils as defined in **Section 48900.2**, 48900.3, or 48900.4, directed toward one or more pupils that has or can be reasonably predicted to have the effect of one or more of the following:

> (A) Placing a reasonable pupil or pupils in fear of harm to that pupil's or those pupils' person or property.

> (B) Causing a reasonable pupil to experience a substantially detrimental effect on his or her physical or mental health.

> (C) Causing a reasonable pupil to experience substantial interference with his or her academic performance.

> (D) Causing a reasonable pupil to experience substantial interference with his or her ability to participate in or benefit from the services, activities, or privileges provided by a school.

(2) (A) "Electronic act" means the creation or transmission originated on or off the schoolsite, by means of an electronic device, including, but not limited to, a telephone, wireless telephone, or other wireless communication device, computer, or pager, of a communication, including, but not limited to, any of the following:

…

> (iii) (I) An act of **cyber sexual bullying**.

> (II) For purposes of this clause, "cyber sexual bullying" means the dissemination of, or the solicitation or incitement to disseminate, a photograph or other visual recording by a pupil to another pupil or to school personnel by means of an electronic act that has or can be reasonably predicted to have one or more of the effects described in subparagraphs (A) to (D), inclusive, of paragraph (1). A photograph or other visual recording, as described above, shall include the depiction of a nude, semi-nude, or sexually explicit photograph or other visual recording of a minor where the minor is identifiable from the photograph, visual recording, or other electronic act.

(III) For purposes of this clause, "cyber sexual bullying" does not include a depiction, portrayal, or image that has any serious literary, artistic, educational, political, or scientific value or that involves athletic events or school-sanctioned activities.

. . .

48900.2-In addition to the reasons specified in Section 48900, a pupil may be suspended from school or recommended for expulsion if the superintendent or the principal of the school in which the pupil is enrolled determines that the pupil has committed sexual harassment as defined in Section 212.5.

For the purposes of this chapter, the conduct described in Section 212.5 must be considered by a reasonable person of the same gender as the victim to be sufficiently severe or pervasive to have a negative impact upon the individual's academic performance or to create an intimidating, hostile, or offensive educational environment. This section shall not apply to pupils enrolled in kindergarten and grades 1 to 3, inclusive.

. . .

48900.4-In addition to the grounds specified in Sections 48900 and 48900.2, a pupil enrolled in any of grades 4 to 12, inclusive, may be suspended from school or recommended for expulsion if the superintendent or the principal of the school in which the pupil is enrolled determines that the pupil has intentionally engaged in harassment, threats, or intimidation, directed against school district personnel or pupils, that is sufficiently severe or pervasive to have the actual and reasonably expected effect of materially disrupting classwork, creating substantial disorder, and invading the rights of either school personnel or pupils by creating an intimidating or hostile educational environment.

What is the Difference Between "Pornographic" and "Obscene?"

- "Pornography," by dictionary definition refers to "sexually explicit videos, photographs, writings, or the like, whose purpose is to elicit sexual arousal" which is included within the broader legal definition of "obscenity" which can also include speech, plays, and other "live" activities.

- Legally, "'Obscene matter'" is the operative term. It is defined as matter, taken as a whole, that to the average person, applying contemporary statewide standards, appeals to the prurient interest, that, taken as a whole, depicts or describes sexual conduct in a patently offensive way, and that, taken as a whole, lacks serious literary, artistic, political, or scientific value." (Penal Code section 311(a))

- Mere possession of obscene material, with an intent to share the material, is a crime [Penal Code section 311.2(a)] with more severe felony penalties if the material depicts a minor. (Penal Code section 311.2(b))

- Simulated sexual acts or images of pubic or rectal areas of minors are included as "sexual conduct" constituting potentially obscene material. (Penal Code section 311.4(d))

Preserve Evidence of Pornographic/Obscene Material for Both School Discipline and Potential Police Reports and Criminal Prosecution

- Place the material and, if found on an electronic device, the pupil's cell phone, lap top, or tablet, in a secure, locked location, so that you can state that from the time you obtained the evidence that you were the sole custodian.

- Contact law enforcement immediately and turn the pornographic material over to them.

- Request a copy of the police report describing the pornographic material for use in an expulsion evidence packet, if applicable.

- If parents want a copy of the pornographic material, provide them with the police report number and direct them to contact law enforcement directly.

Pornographic/Obscene Material, Whether in Physical or Electronic Form, May be Part of an Education Code Suspension and/or Expulsion as Well as Part of Multiple Offenses

- Taking, sending, viewing, or possessing nude, semi-nude sexually explicit digital images violates CA Ed. Code 48900(i) but also constitutes a crime under Penal Code section 311.2.

- Exchanging obscene images of a minor is sexual exploitation under Penal Code sections 311.4 and child abuse under Penal Code section 11165.1.

- Forwarding sexually explicit images may be part of bullying, harassment, or cyberstalking pursuant to CA Ed. Code 48900(r), or sexual harassment pursuant to CA Ed. Code 48900.2.

Mandatory Reporting Applies After Learning of Obscene Images of Minors

- District credentialed and classified employees are "mandatory reporters" if within the scope of their employment they have a reasonable suspicion of abuse of a minor. (Penal Code sections 11165.7(a)(1)-(4), 11165.9)

- Mandatory reporters must report a "reasonable suspicion" of abuse or neglect to local law enforcement or county probation, depending on local procedures. (Penal Code section 11165.9)

- Mandatory reporters must make a telephone report immediately, "or as soon as practicably possible," and follow up with a written report within 36 hours of learning about the suspected violation. (Penal Code section 11166(a))

- The follow up report may include the evidence obtained including the images from the pupil's cell phone. (Penal Code section 11166(a))

- "Reasonable suspicion" does not require certainty that abuse of neglect occurred so long as the suspicion results from facts that would lead a reasonable person, based on training and experience, to suspect child abuse or neglect. (Penal Code section 11166(a)(1))

Pornography/Obscenity Definitions Apply to "Selfies" or "Sexting"

The Penal Code sections listed above would apply to an adult who takes a sexually explicit picture of a minor and shares it via social media or text message. Schoolsite administrators, however, should be aware that minors who take nude or semi-nude selfies and send them to peers, even if done so discretely, have violated not only provision of the Education Code, but state criminal law as well.

Clearly, child pornography laws are designed to protect minors from exploitation caused by others. The criminal justice system, however, will prosecute minors for sending nude or otherwise lurid self-portraits, even when the minors sent the selfies without coercion. There is no exception for taking or distributing sexually explicit pictures of oneself when the object is a minor. A student sending a nude or semi-nude selfie to a boyfriend or girlfriend could be prosecuted for child pornography. Further distribution through social media or direct sharing could subject every individual who received or distributed the images to criminal prosecution.

All questions about procedures for handling child pornography cases should be directed to the Department of Student Services at the District Office.

Questioning Students In Sexual Battery/Assault Cases

CA Ed. Code Sections 48900(n) and 48915(c)(4) designate conduct that amounts to a sexual battery or sexual assault as a mandatory recommendation for expulsion. However, rather than define the terms, the CA Ed. Code references relevant California Penal Code Sections for definitions of the conduct.

48900(n) consists of seven different and unique Penal Code ("PC") offenses and it is up to the site administrator to determine which of the PC offenses the conduct violates, before a student is charged with sexual battery or sexual assault.

For use in cases of a student suspected of violating CA Ed. Code 48900(n):

"Committed or attempted to commit a sexual assault as defined in Section 261, 266c, 286, 287, 288, or 289, or former Section 288a of, the Penal Code or committed a sexual battery as defined in Section 243.4 of the Penal Code."

If a student charged with this offense committed the act at school or at a school-sponsored activity off campus, the administration must recommend expulsion to the Governing Board under CA Ed. Code 48915(c)(4):

> The principal or superintendent of schools shall immediately suspend, pursuant to Section 48911, and shall recommend expulsion of a pupil that he or she determines has committed any of the following acts **at school or at a school activity off school grounds:**"
>
> . . .
>
> (4) Committing or attempting to commit a sexual assault as defined in subdivision (n) of Section 48900 or committing a sexual battery as defined in subdivision (n) of Section 48900."

Sexual Battery

Sexual battery is the most common CA Ed. Code 48900(n) violation on school campuses, as compared to the sexual assaults. (See Chapter 3 – Expulsion Recommendations, for a summary of all of the sexual assaults). There are two types of sexual battery that commonly occur on school campuses, one is a misdemeanor and one is a felony. This distinction is not relevant, as both fall under CA Ed. Code 48900(n), and are subject to a mandatory recommendation for expulsion. However, being aware of the distinction between the two types of sexual battery helps an administrator understand the evidence necessary to prove the two offenses.

Because the CA Ed. Code uses Penal Code sections to define the offense in the school context, investigation of an alleged act under the above sections needs to address the elements of the offense under the Penal Code, even though a school suspension or expulsion is not a criminal proceeding. If at all, a parallel criminal proceeding will be brought by the District Attorney in Juvenile Court, which is totally independent of the District's process.

The Challenge Facing Administrators in These Cases

When investigating an alleged sexual battery, under CA Ed. Code 48900(n), the threshold determination that administrators must make is to conclude whether the touching of an intimate part was intentional. It is often the most challenging element to establish through the facts that the acts were done with "the specific purpose of sexual arousal, sexual gratification, or sexual abuse."

Specific Purpose - Sexual arousal, Sexual gratification, or Sexual abuse

The general standard to determine intent for sexual battery crimes is to look to "[A] defendant's statement of his intent and by the circumstances surrounding the commission of the act.. . . In objectively assessing a defendant's state of mind during an encounter with a victim, the trier of fact may draw inferences from his conduct, including any words the defendant has spoken. . ."*People v. Craig* (1994) 25 Cal.App.4th 1593, 1597.

Sexual Arousal or Gratification

To prove "arousal" and "gratification" in reported California cases on sexual battery, the substantial evidence must support a finding that the act was committed for the purposes of sexual pleasure.

Facts that could support a finding of sexual arousal or gratification of the perpetrator include a male with an erection, exposing himself, or masturbating or attempting sexual arousal of the victim by touching the victim's intimate places or forcing the victim to touch the perpetrator in intimate places. *People v. Dixon*, 75 Cal.App.4th. 935.

Sexual Abuse

"Sexual abuse" needs to be shown by a battery on another person's "intimate part" done either to harm or humiliate that person. Therefore, it is an "either /or" element of the offense. Sexual abuse cases satisfy this element with facts showing intent to hurt or humiliate, which appear to arise more often with school-age students.

With school-age perpetrators, courts more often find "sexual abuse" was present under Penal Code section 243.4(e)(1) to support sexual battery decisions rather than purposeful "sexual gratification" or "arousal."

Even if the perpetrator says nothing during the incident, a verbal or physical reaction by the victim could suggest that the act was intended to be or resulted in physical or psychological pain or humiliation and embarrassment.

"Pain, injury, or discomfort" can be physical or emotional arising from what likely are humiliating and embarrassing public incidents.

A juvenile court conviction of a 14-year-old minor male defendant who pinched the breast of a 16-year-old female victim was upheld with findings that the assault caused her emotional distress and resulted in a significant bruise. *In re Shannon T.*, 50 Cal.Rptr.3d at 565, 567. The court found that the defendant inflicted a sexual battery under § 243.4(e) with the specific purpose of sexual abuse because he first told her, "Get off the phone. You're my ho," and when the victim responded, "Whatever," and walked away, the defendant pursued her, slapped her face, grabbed her arm, and pinched her breast. Id. at 566–67.

Similarly, the court found the minor defendant committed sexual battery when he poked the center of the victim's buttocks, penetrating about an inch. Because the defendant laughed with his companions as he touched the victim and used derogatory language, the court found the evidence demonstrated the defendant's purpose was sexual abuse. *In re A.B.*, 2011 WL 193402, at *1.

Lastly, a middle school student, who slapped his classmate-victim "with an open hand in her crotch area" was guilty of misdemeanor sexual abuse under Penal Code section 243.4(e)(1). The juvenile offender blamed his friends for telling him to do it. The record showed that the victim was "mad, embarrassed, and 'kind of scared'" and chased the defendant, who "ran away laughing." These facts led the court to conclude that the defendant "understood that his action would embarrass and humiliate" the victim. *In re Carlos C.*, 2012 WL 925029 (Cal.Ct.App.2012)

Judicial interpretations of this Penal Code section, which by extension are legally applicable to an Education Code section 48900(n) investigation, hold a perpetrator accountable for "sexual abuse" to support a finding of sexual battery if "any touching of a person's intimate parts [was] in order to cause pain, injury, or discomfort. The perpetrator does not need to achieve any sexual arousal or sexual gratification." *California Criminal Jury Instructions*, Number 938.

Careful questioning can help administrators develop information to show whether in addition to an intentional touching of an intimate part, the facts support the required element that the act was for "the specific purpose of sexual arousal, sexual gratification, or sexual abuse."

The following questions can be edited and selectively used when questioning the student accused of sexual battery, the victim, and witnesses. These questions are not a limit on questioning, but are rather a starting point. The goal is to investigate thoroughly to determine to the greatest extent possible what happened, including the more difficult question of what the perpetrator intended:

Sample Questions to the Suspected Perpetrator:

Do you know [the victim]? (If the answer is "yes") How do you know [the victim]? How long have you known [the victim]? What is your relationship?

Have you ever posted any items relating to [the victim] on social media such as Facebook, Snap Chat, or Instagram? Has [the victim] ever posted any items on social media relating to you? Have you exchanged photos or messages with [the victim] via social media, email, texts, instant messaging, written notes or letters, or any other means? What was said in all of these postings or messages? Do you have access to any of these communications? (If the answer is "yes") Can you provide them to me?

How did you meet up with [the victim] on [date and time of alleged offense]? Why were you in this location? Did you invite [the victim] to meet you? (If the answer is "no") How did you and the victim come to be in the same place at the same time?

At that time did you say anything to [the victim]? Did [the victim] say anything to you? (If the answer is "yes" to either of these questions) What was said--be as complete as you can?

During this incident did you see that [the victim] was angry? During this incident were you aware that [the victim] was scared? During this incident were you aware that [the victim] was embarrassed? During this incident were you aware that [the victim] was humiliated? What did you observe? After the incident did you see that [the victim] was angry? Scared? Embarrassed? Humiliated? What did you observe?

Before this incident were you angry with [the victim]? During this incident were you trying to scare [the victim]? During this incident were you trying to embarrass [the victim]? During this incident were you trying to humiliate [the victim]?

Did [the victim] tell you to stop or not do what you were doing? (If the answer is "yes") What did [the victim] say? What did you say? What did you do?

(If applicable) [the victim] said that you were asked to stop. Why do you think [the victim] said this?

At any time during the incident, did you take off any of your clothes? Did you take off any of [the victim]'s clothes? Did you put your hands on [the victim]'s clothes? Did you put your hands into or under [the victim]'s clothes?

Did you have any negative feelings toward [the victim]? Were you feeling any sexual arousal or desire before, during or after the incident?

What happened next--be as complete as you can?

(Depending on the answer, follow up as needed with as much detail as possible)

Did you touch [the victim]? If yes, how many times? (Obtain details for each touching if more than one occurred on more than one occasion.)

(If the answer is "yes") Where did you touch [the victim]? Did you touch the buttocks? Did you touch the groin area? Did you touch the anus? Did you touch the sexual organ? Did you touch the breast or breasts (If the victim was female)?

Can you show me exactly where you touched [the victim] (use a preprinted outline of the front and back of the body and ask the perpetrator to mark each point of touching with a pen or pencil)?

Did you do anything to keep [the victim] from leaving or getting away, for example, by holding, restraining, blocking, limiting movement, or threats or warnings?

(If the answer to "Did you touch" is "no") We have information that you touched [the victim] on the [specifically state what the victim said].—why did [the victim] say this? And/or why did [number] witness[es] say this (If there are witness statements)?

Did anyone see the incident? Do you know anyone who can support your explanation? Do you know if anybody took photos, audio recordings, or videos of the incident? (If the answer is "yes"), Do you have a copy of the photos, audio recordings, or videos? Who else has a copy of the photos, audio recordings, or videos?

Sample Questions to the Victim:

Things to consider before interviewing the victim:

There are medical, psychological, and mental health consequences for victims of sexual violence. This is often compounded by the age of the victim. Interviewing a child victim of sexual violence is a sensitive matter and consideration must be given to ensuring physical and emotional safety during the interview and maximizing the victim's sense of trust with the interviewer. As such, the gender of the interviewer and their expertise in working with children who have been exposed to traumatic events, are essential considerations for a school administrator. Experienced school counselors are often ideal interviewers. School administrators may also defer to law enforcement resources to conduct the interview of the victim, however, there should be some a discussion to determine "how" and "if" the results of the interview will be shared with school officials, in order to allow the school to gather the evidence necessary to pursue disciplinary action against the alleged perpetrator.

To avoid adding to the victim's trauma, limiting the number of people interviewing the student and/or the number of times s/he has to be interviewed is important. Audio-taping or videotaping the interview are alternatives for reducing the number of times the victims have to be interviewed. Also consider interviewing the alleged victim in a place where s/he feels safe and comfortable.

Do you know [the perpetrator]? (If the answer is "yes") How do you know [the perpetrator]? How long have you known [the perpetrator]? What is your relationship?

Have you ever posted any items relating to [the perpetrator] on social media such as Facebook, Snap Chat, or Instagram? Has [the perpetrator] ever posted any items on social media relating to you? Have you exchanged any photos or messages with [the perpetrator] via social media, email, texts, instant messaging, written notes or letters? What was said in all of these postings or messages? Do you have access to any of these communications? (If the answer is "yes") Can you provide them to me?

How did you meet up with [the perpetrator] on [date and time of alleged offense]? Why were you in this location? Did you invite [the perpetrator] to meet you? Did [the perpetrator] invite you to meet? (If the answer is "no") How did you and [the perpetrator] come to be in the same place at the same time?

At the time did you say anything to [the perpetrator]? Did [the perpetrator] say anything to you? (If the answer is "yes" to either of these questions) What was said--be as complete as you can?

Did [the perpetrator] take off any clothes? Any of your clothes? Put hands into or under your clothes? Put hands into [the perpetrator]'s own clothes.

Was [the perpetrator] showing any signs of sexual arousal? What made you think so? Did you think that [the perpetrator] had negative feelings toward you? Why do you think so?

What happened next--be as complete as you can?

(Depending on the answer, follow up as needed with as much detail as possible)

Did you tell [the perpetrator] to stop or not to do what was happening? (If the answer is "yes") What did you say? What did [the perpetrator] say? What did [the perpetrator] do? (If the answer to the question is "no") Why did you not say anything to make [the perpetrator] stop? If you did not tell [the perpetrator] to stop, was there another way that you tried to communicate that you wanted [the perpetrator] to stop? If yes, how do you believe you communicated that you wanted [the perpetrator] to stop?

Before the incident was [the perpetrator] angry with you? Before the incident were you angry with [the perpetrator]? During the incident was [the perpetrator] angry? During this incident were you angry? Before the incident were you afraid of [the perpetrator]? During this incident were you scared? During this incident were you embarrassed? During this incident did you feel humiliated? How did you feel after the incident? Angry? Scared? Humiliated? Explain how.

Did [the perpetrator] do anything to keep you from leaving or getting away by holding, restraining, blocking, limiting movement, or threats or warnings?

Where exactly were you touched? If yes, how many times? (Obtain details for each touching if more than one occurred on more than one occasion.)

Were you touched on the buttocks? Were you touched in the groin area? Were you touched on or in the anus? Were you touched on your sexual organ? Were you touched on your breast or breasts (If the victim was female)? Can you show me exactly where you were touched (use a preprinted outline of the front and back of the body and ask the victim to mark each point of touching with a pen or pencil)?

(If the victim denies the incident) Why did you make the report that you did? (If there are witnesses or witness statements), Why do you think [the witnesses] said this? And/or why did [number] witness[es] say this (If there are witness statements)?

Did anyone see the incident? Do you know anyone who can support your explanation? Do you know if anybody took pictures, audio recordings, or videos of the incident? (If the answer is "yes"), Do you have a copy of the photos, audio recordings, or videos? Who else has a copy of the photos, audio recordings or videos?

Sample Questions to Witnesses (if there are any):

Do you know [the perpetrator]? Do you know [the victim] (If the answer is "yes" to either one) How long have known [the perpetrator]? How long have you known [the victim]? What is your relationship with [the perpetrator]? What is your relationship with [the victim]?

Have you ever seen postings of any items relating to [the victim] or [the perpetrator] on social media such as Facebook, Snap Chat, or Instagram? Have you ever seen postings of any items relating to [the perpetrator] posted by [the victim] on social media such as Facebook, Snap Chat, or Instagram? Have you ever seen postings of any items relating to [the victim] posted by [the perpetrator] on social media such as Facebook, Snap Chat, or Instagram? If yes, can you describe what you saw? Do you have access to any of these communications? (If the answer is "yes") Can you provide them to me?

Have you ever seen any photos, messages, emails, texts, instant messages, written notes or letters exchanged between [the perpetrator] and [the victim] Do you have access to any of these communications? (If the answer is "yes") Can you provide them to me?

What did you observe on [date and time of alleged offense]? Why were you in this location? Where were you standing or sitting? How far from [the victim] and [the perpetrator]? Was there any interference to your ability to view the incident? Did you move your location during the incident? (If the answer is "yes") Where did you move to? Why did you move?

At the time, did you say anything to [the perpetrator]? [the victim]? Did [the perpetrator] or [the victim] say anything to you? Did [the victim] say anything to anyone? (If the answer is "yes" to either of these questions) What was said--be as complete as you can regarding who said what?

Did you hear [the victim] say to [the perpetrator] to stop or not do what was happening? (If the answer is "yes") What did [the victim] say? What did [the perpetrator] say? What did [the perpetrator] do? What did the victim do?

Did you see [the victim] do anything that would suggest to [the perpetrator] to stop or not do what was happening? (If the answer is "yes") What did [the victim] do? What did [the perpetrator] say in response? What did [the perpetrator] do in response?

Did [the perpetrator] take off any clothes? Any of [the victim]'s clothes? Put hands into or under [the victim]'s clothes? Put hands into or under [the perpetrator]'s own clothes?

Did [the perpetrator] show any signs of sexual arousal? What did you notice to make you think so? Did you think that [the perpetrator] had negative feelings toward [the victim]? Why do you think so?

What happened next--be as complete as you can?

(Depending on the answer, follow up as needed with as much detail as possible)

Did [the perpetrator] do anything to keep [the victim] close to [the perpetrator] by holding, restraining, blocking, limiting movement, or threats or warnings?

Where exactly was [the victim] touched? If yes, how many times? (Obtain details for each touching if more than one occurred on more than one occasion.)

Was there touching on the buttocks? The groin area? On or into the anus? The sexual organ? The breast or breasts (If the victim was female)? Can you show me exactly where there was touching (use a preprinted outline of the front and back of the body and ask each witness to mark each point of touching with a pen or pencil)?

If you know, was [the perpetrator] angry with [the victim] before the incident? If you know, was [the victim] angry with [the perpetrator] before the incident? (If the answer is "yes") How do you know this? During this incident did you see that [the victim] was angry? During this incident did you see that [the victim] was scared? During this incident did you see that [the victim] was embarrassed? During this incident did you see that [the victim] was humiliated? After the incident, was [the victim] angry? Scared? Embarrassed? Humiliated? Be specific about what you saw that made you think the victim felt this way.

Do you know any other witnesses who saw this incident? Did anyone see the incident? Do you know anyone who can support your explanation? Do you know if anybody took pictures, audio recordings, or videos of the incident? (If the answer is "yes"), Do you have a copy of the photos, audio recordings, or videos? Who else has photos, audio recordings, or videos?

Megan's Law Registry – Parent, Guardian or Caregiver

There are occasions when a parent, guardian, or caregiver of a student is a registered sex offender. The district must assess, limit, and supervise the interactions and activities the registered sex offender engages in at school or school activities, including coming to school for such things as open house, teacher conferences, and participation as a volunteer at school or on field trips.

The District, after verification that the parent, guardian, or caregiver is on the Megan's Law list, should place restrictions and conditions on coming to school for legitimate purposes regarding the student, but under no circumstances allow the registered sex offender to volunteer for any school activity involving other students or for field trips. Reasonable precautions should be taken to be assured that the registered sex offender does not come to school without a specific purpose regarding only the student, the school has advance warning, and the registered sex offender is with a staff escort at all times. There should be no opportunity for the registered sex offender to interact with any other student other than her/his child while at school.

Name Appearing on Sex Offender List

Under Penal Code sections 290, and following, individuals convicted of sex offenses must register with the state and provide specific information including their addresses and keep the data current. These code sections also direct the California Attorney General to create and maintain an on-line list of those who registered on what is called "Megan's List." It can be accessed at www.meganslaw.ca.gov.

The District should independently verify the name and address of any individual suspected of being on the list rather than relying upon what parent, community member, or staff, report to the administration.

A registered sex offender is not allowed to volunteer as an aide for certificated employees. CA Ed. Code 35021(a) states this rule:

> Notwithstanding any other law, any person, except a person required to register as a sex offender pursuant to Section 290 of the Penal Code, may be permitted by the governing board of any school district to perform the duties specified in Section 44814 or 44815, or to serve as a nonteaching volunteer aide under the immediate supervision and direction of the certificated personnel of the district to perform noninstructional work which serves to assist the certificated personnel in performance of teaching and administrative responsibilities…

Field trips are permitted under CA Ed. Code 35330 as long as direct supervision of students is by certificated staff. (CA Ed. Code section 35330(a)(4)). Parent chaperones, therefore, are to aid and assist certificated personnel in their field trip duties. Although CA Ed. Code 35021(a) does not deal with field trips, *per se*, it is clear that the law contemplates a volunteer in the school context, parent or not, may not be considered if on the sex offender registry. School districts place control over field trip chaperones in the hands of the principal in line with the CA Ed. Code. Administrative Regulation 6153 states, "The principal shall approve chaperones that are not employees of the district after researching and checking the California Department of Justice Megan's Law website."

School administrators must be aware of these restrictions and ensure that certificated staff understands that they have a responsibility to vet any adults they allow to volunteer in or with their classes.

To be assured that the school district is on sound legal ground and to avoid unreasonable liability risks, the following steps are recommended:

1. Verify that the parent, guardian, or caregiver at the address indicated is in fact on the California Attorney General's Megan List registry as a convicted sex offender. Do not rely upon unconfirmed reports from community members or staff.
2. If the registered sex offender is a caregiver, verify the legal sufficiency of the format and completeness of the caregiver affidavit on file for the subject student. Investigate if there is any question that the student actually resides with the caregiver.
3. If numbers 1 and 2, above, are satisfied, write the registered sex offender and

designate a staff member to contact should the registered sex offender want to come to the school site for any reason. The registered sex offender should be notified that s/he may not come to school without advance arrangement and the reason for coming to the school must be directly related to the subject student. The designated staff member should meet the registered sex offender and escort her/him to and from where s/he needs to be while at school.

4. Under no circumstances should the registered sex offender be allowed to volunteer or participate in any school activity such as providing classroom assistance to certificated staff or helping to chaperone a field trip.

CHAPTER 2: DISCIPLINARY INVESTIGATIONS

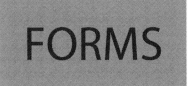

FORMS

WITNESS STATEMENT FORM

School Name _____ Date: _____ Student #:_____

SWORN DECLARATION OF _____
Print name of witness

I, _____ , declare the following:

_____

_____

_____

_____

_____

_____

_____

_____

_____

_____

_____

_____

_____

_____

_____

_____

_____

_____

_____

_____

_____

_____

_____

_____

_____

_____

_____

_____

I have read this declaration and do declare under penalty of perjury and the laws of the State of California that it is true and correct to the best of my knowledge.

Dated: _____
Signature

Student Searches Checklist 2.2

INSERT DISTRICT LETTERHEAD AND/OR LOGO

STUDENT SEARCHES CHECKLIST

This checklist is to be used in conjunction with investigation of incidents warranting the need for student searches.

Name of Administrator completing the report: _____

Student's name: _____ _____ DOB_____ Gender_____

School: _____Grade_____

What facts caused you to have a reasonable suspicion that search of the student or student's belongings, will provide evidence that the student has violated or is violating school rules or the law?

_____

_____

_____

Information from a reliable source:

By whom: _____

Date/Time: _____

Place: _____

What was observed?_____

Suspicious behavior?

Explain_____

Date and time conducted? _____

Location of search: _____

Person(s) present during search: _____

Reason given to the student for the search? _____

Was the student's consent requested? _____Given:_____

What were you searching for? _____

What exactly was searched? _____

Who conducted the search? _____

Title:_____Gender:_____

What did the search yield? _____

What was seized? _____

Was the law enforcement involved? _____If so, name of Officer:_____

Was anything released to law enforcement? _____

Were parent/guardian notified of the search, including the reasons and scope? _____

If so, name of parent: _____

Time notified: _____

Evidence Envelope Coversheet **2.3**

INSERT DISTRICT LETTERHEAD AND/OR LOGO

EVIDENCE ENVELOPE

Student Last Name: _____

Student First Name: _____

DOB: _____ Grade: _____ School: _____

Date of Search: _____

Time of Search: _____

Location of Search: _____

Contents of Envelope: _____

_____

Describe where prohibited items were found (exact location, i.e., left front pocket of shirt):

_____

_____

List Name(s) and Title of Witness(es) to the Search:

_____

_____   _____

Administrators Name: _____ Title: _____

Administrator's Signature: _____ Date: _____

Photocopy evidence for expulsion packet
SEAL THIS ENVELOPE AND SECURE IN A LOCKED LOCATION

OPEN AND PRESENT EVIDENCE AT TIME OF EXPULSION HEARING

Letter to Parent re: Questioning Student　2.4

[LETTERHEAD]

[ADDRESSEE]

Dear　:

This letter is in response to your letter/phone call indicating that the school administration does not have your permission or consent to question your child without your prior approval.

While the District strives to keep parents involved and informed, it is sometimes necessary and appropriate for school officials and law enforcement officers to speak to students without first notifying their parents. The district does not and is not required to obtain parental permission prior to speaking to students regarding school or District issues during school time.

Administrators have the responsibility to gather information necessary to maintain safety, smooth operation, and order to keep the focus on the education mission of the schools. Administrators frequently interview many students for a number of purposes including to ascertain whether disciplinary measures should be taken. Many of these students are tangentially involved or are merely witnesses who do not face disciplinary consequences.

Inherent in the District's obligation to operate schools and supervise students, as well as its legal obligations to respond to and remedy allegations against students or staff, is the ability to speak to students as part of an investigation. This authority has been recognized by the California Supreme Court. In In re Randy G. (2001) 26 Cal.4th. 556, the Supreme Court held that "special needs" exist in the public school context in light of the high governmental interest in education and the need to maintain order in schools, and in light of the minimal intrusion on a minor student who is questioned.

Even if a student is found to have violated the rules, there is no requirement for prior parental notification. The District strictly follows discipline procedures specified in the Education Code. Should interviews uncover a violation of the rules and suspension is warranted, this may follow only under procedures in Education Code section 48911, which calls for advising a student of the charges and evidence and soliciting the student's version of the facts but does not call for notifying parents in advance.

Accordingly, we cannot guarantee your child will never be questioned or spoken to by a school official; as such contact is well within the legal authority of those officials, and we will not be providing prior notice to you in the event we need to question your student. As a parent, you will be informed if a situation arises that requires your consent or participation.

The District does not have the authority to prevent a law enforcement officer from questioning or speaking to a student in the course of the law enforcement officer's duties. If you are concerned about contacts between your child and law enforcement officers, we suggest you address your concerns to the local law enforcement agency.

Sincerely,

Police Questioning and Release Form | 2.5

[NAME] UNIFIED SCHOOL DISTRICT

School: _____

LAW ENFORCEMENT STUDENT QUESTIONING AND RELEASE FORM

Date:	
Student Name:	
Law Enforcement Officer Name:	
▪ Agency	
▪ Badge/Identification No.	
▪ Basis of Authority	

Reason for Questioning:

Arrival Time		Time of Questioning		Time of Departure	

Did student ask for parent/guardian or other adult to be present?	Yes		No	
Did the principal/designee ask officer for permission to contact the parent/guardian prior to the student being questioned?	Yes		No	
▪ Did officer grant permission?	Yes		No	

If permission granted, Name of parent/guardian contacted:	
▪ By whom:	
▪ Time:	
▪ If no answer, what follow up was done?	
▪ What did the parent tell the principal/designee?	

Did the principal/designee ask to remain in room during questioning?	Yes		No	
▪ Did officer grant permission?	Yes		No	
▪ If not, what was the reason given?				

Did the officer take the student into custody?
▪ What time?
▪ Was the parent notified?
▪ If so, provide name of parent notified.
▪ If parent not notified, why not?

_____   _____
Principal/Designee Signature   Date

CHAPTER 3

Expulsion Recommendations

TOOLS FOR THE TRADE

The CA Ed. Code is structured such that it presents the basic disciplinary code of conduct first in section 48900. CA Ed. Code Section 48915 then details more severe instances of conduct listed in 48900 that, if violated, create an increased health or safety hazard for a school such that an expulsion recommendation may be appropriate. There are three types of expulsion recommendations: mandatory, discretionary, and stipulated. (See 3.1 – Sample General Education Expulsion Process Flow Chart at the end of this chapter)

As a practical matter, a recommendation for expulsion should only be made when the law requires it, pursuant to CA Ed. Code 48915(c) – Mandatory Expulsion Recommendations, or when the conduct is so severe that maintaining the student on campus safely is impractical.

School administrators should consider creating a plan for implementing "other means of correction," in lieu of recommending a student for expulsion, when the offense does not require an expulsion recommendation. (See 3.2 – Sample Principal's Report in Lieu of Recommendation for Expulsion Form at the end of this chapter)

Principal's Recommendation For Expulsion

If an expulsion recommendation is required or appropriate under the circumstances, the Principal needs to draft a Principal's Recommendation For Expulsion. (See 3.3 - Sample Principal's Recommendation For Expulsion Form at the end of this Chapter) The Principal's Recommendation should include the following components:

1. The name of the student being recommended for expulsion.

2.   List the CA Ed. Code sections that the student is being charged with.

3.   A summary of the incident. *NOTE – Do not just restate what is written in witness statements. It is appropriate to utilize information from your investigation, including witness statements, but the Principal's recommendation should be an unbiased summary of the facts supporting the expulsion recommendation.

4.   A summary of the facts that support the secondary findings, if applicable.

5.   A summary of the student's relevant disciplinary history.

6.   A summary of the interventions and "other means of correction" that have been tried with the student.

7.   Addition/Optional information about the student's academic performance and attendance.

Expulsion – Due Process

Once a student has been recommended for expulsion, the student's right to due process is again triggered. When a student was only facing a one to five day suspension, her/his due process consisted of an informal conference with the administrator as described in Chapter 1. However, because the expulsion recommendation proposes to take away a significant right of the student, to attend district schools for up to one calendar year, the amount of process that is due to the student increases significantly.

Extension of Suspension

First, the school administrator has the right to extend a student's suspension, beyond the initial five days, pending the expulsion decision by the district's governing board. (CA Ed. Code 48911(g)) This means that a student may be suspended from school for thirty (30) school days or longer, until the governing board makes a decision about the expulsion recommendation. (CA Ed. Code 48918(a)(1)) However, prior to extending a student's suspension pending expulsion, the school administrator <u>must invite the parent/guardian and the student</u> to a meeting to discuss the expulsion recommendation. If this meeting does not occur prior to the expiration of the five day suspension for the same conduct, the student has the right to return to school on day six and remain until the extension of suspension conference is held. Before the administrator can extend a student's suspension, s/he **must** determine that allowing the student to remain at school during the pendency of the expulsion process would <u>cause a danger to persons or property or a threat of disrupting the instructional process</u>. (CA Ed. Code 48911(g)) (See 3.4 – Sample Extension of Suspension

Meeting Checklist Form at the end of this chapter)

If the determination is made to extend a student's suspension pending the outcome of the expulsion process, the student may not attend her/his school, or any school events or activities on any campus within the district. During the period of suspension, the law requires, upon request of the parent, guardian, or other person holding educational rights for the student, that the teacher provide the student with homework s/he would have been assigned for suspensions beyond two days. (CA Ed. Code 48913.5 and 47606.2) The school must provide the parent/guardian with written notice of its decision to extend the student's suspension pending expulsion. (See 3.5 – Sample Letter Extending the Suspension Pending Expulsion Form; See also, 3.6 - Sample Letter Extending Suspension Pending Expulsion - IDEA/Section 504 at the end of this chapter)

If the student is a foster child, her/his attorney and an appropriate representative of the county child welfare agency must be invited to participate in the extension of suspension meeting.

Expulsion Recommendation

Mandatory Expulsion Recommendations – Education Code 48915(c)

There are only five (5) offenses that require a mandatory recommendation for expulsion. If a student engages in one of the five offenses, the student must be suspended and recommended for expulsion. If the governing board finds that there is "substantial evidence" establishing that the student engaged in the conduct, the governing board must expel her/him. The five offenses include:

1. Verified possession of a firearm;

    It is important to know what distinguishes a "firearm" from an "imitation firearm," as possession of an imitation firearm does not require a mandatory recommendation for expulsion.

    California Penal Code 165210 defines "firearm" as "a device, designed to be used as a weapon, from which is expelled through a barrel, a projectile by the force of an explosion or other form of combustion." Therefore, the determining characteristic is whether the weapon uses an explosion or combustion to propel the projectile. If "yes," it is a firearm, requiring a mandatory recommendation for expulsion. If "no," the weapon is an imitation firearm, which does not require a mandatory recommendation for expulsion and would require "secondary findings" to support an expulsion recommendation. (See Discretionary Recommendations For Expulsions for a description of "secondary findings")

2. Brandishing a knife at another person;

    Education Code 48915(g), defines a knife as "… any dirk, dagger, or other weapon with a fixed, sharpened blade fitted primarily for stabbing, a weapon with a blade fitted primarily for stabbing, a weapon with a blade longer than 3 1/2 inches, a folding knife with a blade that locks into place, or a razor with an unguarded blade."

    Be aware that California Penal Code 626.10 definition of knife includes a knife with a blade longer than 2½ inches. Therefore, law enforcement may consider a weapon a knife based on Penal Code, when the weapon, in fact, does not meet the California Education Code definition of a knife.

    If a school is pursuing an expulsion recommendation based on possession or brandishing a knife, it is imperative that there is evidence that the weapon used meets the 48915(g) definition of a knife. Administrators must be clear how and if the weapon meets the definition of a knife.

    Example:

    Student brandishes what the school believes to be a knife. The school pursues a mandatory recommendation for expulsion based on brandishing a knife but the administrator has not specified what characteristics make the weapon a knife. The administrator enters a photo of the knife into evidence during the expulsion hearing. When the characteristics of the knife are examined, it is determined that it does not meet the definition of a knife and the student cannot be expelled for brandishing a knife.

    Even though the weapon is called a knife, the school administrator must examine it and determine what characteristics make it a knife, such as the length of the blade or the fact that the blade locks into place. If the weapon does not meet the definition of a knife, the student can still be expelled, however the expulsion recommendation would have to be based on possession of a dangerous object and on the fact that "due to the nature of the act," brandishing the knife at another student, the student's presence on campus is a danger to the student or others. (CA Ed. Code 48915(a)(1)(B)) These additional charges must have been charged at the same time as the brandishing charge for the case to go forward.

3. Selling a controlled substance;

    Selling any amount of a controlled substance requires a mandatory recommendation for expulsion.

    Examples:

    A student sells hits off his marijuana pipe for $1 per hit. Even though the amount is relatively minuscule, the conduct would require a mandatory recommendation for expulsion.

    A student has a prescription for Adderall. The student sells her Adderall to another student for $5 per pill. The fact that the student has a legal prescription for the controlled substance does not protect her from an expulsion recommendation for selling a controlled substance.

4. Sexual assault or sexual battery;

    CA Ed. Code Sections 48900(n) and 48915(d) designate conduct that amounts to a sexual battery or sexual assault as a mandatory recommendation for expulsion. However, rather than define the terms, the CA Ed. Code references relevant California Penal Code Sections for definitions of the conduct.

    If a student is facing an expulsion recommendation based on sexual battery or sexual assault, the administrator must identify the relevant Penal Code sections the conduct violates and be clear what the elements are of the offense that the school must prove to support a decision to expel the student.

    Sexual Battery

    There are two types of sexual battery that commonly occur on school campuses, one is a misdemeanor and one is a felony. This distinction is not relevant, as both fall under CA Ed. Code 48900(n) and are subject to a mandatory recommendation for expulsion. However, being aware of the distinction between the two types of sexual battery helps to understand the evidence necessary to prove the two offenses.

Misdemeanor Sexual Battery – California Penal Code 243.4(e)(1)

When looking at the definition of any offense, it is useful to think about the definition in terms of elements that must be proved to support an expulsion order. A misdemeanor sexual battery has three elements: 1) touching an intimate part of another person, 2) if the touching is against the will of the person touched, and 3) is for the specific purpose of sexual arousal, sexual gratification, or sexual abuse.

Intimate Part

An "intimate part" is defined by Penal Code to be "the sexual organ, anus, groin, or buttocks of any person, and the breast of a female." So, there must be evidence that an intimate part was touched.

Against The Will of The Person Touched

This element is self-explanatory. The victim did not consent to the touching.

Specific Purpose - Sexual arousal, Sexual gratification, or Sexual abuse

The general standard to determine intent for sexual battery crimes is to look to "[A] defendant's statement of his intent and by the circumstances surrounding the commission of the act.. . . In objectively assessing a defendant's state of mind during an encounter with a victim, the trier of fact may draw inferences from his conduct, including any words the defendant has spoken. . ."*People v. Craig* (1994) 25 Cal.App.4th 1593, 1597.

Sexual Arousal or Gratification

To prove "arousal" and "gratification" in reported California cases on sexual battery, the substantial evidence must support a finding that the act was committed for the purposes of sexual pleasure.

Facts that could support a finding of sexual arousal or gratification of the perpetrator include a male with an erection, exposing himself, or masturbating or attempting sexual arousal of the victim by touching the victim's intimate places or forcing the victim to touch the perpetrator in intimate places. *People v. Dixon*, 75 Cal.App.4th. 935.

Sexual Abuse

"Sexual abuse" needs to be shown by a battery on another person's "intimate part" done either to harm or humiliate that person. Therefore, it is an "either /or" element of the offense. Sexual abuse cases satisfy this element with facts showing intent to hurt or humiliate, which appear to arise more often with school-age students.

A juvenile court conviction of a 14-year-old minor male defendant who pinched the breast of a 16-year-old female victim was upheld with findings that the assault caused her emotional distress and resulted in a significant bruise. *In re Shannon T.*, 50 Cal.Rptr.3d at 565, 567. The court found that the defendant inflicted a sexual battery under § 243.4(e) with the specific purpose of sexual abuse because he first told her, "Get off the phone. You're my ho," and when the victim responded, "Whatever," and walked away, the defendant pursued her, slapped her face, grabbed her arm, and pinched her breast. Id. at 566–67.

Similarly, the court found the minor defendant committed sexual battery when he poked the center of the victim's buttocks, penetrating about an inch. Because the defendant laughed with his companions as he touched the victim and used derogatory language, the court found the evidence demonstrated the defendant's purpose was sexual abuse. *In re A.B.*, 2011 WL 193402, at *1.

Lastly, a middle school student, who slapped his classmate-victim "with an open hand in her crotch area" was guilty of misdemeanor sexual abuse under Penal Code section 243.4(e)(1). The juvenile offender blamed his friends for telling him to do it. The record showed that the victim was "mad, embarrassed, and 'kind of scared" and chased the defendant, who "ran away laughing." These facts led the court to conclude that the defendant "understood that his action would embarrass and humiliate" the victim. *In re Carlos C.*, 2012 WL 925029 (Cal.Ct.App.2012)

These are examples of the factual evidence the school would need to prove to establish that a student's intent in engaging in the conduct was sexual arousal, sexual gratification or sexual abuse.

Felony Sexual Battery – California Penal Code 243.4(a)

A felony sexual battery has four elements, 1) Touching an intimate part of another person, 2) while that person is unlawfully restrained by the accused or an accomplice, and, 3) if the touching is against the will of the person touched and, 4) is for the purpose of sexual arousal, sexual gratification, or sexual abuse.

As compared to a misdemeanor sexual battery, a felony sexual battery requires that the victim be unlawfully restrained and there is no requirement to establish "specific intent," only "intent."

To prove a felony sexual battery, there must be evidence of all four elements.

Unlawfully Restrained

The person must be "unlawfully restrained" during the touching. The general rule is that a person is "unlawfully restrained when his or her liberty is being controlled by words, acts or authority *of the perpetrator* aimed at depriving the person's liberty." *People v. Pahl*, (1991) 226 Cal.App.3d 1651,1661. Effectively blocking or impeding any exit the victim could take could also be considered "unlawful restraint."

See Misdemeanor Sexual Battery (above) for a more detailed analysis of the other three elements of a felony sexual battery. Although the analysis in the sexual arousal, gratification or abuse section is specifically addressing "specific intent," which is an element of a misdemeanor sexual battery, evidence that supports a finding of "specific intent" would also support a finding of "intent" in a felony battery case.

Sexual Assault

If a student allegedly commits or attempts to commit a sexual assault, s/he is subject to a mandatory recommendation for expulsion. It is important for administrators to understand that there are six (6) different offenses that are considered sexual assaults pursuant to CA Ed. Code and you must be clear which offense is being alleged to have been violated. Below are the six offenses that are sexual assaults, however, the definitions are not complete and you MUST refer to the relevant Penal Code ("PC") sections for a comprehensive definition.

PC 261. Rape; "Duress;" "Menace"

(a) Rape is an act of sexual intercourse accomplished with a person not the spouse of the perpetrator, under any of the following circumstances: (See PC for circumstances.)

PC 266c. Inducing consent to sexual act by fraud or fear

Every person who induces any other person to engage in sexual intercourse, sexual penetration, oral copulation, or sodomy when his or her consent is procured by false or fraudulent representation or pretense that is made with the intent to create fear, and which does induce fear, and that would cause a reasonable person in like circumstances to act contrary to the person's free will, and does cause the victim to so act. (See PC for comprehensive definition.)

PC 286. Sodomy

(a) Sodomy is sexual conduct consisting of contact between the penis of one person and the anus of another person. Any sexual penetration, however slight, is sufficient to complete the crime of sodomy. (See PC for comprehensive definition.)

PC 287. Oral copulation

(a) Oral copulation is the act of copulating the mouth of one person with the sexual organ or anus of another person. (See PC for comprehensive definition.)

PC 288. Lewd or lascivious acts involving children

(a) Except as provided in subdivision (i), any person who willfully and lewdly commits any lewd or lascivious act, including any of the acts constituting other crimes provided for in Part 1, upon or with the body, or any part or member thereof, of a child who is under the age of 14 years, with the intent of arousing, appealing to, or gratifying the lust, passions, or sexual desires of that person or the child. (See PC for comprehensive definition.)

PC 289. Penetration by foreign object

(a) (1) (A) Any person who commits an act of sexual penetration when the act is accomplished against the victim's will by means of force, violence, duress, menace, or fear of immediate and unlawful bodily injury on the victim or another person. (See PC for comprehensive definition.)

5.   Possession of an explosive.

Under CA Ed. Code Section 48915, subdivision (h), "the term 'explosive' means 'destructive device' as described in Section 921 of Title 18 of the United States Code." Under this statute, a "destructive device" means "(A) any explosive, incendiary, or poison gas; bomb; grenade; rocket having a propellant charge of more than four ounces; missile having an explosive or incendiary charge of more than one-quarter ounce; mine, or device similar to any of the devices described in the preceding clauses." 18 U.S.C. § 921(a)(4)(A).

Common denominators to the above examples of "destructive devices" are that they are weapons that are actually capable of harm by way of explosion or flammability, with the possible exception of "poison gas." The common definition of "explode" involves bursting violently, expanding with force, and projecting outwards.

Example

A student put a "chemical mixture" in a plastic bottle, which was thrown, kicked, or rolled into a group of students at a crowded assembly. The contents exploded in some fashion, with the cap remaining on the bottle. No one was injured. There were no flames, although some reported smoke. This may have been mist. The school cannot prove it was smoke. The school must determine whether the object constitutes an explosive device, for purposes of determining whether a recommendation of expulsion is mandatory under CA Ed. Code 48915(c).

An explosive device is by definition a destructive weapon, and it appears the school would not have any evidence that the "chemical mixture" in the bottle was destructive or a weapon. Therefore, with the facts given, there does not appear to be sufficient evidence to prove the bottle was an explosive device. If the District could prove that the substance in the bottle was flammable or poisonous, it would be an explosive device. If the weapon does not meet the definition of an explosive, the student can still be expelled. However, the expulsion recommendation would have to be based on possession of a dangerous object and the fact that "due to the nature of the act," throwing a devise that exploded in the middle of a crowded assembly, the student's presence on campus is a danger to the student or others. (CA Ed. Code 48915(a)(1)(B))

These are the only offenses that require that a student to be recommended for expulsion.

Also note that the conduct listed in CA Ed. Code 48915(c) must occur **at school or at a school activity off school grounds** in order for the district to have jurisdiction to recommend an expulsion based on this section. This is a more limited jurisdiction than what applies to CA Ed. Code 48900 violations.

Lastly, the school administrator only needs to prove that a student engaged in the conduct charged in order to support a mandatory expulsion recommendation. (See Appendix for the 2020 version of the CA Ed Code 48915(c) offenses.)

Discretionary Expulsion Recommendations - Education Code 48915(a)

School administrators have discretion to suspend or expel for all conduct violations, except the five listed in CA Ed. Code 48915(c), and discussed above. In light of the data clearly establishing the overuse of exclusionary discipline for all students and, particularly the disproportionate impact of exclusionary discipline on students of color and other marginalized groups, it is important that administrators exercise their significant discretion and understand that just because they can suspend or expel does not mean that they should.

CA Ed. Code 48915(a) lists the following conduct violations that may lead to a recommendation for expulsion:

> (1)(A) Causing serious physical injury to another person not in self-defense;
>
> (1)(B) Possession of a knife or other dangerous object;
>
> (1)(C) Possession of a controlled substance (with exceptions);
>
> (1)(D) Robbery or extortion; and
>
> (1)(E) Assault or battery on a school employee.

However, if the principal or designee determines that expulsion should not be recommended under the circumstances or that an alternative means of correction would address the conduct, a recommendation for expulsion should not be made for these conduct violations.

The idea that students who engage in the above listed behaviors would not be recommended for expulsion represents a shift from the practice of strictly enforcing zero tolerance policies. This shift has been embraced and supported by the state legislature in the form of legal amendments clarifying what constitutes "other means of correction," limitations added to CA Ed. Code 48900(k) removals, and clarification of conduct that does and does not violate CA Ed. Code 48915 offenses.

Also note that the conduct listed in CA Ed. Code 48915(a) must occur **at school or at a school activity off school grounds** in order for the district to have jurisdiction to recommend an expulsion based on this section. This is a more limited jurisdiction than what applies to CA Ed.

Code 48900 violations.

A student may also be subjected to a discretionary recommendation for expulsion for any CA Ed. Code 48900 offense, except 48900(t) – Aiding and abetting, if the school administrator determines that secondary findings exist. However, all CA Ed. Code 48900 expulsion recommendations are subject to the broader jurisdictional statement in CA Ed. Code 48900(s).

Secondary Findings Required To Support Discretionary Expulsion Recommendations

If a student is facing a discretionary expulsion recommendation, in addition to proving that the student engaged in the underlying offense, the administrator must also prove one or both of the following:

> 1) "Other means of correction" are not feasible or have repeatedly failed to bring about proper conduct; or
>
> 2) "Due to the nature of the violation," the presence of the student causes a continuing danger to the physical safety of the pupil or others. (CA Ed Code 48915(b)(1) & (2); 48915(e)(1) & (2))

Examples of the type of evidence that would prove "other means of correction," can be found at CA Ed. Code 48900.5. In order to prove "due to the nature of the violation," the administrator would need to introduce evidence that looked specifically at the conduct for which the student is facing the expulsion recommendation and demonstrate how engaging in the conduct created a danger for the student or others.

For example, a student gets into a fight with another student and beats the student so badly that the student must be hospitalized for serious injuries. If the administrator also produced evidence that teachers attempted to deescalate the student and he ignored their directives and, in fact, began physically attacking the teachers, this evidence could support a finding that due to the nature of the act, the student's presence is a danger.

Evidence of both the underlying CA Ed. Code violation and the relevant secondary finding is required to support a discretionary recommendation for expulsion. (See Appendix for the 2020 version of the CA Ed Code 48915(a) offenses.)

Stipulated Expulsion Recommendations

A stipulated expulsion is basically a process that allows a student to admit guilt and waive her/his right to an expulsion hearing. This is a useful process when a student is not contesting the facts of the conduct violation and has admitted to engaging in the conduct. The value of a stipulated expulsion is that it allows for the expulsion process to be expedited, thus allowing a student to be placed in the alternative setting sooner and minimizing the academic impact of the missed instruction. **The student must sign the stipulated agreement. This is not a right the parent can waive on the student's behalf.** (See 3.9 – Sample Stipulation and Waiver of Expulsion Hearing Form at the end of this chapter)

There is no statutory authority for stipulated expulsions. The validity of the process was upheld in Choplin v. Conejo Valley Unified School District, 903 F.Supp. 1377 (C.D. CA 1995). The case held that a person may waive a constitutional right if it can be established by clear and convincing evidence that the waiver is voluntary, knowing and intelligent and, specifically, that parents may waive the right to a pre-expulsion hearing and consent to discipline, once the student has admitted guilt.

If your district uses the stipulated expulsion process, it is important that the stipulation that is signed clearly delineates the conduct violations the student is admitting to, including the secondary findings, and the rights that the student is waiving by signing the stipulation. The stipulation should be signed by both the parent/guardian and the student.

Administrators in most school districts are responsible to prepare for and present the expulsion case. The process has many procedural requirements that implicate legal concepts, such as due process, rules of evidence, and burden of proof. It is important that school administrators understand how to navigate the expulsion process to ensure that the law is followed and that the rights of students are protected.

Creating The Expulsion Packet

Once the investigation has been completed and it has been determined that an expulsion recommendation is appropriate, the next step for the administrator is to gather all the evidence and create the expulsion packet. Below is a list of the items that should be included in an expulsion packet. (See 3.10 – See Sample Expulsion Packet Checklist Form at the end of this chapter)

- Notice of Suspension
- Principal's Recommendation for Expulsion

- Notice of Meeting to Consider Extension of Suspension

- Notice of Extension of Suspension

- Notice of Hearing Date and Charge Letter (notice)

- Incident reports/witness statements (redacted)

- Physical evidence (weapon, drugs, photos, etc.)

- Interventions and discipline tracker

- Teacher reports/ transcripts/attendance

- Any other relevant documents (e.g. continuance request, police report, "fear" declaration, etc.)

As the administrator assembles the expulsion packet, there are a few items to pay close attention to. First, ensure that the charges listed in the Notice of Hearing are accurate. The Notice of Hearing is the official list of Education Code violations and the district may only proceed at the expulsion hearing on the charges listed in the Notice of Hearing. If the Notice of Hearing lists multiple Code section violations, the administrator should understand the elements that must be proved for each code violation and be prepared to introduce evidence proving each charge.

Second, if witness statements are going to be introduced at the hearing, make sure the names of all students and minors are redacted.

Protocol for Redacting Student Records

Student Records are records maintained by the District which are identifiable to a specific pupil in any form, whether on paper, electronic, audio, video, photographic, or in any other medium. These records are strictly confidential under state and federal law and may be disclosed only under specific circumstances. Records which are disclosable in reference to one student may also include data identifiable to another student or students. For example, if a parent receives a copy of a student record relating to that parent's child, references to all other students in the record must be covered up or "redacted" so that the other students' names cannot be seen.

Apply the following guidelines when redacting student records:

1.   Make a copy, either electronic or otherwise, of each record to be disclosed and do the

following:

a. Review the document to find the names of all students other than the one whose parent will be receiving a copy. On a separate document, make a key for the names of the other students identified in the document and create an anonymous identifier for each, e.g., "Student #1," "Student #2," etc.

b. If you can save the version of the document to be redacted in Word format or as an editable PDF, search for each of the other student's names. Substitute the appropriate anonymous identifier for each of the other students' names in the text. (i.e. Every where Rosa Parks' name shows up, replace it with "Student 1.") If an electronic form of the redacted record will be disclosed, save the final version again and take other steps to ensure metadata revealing the original version is not viewable.

c. If the document cannot be electronically edited, go through and mark out the names of each other student with correction tape or white out, and make a copy of the redacted document. <u>On the copy, write in the anonymous identifier for each name.</u> Sometimes, the names of the other students can be seen or can be uncovered with a hand-redacted document; using the copy should help strengthen the redaction.

d. Proof read each document to be sure that all of the other students' names are redacted. Often, names of other students are missed in the redaction process, so a double check is well worth the effort.

e. Create a complete original set of the unredacted documents and a complete set of the redacted documents in electronic form or hard copies. Label the sets "Unredacted" and "Redacted."

f. When disclosing the records to the parent, be certain the redacted set is produced.

2.   All questions about release of Student Records should be directed to the Department of Student Services at the District Office.

Third, make sure any photos of physical evidence depict what you intend to show. For instance, if a picture of a knife is being introduced to establish that the weapon meets the definition of a knife based on the length of the blade, the photo should have a ruler next to the blade establishing that the blade is longer than 3 ½ inches. Additionally, make sure that any equipment needed for demonstrative evidence, such as audio or video equipment is available and in working condition for the expulsion hearing.

Lastly, if the case has been continued beyond the statutory timelines for any reason, the expulsion packet must include documentation supporting the continuance.

Once you have all the documentary evidence you intend to introduce as part of the expulsion packet, you will need to prepare and organize the packet. While there is no one right way to organize the packet, the objective is to create an expulsion packet that is complete and easy to access. Below are some best practice tips for organizing the expulsion packet:

1. Start with the procedural documents and organize them in chronological order. (e.g., Notice of Suspension, Principal's Recommendation for Expulsion, Extension of Suspension, Notice of Hearing and Charges, Continuation Request, if applicable.) Each document should be a separate exhibit. If there are multiple/amended versions of a document, keep them together in the same exhibit, but in chronological order.

2. Redacted versions of the victim and witness statements should be next. Start with the victim's statement. If there is a handwritten and typed version of the statement, put the handwritten one first, then the typed version. Then add the accused statement, then any remaining witness statements, including "fear declarations." I tend to have the victim's and the accused's statement be separate exhibits and combine the remaining witness statements in a separate exhibit.

3. If there are any pictures of evidence or relevant business records (e.g., picture of a knife, medical records, police report), they would go next, each as its own exhibit.

4. Any relevant student records would be next, (e.g., discipline/intervention tracker, teacher observations, attendance, transcripts) each as a separate exhibit.

5. Copy of the relevant laws, particularly if they are laws other than CA Ed. Code. (i.e. Penal Codes)

Once you have the expulsion packet organized, insert a sheet in between each exhibit with the number of the respective exhibit (e.g., 1, 2, 3, etc). Then number each page of the expulsion packet in the lower right hand corner. You can number the packet continuously from beginning to end, or you can number each exhibit internally. Once the packet is numbered, create your Table of Contents. (See 3.11 – See Sample Expulsion Packet Table of Contents Form at the end of this chapter) This may seem tedious, but if you take the time to organize the expulsion packet in this way, you will find that the process of using and referring to the packet in the hearing is much more efficient and will save time during the hearing.

While the CA Ed. Code does not require that the expulsion packet be provided to the accused prior to the hearing, best practice is to provide the accused a copy of the expulsion packet as soon as it is available in order to give the student and their representative an opportunity to review the evidence to be presented and prepare a defense.

Burden of Proof

The burden of proof required to support an expulsion order is **"substantial evidence."** For an administrator presenting an expulsion case, this means that you must present evidence that "a reasonable mind could accept as adequate to support a conclusion" that the student engaged in the conduct charged.

Additionally, CA Ed. Code states that an expulsion order may not be based solely on "hearsay." **Hearsay**, in a school disciplinary case, is a statement made outside of the expulsion hearing, that is offered in the hearing, by someone other than the declarant, as evidence to prove the truth of the matter asserted. For example, all written witness statements are hearsay because they are statements written outside of the expulsion hearing, that are being offered in the hearing, by someone other than the person who wrote the statement, and they are being offered for their truth regarding the information described in the statement.

Hearsay may be introduced in an expulsion hearing. However, there must also be "direct evidence" to support an expulsion order. **Direct evidence** is evidence offered at the hearing by someone with firsthand knowledge of the incident. Therefore, in addition to written witness statements, there must be a "warm body" testifying at the hearing from firsthand knowledge of the incident, unless there is an admission to the conduct violation by the accused.

If the accused student admits to the charged conduct violation in a written statement, her/his **admission is not hearsay** and the written admission can be relied upon, as direct evidence, to support an expulsion order. The key is to make sure that the admission addresses the conduct violation directly. For instance, if the accused writes, "I did it," that has very little value in proving your case, as it is vague as to what the student is admitting to doing. If the student instead writes, "I sold weed to Tom at school on Monday," that admission could be relied upon to support the expulsion order for selling a controlled substance, even if no one physically testifies at the hearing. **The written admission is direct evidence.** Additionally, the **administrator's testimony at the hearing** that the accused admitted verbally to the same administrator that the student sold weed to Tom at school on Monday **would also be direct evidence.**

Sworn Declaration Process – Obtaining a "Fear Declaration"

Due to the CA Ed. Code's requirement that there be some "direct evidence" to support an expulsion recommendation, districts often encounter the situation where there is a witness to the conduct violation, the witness has written an incident statement (which is hearsay), yet the witness is unwilling to testify. If there is no other direct evidence, the administrator needs to figure out a way to get the witnesses testimony into the hearing as "direct evidence."

At this point, the administrator needs to determine why the witness is unwilling to testify. If it is because the witness does not want to be involved or does not want to "snitch," and the administrator needs the witness' testimony to support the expulsion recommendation, then the administrator would need to find a way to encourage the witness to participate in the process or the expulsion hearing cannot go forward.

However, if testifying at the hearing would cause an <u>unreasonable risk of psychological or physical harm</u> to the witness, the CA Ed. Code allows for the witness to testify via sworn declaration. This means that the witness' incident statement could be admitted into evidence as "direct evidence," an exception to the hearsay rule, and relied upon to support an expulsion order.

The administrator must document what the unreasonable risk of psychological or physical harm is. The documentation could be a written statement by the witness that the accused has a reputation for violence and has threatened to harm the witness in the past. The documentation could also be evidence that since the incident, the witness has suffered severe anxiety, which has manifested in the form of loss of appetite, insomnia, school anxiety, or lowered academic performance. This fear declaration should be separate from the witness' underlying incident statement documenting the conduct violation. (See 3.12 - Sample Fear Declaration at the end of this chapter)

The unreasonable risk of psychological or physical harm could also be established by having the parent of the witness testify at the hearing about how the incident has impacted the witness' psychological or physical health and how the situation would be exacerbated if the witness had to testify at the hearing. Regardless of how the administrator goes about establishing that an unreasonable risk of psychological or physical harm would result, the documentation of the fear declaration must be made part of the expulsion packet or hearing process and be considered during the hearing. (See Chapter 4 – Expulsion Hearings for an explanation of the process for introducing a fear declaration at the expulsion hearing)

CHAPTER **3:** EXPULSION RECOMMENDATIONS

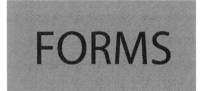

General Education Expulsion Flow Chart **3.1**

STUDENT EXPULSION PROCESS CHART

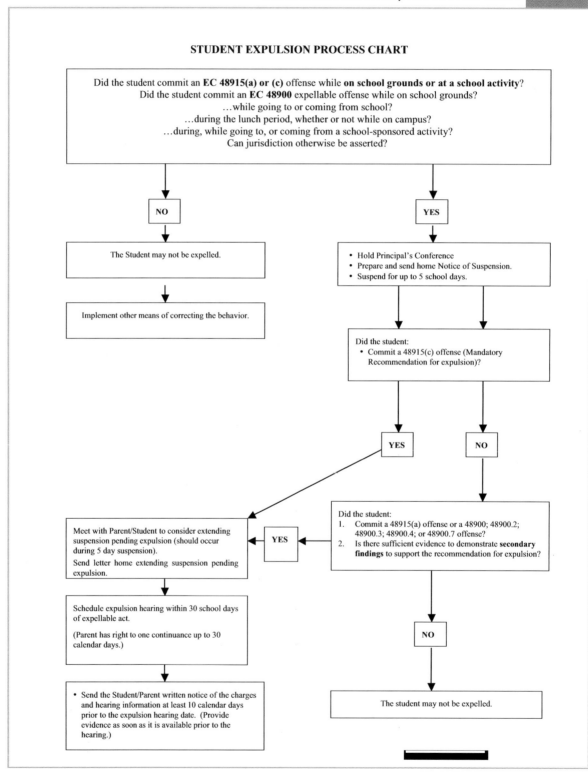

Did the student commit an **EC 48915(a) or (c)** offense while **on school grounds or at a school activity**?
Did the student commit an **EC 48900** expellable offense while on school grounds?
…while going to or coming from school?
…during the lunch period, whether or not while on campus?
…during, while going to, or coming from a school-sponsored activity?
Can jurisdiction otherwise be asserted?

NO

The Student may not be expelled.

Implement other means of correcting the behavior.

YES

- Hold Principal's Conference
- Prepare and send home Notice of Suspension.
- Suspend for up to 5 school days.

Did the student:
- Commit a 48915(c) offense (Mandatory Recommendation for expulsion)?

YES

NO

Did the student:
1. Commit a 48915(a) offense or a 48900; 48900.2; 48900.3; 48900.4; or 48900.7 offense?
2. Is there sufficient evidence to demonstrate **secondary findings** to support the recommendation for expulsion?

YES

Meet with Parent/Student to consider extending suspension pending expulsion (should occur during 5 day suspension).

Send letter home extending suspension pending expulsion.

Schedule expulsion hearing within 30 school days of expellable act.

(Parent has right to one continuance up to 30 calendar days.)

- Send the Student/Parent written notice of the charges and hearing information at least 10 calendar days prior to the expulsion hearing date. (Provide evidence as soon as it is available prior to the hearing.)

NO

The student may not be expelled.

Principal's Report in Lieu of Recommendation for Expulsion   3.2

INSERT DISTRICT LETTERHEAD AND/OR LOGO

Principal's Report in Lieu of Recommendation for Expulsion

(Per Education Code Section 48915)

Student Name: _____ DOB: _____ Ethnicity: _____

Special Ed: Yes_____ No _____   504: Yes _____ No _____

Grade: _____ School: _____ on _____

committed the following suspension/expulsion offense as set forth in Education Code 48915(a) (Conduct must have occurred at school or at school activity off campus):

Check at least one of the following:

(a)(1)(A)   Causing SERIOUS PHYSICAL INJURY to another person, except in self-defense.

(a)(1)(B)   Possession of any KNIFE or other DANGEROUS OBJECT of no reasonable use to the pupil.

(a)(1)(C)   Unlawful possession of any CONTROLLED SUBSTANCE except the following:

  (i)   The first offense for the possession of not more than one avoirdupois ounce of marijuana, other than concentrated cannabis.
  (ii) The possession of over-the-counter medication for use by the pupil for medical purposes or medication prescribed for the pupil by a physician.

(a)(1)(D)   ROBBERY OR EXTORSION.

(a)(1)E)   ASSAULT OR BATTERY on a school employee.

The student was suspended from school for committing the above named offense. The principal or the superintendent of school shall recommend the expulsion of a pupil for any of the following acts committed at school or at a school activity off school grounds, **unless the principal or superintendent determines that expulsion should not be recommended under the circumstances of that an alternative means of correction would address the conduct:**

OTHER MEANS OF CORRECTION

In lieu of recommending the above named student for expulsion, the following other means of correction plan was developed on _____.

     Date

Plan: (Specific) _____

       (Attach plan) _____

_____   _____

Name of Administrator   Signature   Date

Principal's Recommendation for Expulsion **3.3**

Principal's Recommendation for Expulsion
PRINCIPAL'S RECOMMENDATION
FOR EXPULSION

Student:
Grade:
Date of Birth:
School:

Principal's Recommendation:

That the Administrative Panel recommends expulsion of [Student] to the Board of Education of the [NAME] Unified School District.

Principal's recommendation is for violation of Education Code Section(s): **(List exact Code numbers and then write out below.)**

This recommendation is made on the following facts:
On [DATE], [STUDENT],
        List the essential facts of the case.

If there is a 48915 offense add this section:
This recommendation is also made pursuant to Education Code 48915(c)(1), which is a mandatory recommendation for expulsion.

At the end of the Principal's narrative you must add facts that support the determination that secondary findings exist:
1. Other means of correction are not feasible or have failed to brig about proper conduct:
    Add relevant facts

2. That due to the nature of the act, [STUDENT] presents a continuing danger to the physical safety of him/herself or others:
    Add relevant facts

Discipline History: **Highlight disciplinary history relevant to the offense charged**

Previous Interventions:
Add summary of interventions provided to change student behavior.

Academic Performance:
Add relevant student academic information (GPA, Grades, etc)

Attendance
Add attendance information

Submitted by:

_____   _____

Principal   Date

Extension of Suspension Meeting Checklist **3.4**

INSERT DISTRICT LETTERHEAD AND/OR LOGO

Extension of Suspension Meeting

Date: _____

Who attended the meeting?

Student: Yes _____ No _____

Name: Relationship:

_____   _____

_____   _____

_____   _____

Extension was done by phone: Date: _____

Name: Relationship:

_____   _____

No Show: _____

1. The extension was determined to be necessary because:

    _____ The pupil's presence at the school would cause a danger to persons or property.

    _____ The presence of the pupil would pose a threat of disrupting the instructional process.

2. _____ The suspension is extended to the date that the board renders its decision. (E.C. 48911 (g))
3. _____ The suspension was not extended.
4. _____ Special Education Students: The manifestation determination IEP has been or will be held within 10 school days of the decision to recommend expulsion.

_____   _____

Signature of Administrator   Date

[DISTRICT LETTERHEAD]

LETTER EXTENDING SUSPENSION
PENDING EXPULSION

[Date]

[Address]

Re: [Student's Name]
        [Student's Birth Date]

Dear _____:

     The principal of [School Name] has recommended the expulsion of your [son/daughter/grandson/granddaughter], [Student's Name]. The Education Code sections on student suspension and expulsion were explained to you and [Student] during a meeting held in [Administrator's Name] office on [Date]. The expulsion process follows the law as outlined by the Education Code.

     The incident of [Date], described in the attached Notice, demonstrates a clear breach of discipline and defiance of school rules and regulations by [Student's Name]. Therefore, I am extending the suspension until a decision on expulsion is reached by the Board of Education.

     I have determined that [Student's] presence at school would [select relevant basis: cause a danger to persons or property and/or cause disruption of the instructional process]; therefore, [Student] is to remain away from school at all times during this suspension period.   Arrangements for obtaining classwork to be completed at home may be made with [Student's] counselor or school administrator. Supervision of the pupil during the suspension is the responsibility of the parent or guardian.

     It is important that you and [Student] meet with [Administrator] as soon as possible to discuss the Statement of Charges and the hearing process. Please call [Enter phone number] to make an appointment.

              Sincerely,

              [Signature]
              [Title]

cc:

Letter Extending Suspension - IDEA/Section 504   **3.6**

[Date]

[Address]

Re: [Student's Name]
       [Student's Birth Date]

Dear _____:

     The principal of [School Name] has recommended the expulsion of your [son/daughter/grandson/granddaughter], [Student's Name]. [Student] is a student with a disability pursuant to the IDEA or Section 504. Therefore, before expulsion proceedings can be considered, [Student] is entitled to have an IEP or Section 504 team meeting within ten (10) school days of the date the expulsion was recommended to determine whether there is a relationship between the reported misconduct and [Student's] disability.

     The Education Code sections on student suspension and expulsion were explained to you and [Student] during a meeting held in [Administrator's Name] office on [Date]. The expulsion process follows the law as outlined by the Education Code.

     The incident of [Date] demonstrates a clear breach of discipline and defiance of school rules and regulations by [Student's Name]. Therefore, I am extending the suspension pending expulsion and until the IEP or Section 504 team has determined whether there is a relationship between the misconduct and [Student's] disability. If the IEP or Section 504 team determines that there is not a relationship between the conduct and [Student's] disability, the suspension will continue until a decision on expulsion is reached by the Board of Education.

     I have determined that [Student's] presence at school would [Select relevant basis: cause a danger to persons or property and/or cause disruption of the instructional process]; therefore, [Student] is to remain away from school at all times during this suspension period. Beginning on the eleventh day of removal in a school year, [Student's] IEP will be implemented to the extent necessary to enable [him/her] to appropriately progress toward achieving the goals set out in [Student's] IEP, as determined by the IEP team. [The provision of educational services is not required for Section 504 students]

                  Sincerely,

                  [Signature]
                  [Title]

Letter Rescinding Expulsion Recommendation **3.7**

[Date]

[Address]

Re: [Student's Name]
        [Student's Birth Date]

Dear _____ :

This letter is to inform you that the [insert name of district] Unified School District has reconsidered its decision to recommend [insert student name] for expulsion. Therefore, all further disciplinary action will be terminated and [Student] will be allowed to return to his/her school of attendance. However, prior to returning to school, you and your child must meet with me and the site administrator to discuss the terms of his/her return to school.

The meeting has been scheduled for [date] at [time] at [location of meeting]. If you are unavailable during at the proposed date and time, please call me at [insert phone number] to schedule a mutually agreeable meeting time.

.

Sincerely,

[Signature]
[Title]

Letter Rescinding Expulsion Recommendation - IDEA/Section 504　3.8

[Date]

[Address]

Re:　[Student's Name]
　　　[Student's Birth Date]

Dear _____:

　　　The IEP or Section 504 team met on [Date] and determined that there was a relationship between the reported misconduct and [Student's] disability. Therefore, all disciplinary action will be terminated and [Student] will be returned to his/her previous placement.

.

　　　　　　　　　　　　　　Sincerely,

　　　　　　　　　　　　　　[Signature]
　　　　　　　　　　　　　　[Title]

**Stipulation and Request for Waiver of Expulsion Hearing
with Recommendation for Expulsion**

To: ********, Superintendent
        ********** Unified School District

Re: Name of Student
        School
        Principal Recommending Expulsion

[Student Name Full], student, and [Parent Name], parent of student, acknowledge meeting with [Director or designee] on [meeting date]. We have been informed of and understand the right to due process with regard to the expulsion recommendation against [name of student] by [name of principal], of the ******** Unified School District.

Moreover, we received a copy of the Notice of Expulsion and Charges dated [Charge ltr date] and understand the contents of that notice.

We understand that the expulsion hearing has been scheduled for [Day/Date of Hearing], at [Time], in the [Name of District Office], located at [Address of District Office], California. In particular, we have been informed and understand that we have the right to a full evidentiary hearing, the right to appear in person or employ and be represented by counsel at this hearing, the right to inspect and obtain copies of all documents to be used at the hearing, the right to confront and question all witnesses who testify at the hearing, the right to question all evidence presented, and to present oral and documentary evidence on [student's name]'s behalf, including witnesses. We have received a written copy of these rights. We have also received a written description of the charges that led to the recommendation for expulsion, copies of applicable provisions of the California Education Code and District Rules and Regulations governing expulsions.

We stipulate and agree that [name of student] is subject to expulsion from the District for having committed acts in violation of Education Code section _____ [description of statutory offense]. [If applicable, Education Code section 48915] We further stipulate that [Select relevant basis: other means of correction are not feasible or have repeatedly failed to bring about proper conduct or that due to the nature of the violation, the presence of the pupil causes a continuing danger to the physical safety of the pupil or others].

After careful consideration, we voluntarily request a waiver of the expulsion hearing before the ******** Unified School District Hearing Panel, located at [address]. We understand that the purpose and function of the waived hearing would have been for fact-finding and to submit recommendations to the Board of Education when the Board meets to deliberate and act on this matter. In addition to waiving the expulsion hearing, we also request that all legal time lines in this matter be waived.

We understand that an expulsion recommendation will be submitted to the Board of Education for its review and final action. The District administration will recommend that [student's name] be expelled for [one/two semester(s); one calendar year], through [date].

We understand that the Board of Education will ensure that an education program is provided to [student's name] for the period of the expulsion. In addition we understand that the Board of Education will recommend a plan of rehabilitation for [student's name]. This rehabilitation plan may include, but not be limited to, periodic review as well as assessment at the time of review for readmission. The plan may also include recommendations for improved academic performance, tutoring, special education assessments, job training, counseling, employment, community service, or other rehabilitative programs.

We understand that at the conclusion of [student's name] expulsion term, [he/she] shall be reviewed for readmission to a school maintained by the District or to the school [student's name] last attended. Upon completion of the readmission process, the Board of Education will readmit [name of student], unless the Board of Education makes a finding that the pupil has not met the conditions of [his/her] rehabilitation plan or continues to pose a danger to campus safety or to other pupils or employees of the District.

By requesting this Waiver of Hearing on Expulsion, we acknowledge that, should the Board of Education vote not to accept the administration's recommendation, we retain the right to withdraw this Waiver of Expulsion Hearing and have the matter heard by the ******** Unified School District Hearing Panel

EXPULSION REHABILITATION PLAN:

[ADD TERMS OF REHAB PLAN]

[Name of Student]   Date

[Parent]   Date

[Parent]   Date

INSERT DISTRICT LETTERHEAD AND/OR LOGO

Expulsion Packet Checklist

_____ Notice of Suspension Form

_____ Principal Summary/Recommendation For Expulsion

_____ Letter Extending Suspension Pending Expulsion

_____ Notice of Hearing and Charges Letter

_____ Incident Report(s)/ Witness Statements (Staff and students) (Redacted)

_____ Evidence (Photos, weapon, police reports, medical records, etc.)

_____ Interventions AND Discipline History

_____ Student Status reports

_____ Grade Reports/ Transcripts/Attendance

_____ Request for Continuance, if applicable

**INDEX OF ATTACHMENTS INCLUDED IN
THE RECOMMENDATION FOR EXPULSION OF
[STUDENT NAME]**

BEFORE THE [DISRICT] UNIFIED SCHOOL DISTRICT ADMINISTRATIVE EXPULSION PANEL

[DATE]

Exhibit	Description	Page #
1	Suspension Letter & Notice of Suspension	
2	Principal's Recommendation For Expulsion	
3	Notice of Extension of Suspension	
4	Notice of Expulsion Hearing and Charges – Dated ???	
5	Victim Statement	
6	Accused Statement	
7	Witness Statements	
8	Photo of Evidence	
9	Police Department Memo, if applicable	
10	Student Discipline Report: Referrals/Suspensions/Interventions	
11	Parent Request for Continuance	
12	School Attendance Record	
13	Transcript Of Student's Grades/Student Data	

Fear Declaration of Student 1
[Date]

I am a 17 year old student at Sunrise school. This incident has had a big impact on me. I had a difficult time finishing the school year. I was really sad and depressed. I felt like somehow it was my fault. I sometimes felt suicidal because I could not stop thinking about what happened, replaying it over and over in my mind. I was originally excited about being at Sunrise. But, after the incident my grades went down a lot, I could not focus on anything that was happening in class and I would just sit there. I am constantly crying, it just happens and I can't control it. Things I used to like to do, I don't do anymore. I don't have a lot of energy and I want to sleep a lot. On nights before I have meetings for this incident, I am not able to sleep at all due to anxiety and I just freak out. My moods are all over the place and I am angry a lot more than I use to be. Little things trigger me that didn't use to and make me angry. I sometimes take my anger out on my brothers and my mom. It sometimes feels like the anger is trapped inside of me and I have no were else to put it.

Mark has been picking on me since the incident, even after the principal told him not to. Other students make comments so I can hear about how girls lie about being raped. I feel unsafe around guys now because I assume they are going to touch me in some kind of way without my permission. It is also hard to trust people because of this.

When I think about testifying at the hearing I get afraid and freak out. I get sad and depressed. My mind wants to shut down. I stress out and go numb and I would not be able to talk or say what I need to say. If I have to testify, I am not going to be well. I would not be able to continue with my day to day life. I have had panic attacks thinking about the incident and also testifying. At the hearing when perpetrator's mother said that I was mentally ill and that I was lying, and because he was black, I felt attacked and it made me feel less confident about testifying. I already have a hard time believing that it was not my fault. If I have to testify in person I am sure that I would not be able to do it and tell my story. I already feel bad about myself and this makes me feel worse.

It is really important to me that I can tell my side of the story and if I have to testify, I will not physically or emotionally be able to do it.

I declare the forgoing statement is true and accurate under penalty of perjury.

_____

CHAPTER 4

Expulsion Hearings

TOOLS FOR THE TRADE

Expulsion Hearing Process - Generally

If a student is being recommended for expulsion, it is imperative that the administrator understands the applicable rules and procedures in order to ensure compliance with the law. School administrators in most school districts are responsible for presenting the expulsion case. The process has many procedural requirements that implicate legal concepts, such as due process, rules of evidence, and burden of proof. Administrators, parents/guardians and advocates need to understand how to navigate the expulsion process to ensure that the law is followed and that the rights of the student are protected.

Generally speaking, the expulsion hearing should follow fairly common steps. The chair of the hearing body or the expulsion hearing facilitator will read a script that identifies the student and the charges against her/him. (See 4.1 - Sample Admin Panel Expulsion Hearing Script at the end of this chapter) S/he will identify the date and location of the hearing and introduce the members of the hearing body and summarize the hearing process. Typically, both sides are given the opportunity to provide "Opening Statements." The purpose of the opening statement is to summarize each party's position and the evidence that the parties intend to present to support their respective cases. The opening statements are not evidence and there should be no discussion of the opening remarks.

Following the opening statements, the District will present its witnesses and evidence. After each witness' testimony, the parent/guardian or the student's representative may cross-examine the witness. Reexamination and re-cross-examination is often permitted. At the end of re-direct and re-cross-examination, members of the hearing body may ask clarifying questions.

It is important that the administrative hearing panel members NOT "take over" the questioning of the witnesses. It is the responsibility of the school site administrator to prove the school's case and the panel members should not become "advocates" for the schools case. The panel members are impartial fact finders for the District's Governing Board and should avoid acting in a way that would suggest that they are invested in a particular outcome.

After the school has concluded its case, the parent/guardian or the student's representative may present testimony and exhibits. After direct examination of each of the student's witnesses, the school will have the opportunity to cross-examine the witnesses. After re-direct and re-cross, members of the hearing body may ask clarifying questions.

The parties may only call witnesses to offer "relevant" evidence regarding the allegations against the student. "Relevant" evidence is defined by CA Ed. Code as, "…the kind of evidence upon which reasonable persons are accustomed to rely in the conduct of serious affairs." (CA Ed. Code 48918(h)(1))

The parent/guardian or the student's representative may also offer "character" evidence in the form of witness testimony or documents. "Character" evidence is commonly introduced to show a student's character or disposition and is often used to make a case for leniency or compassion.

The accused student has the right to testify on her/his behalf or not to testify. If the accused student chooses to testify, s/he will be required to answer questions on cross-examination by the school following her/his direct testimony. The accused student is required to answer the cross-examination questions or risk having the entirety of her/his testimony stricken from the record.

The accused student has the constitutional right not to testify under the Fifth Amendment of the Constitution. If the accused student chooses to exercise her/his right not to testify, the hearing body cannot hold her/his refusal against her/him nor can it presume that s/he engaged in the conduct charged as a result of refusing to testify.

Any testimony provided by the accused student in an expulsion hearing is expressly deemed to be a privileged communication protected by subdivision (b) of Section 47 of the Civil Code.

(CA Ed. Code 48918.6)

Either side may present rebuttal evidence. After all the evidence has been submitted, each party will have the opportunity to make a closing statement. These closing statements summarize each party's position and request that the hearing body reach the conclusion in favor of the party. The remarks made during closing statements are not evidence and should not be considered by the hearing body when deliberating.

Expulsion Hearing Procedural Requirements

CA Ed. Code 48918 lists the procedural requirements applicable to expulsion hearings. These procedural requirements must be adhered to in order to ensure that the student receives her/his due process rights.

While not exhaustive, below is a list of some of the relevant procedural requirements to keep in mind as the expulsion hearing process moves forward. For a comprehensive list of the rules governing expulsion procedures, refer to CA Ed. Code 48918.

- The expulsion hearing is to be held within 30 school days after the date that the principal or the superintendent determines that the student has committed any act in violation of § 48900, unless the parent/guardian requests, in writing, that the hearing be postponed. (CA Ed. Code § 48918(a)(1))

- The student is entitled to one postponement of the expulsion hearing (for any reason), for a period of not more than thirty (30) calendar days. (CA Ed. Code § 48918(a)(1))

- Notice of the hearing must be provided to the family at least 10 days prior to the hearing. (CA Ed. Code § 48918(b))

- The student has the right to be represented by counsel or a non-attorney advisor. (CA Ed. Code 48918(b)(5))

- The student has the right to inspect and obtain copies of all documents to be used at the hearing. (CA Ed. Code 48918(b)(5))

- The student has the right to confront and question all witnesses who testify at the hearing. (CA Ed. Code 48918(b)(5))

- The student has the right to question all other evidence presented. (CA Ed. Code

48918(b)(5))

- The student has the right to present oral and documentary evidence on her/his behalf, including witnesses. (CA Ed. Code 48918(b)(5))

Foster Children – Required Notice

If the student is a foster child and the recommended expulsion is discretionary, notice of the expulsion hearing **must** be provided to the foster child's attorney and an appropriate representative of the county child welfare agency at least ten (10) calendar days before the date of the hearing. (CA Ed. Code 48918.1(a)(1)) If the foster child is facing a mandatory recommendation for expulsion, the school **may** provide notice of the expulsion hearing as described above. (CA Ed. Code 48918.1(a)(2)) It is recommended that notice is provided to the foster child's attorney and social worker, regardless of whether the expulsion recommendation is discretionary or mandatory to ensure that the rights of the foster child are protected.

Homeless Children – Required Notice

If the student is a homeless child and the recommended expulsion is discretionary, notice of the expulsion hearing **must** be provided to the district's liaison for homeless children at least ten (10) calendar days before the date of the hearing. (CA Ed. Code 48918.1(b)(1)) If the homeless child is facing a mandatory recommendation for expulsion, the school **may** provide notice of the expulsion hearing as described above. (CA Ed. Code 48918.1(b)(2)) It is recommended that notice is provided to the district's liaison for homeless children, regardless of whether the expulsion recommendation is discretionary or mandatory to ensure that the rights of the homeless child are protected.

Continuance Requests

The law only allows a continuance of the expulsion hearing by request of the parent or order of the district's Governing Board. If the expulsion hearing is not held within thirty school days, and there is no request for a continuance by the student or the school, the district will lose jurisdiction to expel the student.

Parents have an absolute right to one continuance of the expulsion hearing, for any reason, up to the start of the hearing. The request must be written and can be a letter or email. Additionally, if the parent has made a verbal request for a continuance and the timing does not allow for receipt of a written request prior to the start of the hearing, the administrator can send an email confirming the parents request for a continuance, indicating the name of the person, time and date the verbal request was made, and include the confirming email in the expulsion packet to document compliance with procedural timelines. (See 4.2 - Sample Parent Request for Continuance at the end of this chapter)

The district can request a continuance from the governing board if there is "good cause" for the continuance. A typical example of "good cause" for a district request for a continuance is that the student needs to be assessed for special education pursuant to "Protections For Students Not Yet Eligible For Special Education" under the Individuals with Disabilities in Education Act ("IDEA"), and the assessment will not be completed prior to the expiration of the expulsion hearing timelines. (See Chapter 5 for details relating to this process) The district could go forward with the expulsion in this scenario, however, if the student is found to be eligible for Special Education and the conduct is determined to be a manifestation of the student's disability, the expulsion order would have to be vacated.

In the interest of minimizing stress and conflict with the family and conserving valuable human resources, it is typically more prudent to obtain a continuance of the expulsion hearing pending the outcome of the special education assessment and move forward with the expulsion hearing if the student is not eligible for special education or Section 504 and/or the conduct is not a manifestation of the student's disability.

School districts should establish a simple process for submitting continuance requests to the Governing Board. It is recommended that the district create a form template, that allows for the case specific facts to be included, the request is then signed by the President of the Governing Board, either granting or denying the continuance request. (See 4.3 - Sample District Request for a Continuance at the end of this chapter) The authority to grant a continuance request for "good cause" can and should be delegated to a board member to avoid the challenges of having the action taken by the entire board during a board meeting.

Subpoenas For Personal Appearance Of Witnesses At The Expulsion Hearing

Prior to the start of the hearing, the governing board of the school district may issue subpoenas for the personal appearance of percipient witnesses (i.e. witnesses with first hand knowledge of the incident) at the hearing, at the request of either the site administrator presenting the case or the student. (CA Ed. Code 48918(i)) (See 4.4 - Sample Governing Board Subpoena at the end of this chapter)

<u>Once the hearing begins</u>, the entity hearing the case may issue subpoenas, upon request of either the county superintendent of schools, the site administrator presenting the case or the student.

If either the site administrator presenting the case or the student <u>objects</u> to the issuance of subpoenas, the governing board of the school district may consider the objection in closed session, or in open session, if requested by the student before the meeting. The decision of the governing board of the school district in response to an objection to the issuance of subpoenas shall be final and binding.

Procedure For Responding To Request To Issue Subpoena For Personal Appearance

<u>Student Request for Subpoena</u>

As part of the expulsion hearing process, the student's representative may request that certain witnesses be made available to testify at the hearing. If the requested witness is an adult staff member of the district, there is no need for a subpoena. It is the responsibility of the site administrator to make the staff member available for the hearing.

If the requested witness is a minor student, to the extent the student knows a specific student witness, the student's representative should contact the witness and/or her/his family directly to determine if the witness is willing to testify on behalf of the student. If the student witness is willing to testify on behalf of the accused student, there is no need for site administration intervention and the accused student should coordinate with the witness to be available for the hearing.

If the student witness is not willing to testify on behalf of the accused student or the accused student does not know the identity of a particular student witness, then the following steps should be followed. **Please note that the identity and confidential information of a minor student witness should never be disclosed to the accused student or her/his representative without consent of the parent/guardian of the student witness or pursuant to a legal exception.**

1. Determine if the requested witness is a "percipient witness," meaning the witness has

first hand knowledge of the incident.

2. If the witness is not a percipient witness, a subpoena cannot be issued to compel the appearance of the witness and the student's representative should be informed that the requested witness will not be made available to testify at the hearing.

3. If the witness is a percipient witness, the site administrator should contact the parent/guardian of the student witness and inform her/him that their student has been requested to testify as a witness in an expulsion hearing by the accused.

   a. If they agree to allow the student to be a witness, the site administrator should coordinate with the student's representative the time for the witness to testify at the hearing.

   b. If they do not agree to allow the student to be a witness, the site administrator should inform the accused student's representative and direct her/him to make a written request to the governing board for a subpoena to compel the witness' testimony at the hearing.

   c. If the accused student's representative submits a written request for a subpoena, the witness' family should be informed of the subpoena request and provided with information to object if they believe that their student would suffer and unreasonable risk of psychological or physical harm if compelled to testify via subpoena.

   A subpoena cannot be issued to compel the personal attendance of a witness at the hearing, if the entity hearing the case determines that a percipient witness would be subject to an unreasonable risk of harm by testifying at the hearing. However, that witness may be compelled to testify by means of a sworn declaration as provided for in subdivision 48918(f). (See Chapter 3 – Sworn Declaration Process – Obtaining a Fear Declaration)

The process for a site administrator to request a subpoena to compel the attendance of a witness is essentially the same as the process outlined above for the accused student. The main difference is that the site administrator will know the identity of the student witness.

Serving the Subpoena

Once a subpoena is issued, it will need to be served on the witness. Service of a subpoena can occur anywhere in the state and must follow the procedures outlined below:

1. Deliver a copy to the witness personally, giving or offering to the witness at the same time, if demanded by him or her, the fees to which he or she is entitled for travel to and from the place designated, and one day's attendance there.

2. The service shall be made so as to allow the witness a reasonable time for preparation and travel to the place of attendance.

3. The service may be made by someone who is over the age of 18 and not a party to the action.

4. If service is to be made on a minor, service shall be made on the minor's parent, guardian, conservator, or similar fiduciary, or if one of those persons cannot be located with reasonable diligence, service shall be made on any person having the care or control of the minor or with whom the minor resides or by whom the minor is employed, and on the minor if the minor is 12 years of age or older.

5. If the minor is a ward of the court and the minor is not in the custody of a parent or guardian, regardless of the age of the minor, service **also** shall be made upon the designated agent for service of process at the county child welfare department or the probation department under whose jurisdiction the minor has been placed.

All witnesses appearing pursuant to subpoena, other than the parties or officers or employees of the state or any political subdivision of the state, shall receive fees, and all witnesses appearing pursuant to subpoena, except the parties, shall receive mileage in the same amount and under the same circumstances as prescribed for witnesses in civil actions in a superior court. <u>Fees and mileage shall be paid by the party at whose request the witness is subpoenaed.</u> Check with your district's legal counsel to determine what the appropriate fees and mileage rates are.

Providing Expulsion Packet to Parent/Guardian or Attorney/Advocate

The student has a right to examine the evidence against her/him. It is recommended that the site administrator finalize the expulsion packet and provide it to the student's representative at least ten (10) days prior to the hearing, with the Notice of Hearing. The law does not require that the expulsion packet is provided to the family prior to the hearing, however, best practice and fairness support making the packet available once it is ready.

Keep in mind that the expulsion packet is comprised of confidential student records and, therefore, can only be disclosed to a person who has a right to access the records, like a parent/guardian, or to someone who has been authorized to access the records. If the student is represented by a parent/guardian, there is no formal process required to provide them with the expulsion packet. The parent/guardian has an absolute right to access the student records contained in the expulsion packet.

However, if the expulsion packet is being provided to legal counsel for the student, the district must first obtain a Notice of Representation from the attorney AND an Authorization for Release of Records signed by the parent or guardian authorizing the disclosure to the attorney, prior to releasing the expulsion packet to the attorney. Similarly, if the student is represented by a non-attorney adviser, the district must obtain an Authorization for Release of Records signed by the parent or guardian, authorizing the disclosure to the advocate prior to releasing the expulsion packet. (See 4.5 - Sample Release of Information Form at the end of this chapter)

Governing Board Hearing Or Administrative Panel Hearing

The law requires the Governing Board to conduct the expulsion hearing in a session closed to the public, unless the parent/guardian requests, in writing, at least five (5) days prior to the date of the hearing, that the hearing be conducted at a public meeting. (CA Ed. Code 48918(c)(1)) Instead of conducting the hearing itself, the Governing Board may designate a hearing officer or appoint an impartial administrative panel ("Panel") to conduct the hearing. (CA Ed. Code 48918(d))

In most districts, particularly larger districts with a large number of expulsion hearings, the Governing Board typically appoints a Panel to conduct the hearing. The Panel must consist of three or more certificated persons, none of whom is a member of the Governing Board or employed on the staff of the school where the student is enrolled. (CA Ed. Code 48918(d))

Presenting An Expulsion Case

General summary

It is the job of the site administrator presenting the case to prove by **substantial evidence** that the accused student engaged in conduct that violates the CA Ed. Code. This standard requires the site administrator to "provide enough evidence that a reasonable mind could accept as adequate to support a particular conclusion."

Additionally, if the offense is not a mandatory recommendation for expulsion, the site administrator must also prove one of the secondary findings: 1. Other means of correction are not feasible or have repeatedly failed to bring about proper conduct, or 2. Due to the nature of the act, the student's presence is a continuing danger to the student or others.

While technical rules of evidence do not apply, legal rules and concepts govern the expulsion hearing process. Administrators are encouraged to make time to properly prepare for the hearing, ensuring that you understand the laws and process you must follow and ensuring that the accused student receives due process. Proper preparation includes meeting with and preparing your witnesses prior to hearing, preparing witness questions in advance of the hearing, and drafting an opening statement.

Sample Opening Statement

Below is a sample opening statement in a drug selling case.

The evidence will show that on Friday, November 19, 2019, STUDENT was in class on the HS campus texting with at least one other student, who was also at school, attempting to arrange the sale of a pre-packaged amount of marijuana. The evidence will show that his text messages were actually being intercepted by the SRO on campus, who was in possession of the other student's cell phone based on a separate incident that was being investigated.

Based on the text messages sent by STUDENT, SRO concluded that there was reasonable suspicion to suspect that STUDENT was in possession of drugs on campus that he was attempting to sell to other students. The administrators then located STUDENT in his class and escorted him to the office.

You will hear testimony from SRO that STUDENT was searched and 9 individually packaged baggies containing marijuana were found in a medicine bottle tucked under his shirt. You will see pictures of the evidence confiscated from the STUDENT. You will also hear testimony from ADMINISTRATOR and SRO that STUDENT admitted, both verbally and in writing, that he was selling marijuana to make money. You will see a copy of STUDENT'S written admission.

STUDENT's conduct violated Education Code sections 48900 (c) offered, possessed or sold a controlled substance and 48915(c)(3) selling a controlled substance. The evidence will also show that other means of correction are not feasible or have repeatedly failed to bring about proper conduct **and** that due to the nature of this act, STUDENT's presence on campus is a danger to himself and other.

Preparing witnesses

Preparing your witnesses is an essential part of your preparation. Once you determine which witnesses you need to call for your case, you should begin by reviewing their written statement, noting what information they have personal knowledge about and which aspects of your case they can help prove. ***Clarity about the elements of each offense you must prove is essential at this point, as it will drive your preparation interview**. In your prep meeting with the witness, you should review their statement with them, asking clarifying questions as appropriate and filling in the details of their account as best you can. You should also explain the expulsion hearing process to them and answer their questions about what to expect.

After your meeting with the witness, you should draft your witness questions, focusing in on questions that will illicit responses that are based on first hand knowledge and address the elements of your case.

Drafting Witness Questions And Questioning Witnesses

Effectively questioning witnesses requires a strong understanding of the charges you must prove, the evidence you want to introduce, and how your witnesses testimony will support the case you are trying to prove. Witness questions should be drafted prior to the hearing and drafted in a way that allows the witness to tell a story. On direct examination, you want to stay away from leading questions, which are typically questions that must be answered with a "yes" or "no."

Do not start your questioning by having the witness refer to their witness statement that is in the expulsion packet. As much as you can, you want the witness to answer your questions based on what they remember of the incident. It is much more persuasive to have the witness testify based on memory, than to have the witness read a statement that the panel is capable of reading. If you need to refresh the witness' recollection or if there is important information in the witness' written statement, you can have the witness refer to their statement, but the majority of their testimony should be based on memory.

Below are some points to keep in mind as you draft your witness questions and question the witness at the hearing.

1. Foundation (e.g. occupation, work experience, duties, grade, etc.). Always start with foundational questions. They introduce the witness to the panel, who may have no idea who the person is. They allow the witness to "settle down," as the questions are

easy to answer. They also allow you to establish a rhythm with the witness, allowing them to get comfortable with the questioning.

2. <u>Only testify based on personal knowledge</u>. Generally speaking, witnesses should only be questioned on topics about which they have first hand knowledge. The purpose of having a "live" witness testify is to present "direct evidence." This purpose is undermined when questions lead to answers that are hearsay. Therefore, be clear which aspects of your case the witness has first hand knowledge about and focus your questions on those issues.

3. <u>Be clear about which aspect of your case each witness' testimony goes to</u>. Similar to bullet 2 above, understand which elements of your case the witness' testimony proves. For example, if the witness saw the injuries, can the witness describe them with sufficient detail to establish that the injuries meet the definition of "serious bodily injury?" If all the witness can testify to is that s/he "saw a lot of blood on the victim," that detail would not be sufficient to prove that the injuries met the definition and that witness' testimony on that issue would not be enough to prove that element of your case. However, if that same witness also saw the accused student attack the victim unprovoked, the witness would have valuable testimony for the charge of "willful use of force, not in self defense" and your questioning should focus on that element of the case with that particular witness. You would then need to find a witness or evidence that actually establishes that the injuries that resulted meet the definition of "serious bodily injury." This could be in the form of testimony by a witness who has first hand knowledge of the seriousness of the injuries or the introduction of medical records that describe the seriousness of the injuries.

4. <u>Have the witnesses authenticate their statements</u>. After you have had the witness testify based on memory, it is a good practice to have the witness authenticate their written statement, if there is one in the expulsion packet. This allows the panel to see that the witness also wrote a statement contemporaneously with the incident when the facts were fresh in her/his mind. It also lets the panel know that there is a statement consistent with the testimony they just heard that they can review while in deliberations, if so desired.

5. <u>Specifically direct the witness (and the panel via the witness) to the exhibits relevant to the witness' testimony</u>. For example, if the witness is the police officer who confiscated the drugs and tested the drugs, it would be appropriate for you to direct the officer to

the picture of the drugs in the expulsion packet to authenticate that the substance in the picture is what was confiscated from the accused student and that the drugs were tested by the officer with a positive test result. (See Sample SRO questions below)

6. Oral testimony required for verbal admissions. If an accused student provides a written statement admitting to the offense, that written statement is not hearsay and can be introduced as direct evidence and relied on to support an expulsion order. However, if the student verbally admitted to the offense but did not write a statement, the person who heard the admission should write her/his own statement detailing the accused's admission and that the accused refused to write a written statement. That statement should be entered into the expulsion packet, but remember it is hearsay. In order to get the accused's verbal admission into evidence as direct evidence, the person who heard the admission must testify at the hearing about the admission. This testimony about the admission by the person who heard it is not hearsay and can be relied on to support an expulsion order.

7. Do NOT have witnesses read their statements. Everyone in the hearing room can read. Having the witness read her/his statement verbatim undermines the credibility of the witness' testimony and is ultimately a waste of time. Have the witness authenticate her/his statement AFTER s/he has completed testifying based on memory.

Below are examples of witness questions for an SRO and site administrator using the same case facts used in the sample opening statement above:

Sample SRO questions

1. State your occupation?
2. Who is your employer?
3. How long have you been employed as a police officer? How long with ??????
4. What are the duties of your position as a SRO?
5. Are you assigned to a particular school? What school?
6. On Friday, November 19, 2019, were you on duty? Did you respond to a call at High School? What was the nature of the call?
7. What did you observe when you arrived at HS?
8. How were you able to identify STUDENT?
9. Did you write a report summarizing this incident? (Ex 6) Can you identify what this is? Does this accurately reflect the events that occurred during your investigation?

10. P. 8 (screenshot of text exchange) – identify what this is? At the time of this text exchange, where you on campus? Was STUDENT on campus? In your professional opinion, what was this text exchange about?

11. What actions did you take based on this exchange?

12. Did you search STUDENT? Was your search based on probable cause or reasonable suspicion? Describe the evidence you relied on to support your search?

13. Did you find anything during your search? What did you find? (P. 9) Explain what this picture is? Did you take it?

14. What was in the bag? Did you do any tests to verify that they contained marijuana? What were the results of the test?

15. Did STUDENT make any statements in your presence? What did he say?

16. Was the way the drugs were packaged consistent with STUDENT's admission that he was selling the marijuana? Explain?

17. What did you do with the drugs once they were taken from STUDENT?

18. Did STUDENT give you a written statement?

Sample Assistant Principal Questions

19. State you occupation?

20. Who is your employer? How long with USD?

21. How long have you been employed as an Assistant Principal?

22. What are the duties of your position as an assistant principal?

23. Are you aware of an incident that occurred on Friday, November 19, 2019 involving STUDENT?

24. What is your understanding of the incident? How did you learn about the incident?

25. Once you learned of the incident, what did you do? Where was STUDENT found prior to being brought to the office?

26. Did you interview STUDENT as part of your investigation? What did he say during the interview?

27. Did STUDENT provide a written statement? (Ex 7, p. 10) Please identify what this document is? Did STUDENT write this? What date was this statement written on?

28. Where you present when SRO searched STUDENT? Do you recall what was found? Explain?

29. Did you write a statement? (Ex 7, p.11) Is your statement true and accurate to the best

of your knowledge?

30. Are you aware of how STUDENT came to be identified as someone selling marijuana on campus? Explain?

31. Did you know STUDENT prior to this incident? How?

32. How would you describe him?

33. Ex 8 pp 12-17 (Discipline tracker) – Identify? There are multiple entries in the discipline tracker that refer to items that show defiant and disrespectful behavior by STUDENT. Can you explain?

34. Has the site done anything to try to address these behaviors? What was done? Where they effective in improving STUDENT's behavior?

35. Do you believe that STUDENT's act of selling marijuana on campus makes him a danger to himself or others? Explain?

Using Documentary Evidence in the Expulsion Packet

The expulsion packet contains the documentary evidence you need to establish compliance with procedural requirements and to support the factual elements of your case. You should be thoughtful not only about what goes into the packet but also how the packet is organized. In addition to their personal notes, these are the only documents and evidence the panel will take with them into deliberations, so make sure the panel knows which documents to focus on.

As a practical matter, the expulsion packet is typically admitted into evidence in its entirety, unless there is an objection. However, without supporting testimony, the documents do not have context. Given that most administrative panels are not provided with the expulsion packet prior to the hearing, it is the job of the site administrator presenting the case to highlight the documents in the packet that are important to your case during the hearing. (Keep in mind that the site administrator presenting the case is not a witness, unless s/he is sworn in to testify and is subject to cross- examination.) The best way to prepare to highlight the documents you want the panel to focus on is to determine, prior to the hearing, which of the witnesses that you intend to call, have the requisite first hand knowledge to authenticate the documentary evidence you want to highlight.

For example, using an officer to introduce the picture of a firearm and to authenticate that the weapon in the picture is what was confiscated from the accused AND that it meets the definition of a firearm, is an appropriate way to introduce the photo of the firearm. However, using the officer to discuss the student's discipline tracker, when the officer has no first hand knowledge of the previous discipline or intervention, would not be an appropriate way to introduce the discipline tracker. Conversely, having the administrator introduce the photo of the firearm can prove that the weapon pictured in the photo was the weapon confiscated from the accused. However, unless the administrator has specific expertise about firearms, s/he would not be able to establish that the weapon met the definition of a firearm, except by hearsay (The officer told her/him that it was a firearm).

Student Production of Evidence

The parent/guardian or the student's representative has a right to introduce evidence at the hearing. If the student is unrepresented, it is likely that the family is unaware of this right. The family should be encouraged to bring any documents to the hearing that they believe are relevant to the case. If the family does not bring the appropriate number of copies, the district should make copies prior to the start of the hearing and distribute them, as appropriate.

Logistics of the Hearing

The expulsion hearing should be thought of like a trial. The various administrators involved in the process, whether presenting the case or sitting on the panel, should maintain a high degree of professionalism at all times. This means that if one of the panel members is a good friend of the site administrator presenting the case, they should not be having informal social conversations in the hearing room, even if the hearing has yet to start. Remember that the student and the parents/guardian are already intimidated and untrusting of the process. If they observe the person who is essentially prosecuting the case socializing with the person judging the case, it creates the appearance of impropriety and unfairness. Also remember that the expulsion hearing is a very stressful process and seeing the folks in authority joking and laughing undermines the seriousness of the proceedings for the family.

The physical layout of the hearing room should be set up like a courtroom, if possible. The panel members should be at one table facing the parties. The site administrator would be at one table, facing the panel, and the student and her/his representatives should be at a separate table, facing the panel. The witness should be at a separate table, furthest away from the accused student. This is typically in between the site administrator's table and the panel's table.

The hearing is required to be recorded. The recording should be set up as close to the witness stand as possible, as <u>the only relevant testamentary evidence is what is provided by a witness, who is sworn in and subject to cross-examination</u>. Therefore, the most important dialogue that needs to be captured on the recording is what is being said by the witnesses. Similarly, the expulsion packet provided for use by the witnesses during the hearing is the official documentary record of the proceeding. The witness copy of the expulsion packet can be marked up by witnesses, at the direction of the person doing the questioning, as part of their testimony. If there is an appeal to the county board of education, it is the witness copy of the expulsion packet that should be part of the record on appeal.

Authority of the Administrative Panel

In districts where a Panel conducts the expulsion hearing, they act as the Governing Board's fact finders and, within three days after the hearing, they must decide whether to recommend the expulsion of the student to the Governing Board. If the Panel decides not to recommend the student's expulsion, the expulsion proceedings must be terminated and the student must be immediately reinstated and permitted to return to the classroom instructional program from which the referral was made, unless the parent/guardian requests another placement in writing. (CA Ed Code 48918(e))

Historically, if the Panel found that there was "substantial evidence" to support the expulsion recommendation, it was required to recommend the student's expulsion to the Governing Board and it was up to the Governing Board to decide whether to order the expulsion. However, recent amendments have extended the Panel's authority to decide not to recommend the expulsion of a student who it has found to have committed a mandatory CA Ed. Code 48915(c) offense. In this situation, the student must be reinstated and may be referred back to her/his prior school, another comprehensive school, or involuntarily transferred to a continuation school in the district. (CA Ed. Code 48918(d))

In either case, the decision of the Panel not to expel is final and does not progress to the Governing Board.

If the Panel recommends the student for expulsion, it must draft findings of fact in support of its recommendation to be submitted to the Governing Board for its consideration. The Panel's findings must be based solely on the evidence presented at the expulsion hearing. (CA Ed. Code 48918(f)(1))

<u>Introducing a Fear Declaration in the Expulsion Hearing</u>

Once the school administrator has obtained the "fear declaration" (See Chapter 3 – Obtaining The Fear Declaration), the documentation of the fear declaration must be made part of the expulsion packet to be considered during the hearing. At some point during the expulsion hearing, the administrator must request that the Governing Board or the Panel (whichever body is hearing the case) consider the fear declaration and make a determination regarding whether there is an unreasonable risk of psychological or physical harm if the witness is forced to testify. The accused student has the right to refute the evidence and argue that an unreasonable risk of psychological or physical harm does not exist. At the conclusion of the arguments, the hearing body must make a determination either way.

If the hearing body determines that there **is not** an unreasonable risk of psychological or physical harm, the witness' underlying incident statement may be admitted into evidence, but only as hearsay, and it cannot be relied on solely as a basis to support an expulsion order against the accused student. However, if the hearing body determines that there **is** an unreasonable risk of psychological or physical harm, the witness' underlying witness statement may be admitted into evidence as "direct" evidence, and may be relied on as the only direct evidence to support an expulsion order against the accused student.

The hearing body must clearly state on the record its findings and specifically identify the written incident statement it is admitting as direct evidence. It is important to note that the value of this process is dependent on the content of the underlying written incident statement, because only what is written in that statement will be admitted into evidence as direct evidence. For instance, if the underlying written incident statement says, "I saw Tom do it," the introduction of that observation does not prove the conduct violation. If, instead, the underlying written incident statement says, "I saw Tom tackle Bob from behind and begin punching him in the head," this observation goes directly to proving the conduct violation and makes it worthwhile to utilize the fear declaration process to get it admitted as direct evidence.

Administrative Panel Deliberations

Once the site administrator and the student have completed the presentation of their respective cases and their closing statements, the Panel will adjourn and go into deliberations. During the hearing, the Panel members should have been taking notes about the evidence that was presented and beginning to form opinions about the adequacy of the evidence. (See 4.6 - Sample Panel Note-Taking Form at the end of the chapter) In deliberations, the Panel members should review each charge and discuss the evidence that was presented to support or refute the charges, including the secondary findings. The Panel members should then agree on one set of factual findings, for each offense charged, and create their Findings of Fact document to submit to the Governing Board, assuming that their recommendation is for expulsion.

When drafting their Findings of Fact, each charge should be broken down into its respective elements, and the facts should be presented that support each element of the offense. The Panel members should consider which of the facts, including documentary/physical evidence, that were produced at the hearing, are relevant to the elements of each charge and present them in a simple organized fashion. (See 4.7 - Sample Findings of Fact and Conclusions of Law at the end of this chapter)

If the Panel's recommendation is NOT to expel, they do not need to create a Finding of Fact document. All Panel members must participate and vote on the expulsion recommendation.

Authority of the Governing Board

Whether the expulsion hearing is conducted by the Governing Board or the Panel, the final action to expel a student can only be taken by the Governing Board in a public session. (CA Ed. Code 48918(j)) Typically, the Governing Board will assign a number to the accused student's case for posting on the public agenda.

When the Governing Board receives a recommendation to expel for a mandatory violation, whether in the form of a Panel recommendation or a Stipulation signed by the accused student and the parent/guardian, if the Governing Board agrees that there is substantial evidence to support the expulsion recommendation, the Governing Board must expel the accused student. (CA Ed. Code 48915(d)) If the accused student has admitted to the conduct violation(s), there is, by definition, substantial evidence that the accused student engaged in the conduct charged.

If the Governing Board receives a recommendation to expel for a discretionary violation, whether in the form of a Panel recommendation or a Stipulation signed by the accused student and the parent/guardian, the Governing Board always has the discretion to choose to expel or not to expel, even if the Governing Board believes that the accused student engaged in the charged conduct. (CA Ed. Code 48915(b))

Board Expulsion Orders

Discretionary Offenses

If the accused student is expelled for a <u>discretionary</u> act, the Governing Board must set a date for the student to be reviewed for readmission no later than the last day of the semester following the semester in which the expulsion occurred. If the expulsion is ordered during the summer session or the intersession period of a year-round program, the Governing Board must set a date, not later than the last day of the semester following the summer session or intersession period in which the expulsion occurred, when the accused student must be reviewed for readmission. (CA Ed. Code 48916(a))

Mandatory Offenses

If the accused student has been expelled for a <u>mandatory</u> act, pursuant to CA Ed. Code 48915(c), the Governing Board must set the review for readmission date one year from the date the expulsion occurred. However, the Governing Board may set an earlier date to review the accused student's readmission on a case-by-case basis. (CA Ed. Code 48916(a))

Rehabilitation Plan

The Governing Board must also recommend a plan of rehabilitation (Rehab Plan) for the accused student at the time of the expulsion order, which may include, but not be limited to, periodic review as well as assessment at the time of review for readmission. The plan may also include recommendations for improved academic performance, tutoring, special education assessments, job training, counseling, employment, community service, or other rehabilitative programs. (CA Ed. Code 48916(b))

The terms of the rehab plan should take into consideration the offense(s) and the needs of the student. While it is appropriate to include aspirational terms that address attendance and grades, **it is inappropriate to deny readmission based solely on not meeting the attendance and grade components of the Rehab Plan**. For instance, a student whose attendance or grades does not meet the aspiration stated in the rehab plan should NOT be refused readmission, if the other, more substantive terms, like counseling and community service have been met.

It is essential to keep in mind that expelled students are still YOUR students and the emphasis should be on designing a rehab plan that is truly rehabilitative, not focused on punishment.

Consequently, the desired expectation is that the expelled student will return to the district once the expulsion order has terminated and will be given a "fresh start" when she/he returns. Do not use failure to comply with aspirational terms of the rehab plan as a barrier to keep students from being readmitted into the district.

Below are some examples of rehab plan terms that should be considered. The list is not exhaustive and should be modified as needed. Additional terms may be developed to meet the circumstance of a particular student and her/his offense.

- Satisfactory behavior: No violations of Education Code sections 48900, *et seq.* Commit no criminal acts while under the jurisdiction of the alternative educational placement.

- Satisfactory academic progress: Maintain a C average (or equivalent). Receive no failing grades.

- Satisfactory attendance: Be present for at least 90% of the school time at the educational program specified for the duration of this expulsion and no School Attendance Review Board (SARB) referrals.

- Stay off and away from school sites: Not be on or in the vicinity of any public school campus other than the one assigned during the period of the expulsion from the school district without the prior written permission from the Assistant Superintendent for Student Services and/or as required by the Student's program at the assigned educational program. The decision to grant or deny any such permission is final and cannot be appealed.

- Counseling: Complete one hour per week of counseling at family expense for the duration of the expulsion for a minimum of [20] sessions. This requirement can only be waived if the family cannot afford professional counseling services and services cannot be secured with the assistance of the District's Student Services Department at no or acceptable cost to the District. This must be completed before [date at least two weeks before the date set for review for consideration of readmission].

- Specialized course work: Satisfactorily completion at family expense of a course pre-approved by the District's Student Services Department on [e.g., anger management, sensitivity training, etc.] for minimum of [5] one-hour sessions.

This requirement can only be waived if the family cannot afford the course and services cannot be secured with the assistance of the District's Student Services Department at no or acceptable cost to the District. This must be completed before [date at least two weeks before the date set for review for consideration of readmission].

- Community Service: Satisfactorily complete a community service activity pre-approved by the District's Student Services Department for a minimum of [10] hours.

- Academic tutoring: Satisfactorily complete academic tutoring at family expense in the area of [e.g., language arts, mathematics, etc.] through a source pre-approved by the District Student Services Department for a minimum of [20] hours. This requirement can only be waived if the family cannot afford academic tutoring and tutoring cannot be secured with the assistance of the District's Student Services Department at no or acceptable cost to the District. This must be completed before [date at least two weeks before the date set for review for consideration of readmission].

- Employment outside of school: Satisfactorily continue employment with [name of employer] for a minimum of [10] hours per week during the period of expulsion. This requirement may be waived by the District's Student Services Department if the employment is no longer available for reasons outside of the Student's control and alternate employment cannot be reasonably found.

- Rehabilitation Program: Satisfactorily participate in a [drug/alcohol] rehabilitation program at family expense pre-approved by the District's Student Services Department for a minimum of [10] hours. This requirement can only be waived if the family cannot afford a professional rehabilitation program and services cannot be secured with the assistance of the District's Student Services Department at no or acceptable cost to the District. This must be completed before [date at least two weeks before the date set for review for consideration of readmission].

- Special Education Assessment: Student's parents agree to sign an Assessment Plan for Student to be assessed to determine qualification for special education and services and Student agrees to cooperate and participate in the assessments.

- Reviews of progress: The educational program where the student is placed, as well as the District's Department of Student Services will make periodic reviews of progress, as well as an assessment at the time of termination of the expulsion, to determine if the requirements of the Expulsion Rehabilitation Plan are fulfilled.

If the student is expelled for reasons relating to controlled substances, or alcohol, the Governing Board may require the student, prior to returning to school, to enroll in a county-supported drug rehabilitation program. However, student cannot be required to enroll in a rehabilitation program pursuant to this section without parental/guardian consent. (CA Ed. Code 48916.5)

The accused student and her/his parent/guardian must also be provided with a description of the readmission procedure at the time the expulsion order is entered. (CA Ed. Code 48916(c))

Suspended Enforcement Of The Expulsion Order

If the Governing Board decides to expel the accused student, they may also decide to suspend the enforcement of the expulsion order for a period of not more than one calendar year. During the period of the suspended enforcement of the expulsion order, the accused student is considered to be on probationary status. (CA Ed. Code 48917(a) & (c)) Many people, administrators and parents alike, mistakenly use the language "suspended expulsion" and believe that when this process is utilized, the student is not expelled. It is important to note that pursuant to a suspended enforcement of an expulsion order, the student is still expelled and will have an expulsion on her/his disciplinary record. The distinction, however, is that the student will be allowed to attend district schools while expelled.

As a condition of the suspended enforcement of the expulsion order, the accused student may be assigned to a school, class, or program that is deemed appropriate for her/his rehabilitation. The rehabilitation program to which the student is assigned may provide for the parent/guardian's involvement in the student's education in ways that are specified in the rehabilitation program. However, the parent/guardian's refusal to participate in the rehabilitation program cannot be considered by the Governing Board in determining whether the accused student has satisfactorily completed the rehabilitation program. (CA Ed. Code

48917(a))

The Governing Board, not an administrator, may revoke the suspended enforcement of the expulsion order under this section if the accused student commits any CA Ed. Code 48900 violation or violates any of the district's rules and regulations governing pupil conduct. The school administrator may make a recommendation to the Governing board requesting that they revoke the suspended enforcement of the expulsion order, and, if the Governing Board chooses to revoke the suspension of an expulsion order, the accused student may be expelled under the terms of the original expulsion order. (CA Ed. Code 48917(d)) School administrators are encouraged to be reasonable and fair when they consider recommending that a student's suspended enforcement be revoked. Students will make mistakes, engage in minor rule violations, and/or fail to comply with attendance or minimum grade requirements in the rehabilitation plan. These minor violations should not lead to a recommendation for revocation of the suspended enforcement of the expulsion order.

If the accused student satisfactorily completes the rehabilitation plan, the Governing Board must reinstate the student in a school of the district and _may_ also order the expungement of any or all records of the expulsion proceedings. (CA Ed. Code 48917(e))

School administrators should inform parents that a decision of the Governing Board to suspend the enforcement of an expulsion order does not affect the time period and requirements for the filing of an appeal of the expulsion order with the county board of education required under CA Ed. Code 48919.

Notice of Decision To Expel

The district must send the parent/guardian a written notice of any decision to expel or to suspend the enforcement of an expulsion order during a period of probation and the notice must include all of the following:

(1) Notice of the right to appeal the expulsion to the county board of education.

(2) Notice of the education alternative placement to be provided to the student during the time of expulsion.

(3) Notice of the obligation under subdivision (b) of Section 48915.1, upon the accused student's enrollment in a new school district, to inform that school district

of the student's expulsion. (CA Ed. Code 48918(j))

Educational Options During Expulsion

If the Governing Board expels the accused student, it must refer the student to a program of study that meets all of the following conditions:

(1) Is appropriately prepared to accommodate pupils who exhibit discipline problems.

(2) Is not provided at a comprehensive middle, junior, or senior high school, or at any elementary school.

(3) Is not housed at the schoolsite attended by the pupil at the time of suspension. (CA Ed. Code 58915(d))

In many situations, the educational placement available to an expelled student is provided through the County in its Community Day School Program ("CDS"). However, many districts have a CDS or Alternative School option within the district.

If the accused student is expelled from the school district for an act other than a CA Ed. Code 48915 (a) or (c) violation, the parent/guardian may request enrollment in another school district where they have either established legal residence or have an inter-district agreement. (CA Ed. Code 48915.1(a)) The parent/guardian **must** inform the new district of the student's status as an expelled student with the previous school district. (CA Ed. Code 48915.1(b))

The Governing Board of the new school district may make a determination to deny enrollment to the accused student, after a hearing, if it determines that the student poses a potential danger to either the pupils or employees of the new school district. (CA Ed. Code 48915.1(c))

The Governing Board of the new school district may consider the following options when making its determination whether to enroll the accused student:

(1) Deny enrollment.

(2) Permit enrollment.

(3) Permit conditional enrollment in a regular school program or another educational program. (CA Ed. Code 48915.1(d))

If the Governing Board of the new district determines that the accused student does not pose a danger to either the pupils or employees of the school district, it must permit the student to enroll in a school in the school district during the term of the expulsion. (CA Ed. Code 48915.1(e))

If the accused student is expelled from the school district for an act listed in CA Ed. Code 48915 (a) or (c), s/he is not allowed to enroll in any other school or school district during the period of expulsion unless it is a county community school pursuant to subdivision (c) of Section 1981, or a juvenile court school, as described in Section 48645.1, or a community day school pursuant to Article 3 (commencing with Section 48660) of Chapter 4 of Part 27. (CA Ed. Code 48915.2)

Readmission – Generally

At the conclusion of the expulsion period, the parent/guardian may apply for the student's readmission into the district. The Governing Board must readmit the student, unless they find that the student has not met the conditions of the rehabilitation plan or continues to pose a danger to campus safety or to other pupils or employees of the school district. (CA Ed. Code 48916(c))

If the Governing Board denies the student's readmission it must make a determination either to continue the student's placement in the alternative educational program initially selected for the student during the period of the expulsion order or to place the student in another program that may include, but need not be limited to, serving expelled pupils, including placement in a county community school. (CA Ed. Code 48916(d))

The Governing Board must provide the parent/guardian and the student with written notice describing the reasons for denying the student's readmittance into the regular school district program. The written notice shall also include the determination of the educational program for the student. The student must enroll in that educational program unless the parent/guardian choose to enroll the student in another school district. (CA Ed. Code 48916(e))

Process For Readmission From Expulsion Order

A Governing Board's Expulsion Order will contain a rehabilitation plan and a date for review of the student for readmission to a school in the District. Before that date, allowing for time to prepare a written report to be included in the Board member's packet for the meeting when the review is on the Board agenda, the Superintendent or designee shall do the following:

1. Hold a conference with the parent/guardian and the student.

2. At the conference, determine whether to recommend readmission to the Board by taking into consideration the student's rehabilitation plan and doing the following:

   a. Review each provisions of the student's rehabilitation plan to verify that they have been met.

   b. Look for substantial compliance of all substantive provisions in the rehabilitation plan. You may weigh any significant shortfall, particularly, serious behavioral infractions, unsatisfactory participation in a counseling program or community service, if required, as a potential basis for recommending against readmission. However, poor attendance or poor grades should **NEVER** be the sole basis for denying readmission.

   c. Evaluate whether the student poses a present danger to the safety of students or staff, weighing the nature of the offense that led to the expulsion and behavior during the period of expulsion, to consider the risk, if any, in the school environment. No student, however, shall be denied readmission into a District school based solely on the student's arrest, adjudication by a juvenile court, formal or informal supervision by a probation officer, detention in a juvenile facility, enrollment in a juvenile court school, or other such contact with the juvenile justice system.

   d. Review school regulations and require the student and parent or guardian to indicate their willingness to comply with these regulations in writing.

3. Prepare and transmit a written recommendation to the Board with a recommendation regarding readmission, supported by conclusions reached after meeting with the parent or guardian and student.

4. The Board shall consider this recommendation in closed session. If a written request for open session is received from the parent or guardian or adult student, it shall be honored to the extent that privacy rights of other students are not violated.

5. If the readmission is granted, the Superintendent or designee shall notify the student and parent or guardian, by registered mail, of the Board's decision regarding readmission.

6. The Board may deny readmission only if it finds that the student has not satisfied conditions of the rehabilitation plan or that the student continues to pose a danger to

campus safety or to other district students or employees.

7. If the Board denies readmission of a student, the Board shall determine either to continue the student's placement in the alternative educational program initially selected or to place the student in another program that serves expelled students, including placement in a county community school.

8. The Board shall provide written notice to the expelled student and parent or guardian describing the reasons for denying remittance into the regular program. This notice shall indicate the Board's determination of the educational program. The student shall enroll in that program unless the parent/guardian chooses to enroll the student in another school district.

CHAPTER **4**: EXPULSION HEARINGS

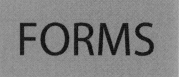

FORMS

******** UNIFIED SCHOOL DISTRICT
ADMINISTRATIVE PANEL HEARING SCRIPT
STUDENT EXPULSION HEARING

I. <u>INTRODUCTORY STATEMENT</u>

This is an Administrative panel hearing to consider the administration's recommendation that (Student's Name) enrolled at (Name of School) be expelled from the ******* Unified School District. Student is being charged with violating the following Education Code Sections: (List code sections)

This hearing is being held on (Date) at (Time) in the (Place).

My name is (Name), I am the Chairperson for the Administrative Panel. Present with me are (Panel member's names).

My role is to structure and clarify these proceedings. The Panel will be ruling on objections made during the hearing. The Panel will not rule until each party has had an opportunity to express its position with regard to the objection. The Panel may consult off the record with members of the Panel, representatives of the District and the student prior to making a ruling.

The decision of the Panel to recommend expulsion of a pupil may only be based upon substantial evidence relevant to the charges against the student and submitted at the hearing, no evidence to expel may be based solely upon hearsay evidence. The Panel may, upon a finding that good cause exists, determine that the disclosure of either the identity of a witness or the testimony of that witness at the hearing, or both, would subject the witness to an unreasonable risk of psychological or physical harm. In that event, the testimony of such witness may be presented at the hearing in the form of a sworn declaration, which shall be examined only by the panel. Copies of the declaration deleting the name and identity of the witness shall be made available to the student.

Each party will be given an opportunity to make a brief opening statement. The purpose of the statement is to summarize each party's position and the evidence, which it intends to present to support that position. These statements are not evidence and there will be no discussion of the opening remarks.

Following the opening statements, the District will present witnesses and evidence. After each witness' testimony, the student or his representative may cross-examine the witness. Reexamination and re-cross-examination is permitted. At the end of direct and cross-examination, panel members may ask clarifying questions.

After the District has concluded its case, the student or his representative may present testimony and exhibits. After the direct examination of each witness, the District has the opportunity to cross-examine the witness, panel members may ask clarifying questions. Either side may present

Panel Chairperson's Script
Expulsion Hearing
Page 2

rebuttal evidence.

After all the evidence has been submitted, each party will have the opportunity to make a closing statement. These statements summarize each party's position and request that the panel reach the conclusion in favor of the party. This hearing will be closed[1]/ to the public.

Before we begin, let me ask the representatives of the District and the student to identify themselves for the record, beginning with the District. (Representatives and parties identify themselves.)

Witnesses will be excluded.

Does either side have any questions before we begin?

II. PRESENTATION OF CASE

To District Representative: Do you wish to make an opening statement?

(Response)

Please proceed.

(District's Opening Statement)

[This should not include the presentation of any evidence. Opening Statements are not testimony but only a party's summary of its case and recommendation as to what finding the panel should reach.]

To STUDENT: Do you wish to make an opening statement or reserve it for the beginning of your case?

(Response)

Please proceed.

(Student's Opening Statement)

A. Examination of Witness/Oath (To Be Given to Each Witness)

These procedures do not call for witnesses to take an Oath prior to giving testimony. However, each witness is expected to tell the truth. Will you do so?

(I will)

(Direct examination then proceeds.)

---

[1]/Unless parent requested that the hearing be open at least five days prior to the hearing.

Panel Chairperson's Script
Expulsion Hearing
Page 3

B. <u>Cross Examination/Redirect
Examination/Re-cross Examination/Etc.</u>

Is there any (Cross-examination)?

Is there any (Redirect examination)?

(Continuing examination until both sides finish examining the witness.)

Does the panel wish to direct any questions to the witness?

C. <u>The Completion of District Case</u>

Has the District completed its case?

(Response)

D. <u>Beginning of Student's Defense</u>

_____, please call your _____

(first) (second, etc.) witness.

(Repeat as stated above direct examination/cross-examination, opportunity for Board to ask

questions.)

E. <u>Completion of Student Case/Rebuttal</u>

Have you completed your case?

(Response)

Is there any rebuttal evidence the District wishes to present?

(Response)

Please proceed.

_____ do you wish to call any additional witnesses?

(Response)

F. <u>Closing Statements</u>

To District Representative: Would you like to make a closing statement?

To Student's Representative: Would you like to make a closing statement?

(Student's closing statement)

III. <u>CHAIRPERSON'S FINAL STATEMENT</u>

The Panel will adjourn to closed session to deliberate on this matter.

Thank you all for your cooperation.

The hearing is adjourned.

Panel Chairperson's Script
Expulsion Hearing
Page 4

IV. <u>PANEL RECONVENE TO ISSUE DECISION, if applicable based on district practice</u>

Recommending Expulsion

Having found the allegations to be true based on the evidence presented, the Panel recommends that [Student Name] be expelled from the [District] Unified School District. The Governing Board will take final action in public session as to whether (Student) shall be expelled at its next scheduled board meeting.

[The Panel further recommends that enforcement of [Student's name] expulsion order suspended for the duration of the expulsion.] *Use if appropriate.

Not Recommending Expulsion

The Panel finds that the suspension will be the extent of the discipline and [Student's name] will not be recommended to the Governing Board for expulsion and no further action will be taken.

INSERT DISTRICT LETTERHEAD AND/OR LOGO

Request by Parent or Guardian for Postponement of Administrative Hearing

In the matter of the suspension and possible expulsion of:

_____

(Student Name)

_____

(Grade)

_____

(School)

To: Governing Board and Superintendent, [NAME] Unified School District

The undersigned parent or guardian of the above-named pupil hereby requests postponement in the possible expulsion of said pupil to be held on _____ .

I*n making this request the undersigned acknowledges that the pupil and parent or guardian has the right* to a hearing within 30 school days of the date the principal or the superintendent of school determined that the pupil has committed any of the acts enumerated in Section 48900-48915 of the Education Code, and hereby waives the right to such hearing within this time limit. (Ed Code 48918).

The undersigned acknowledges that decision of the governing board whether to expel the above named pupil shall be made within ten (10) school days following the conclusion of the hearing, unless the pupil requests in writing the decision to be postponed.

_____   _____

Parent/Guardian (Print Name)   Date

_____   _____

Parent/Guardian (Signature)   Date

District Request For Continuance **4.3**

INSERT DISTRICT LETTERHEAD AND/OR LOGO

DISTRICT REQUEST FOR CONTINUANCE

To: [District] Governing Board

From: [Name and position of person making request on behalf of district]

Date:

Re: Expulsion of [Student Name] – Request for Continuance

Dear Board Members:

The [Name] Unified School District respectfully requests that the governing Board grant a continuance of the administrative panel hearing to [insert new date or pending completion of special education assessment, etc.].

[Student] was involved in an incident on [Date of Incident]. On [Insert date of Principal's recommendation], the Principal of [name of school] recommended [student] for expulsion. The administrative panel hearing was scheduled to for [Date of originally scheduled hearing].

[State reason for request and facts supporting a finding of good cause]

Therefore, the District believes that good cause exists and respectfully requests that the governing Board grant a continuance of this matter to [insert new date].

Postponement of the hearing is:

Approved_____   Denied _____

_____   Date: _____

President of the Governing Board

Governing Board Subpoena and Declaration Form **4.4**

BEFORE THE GOVERNING BOARD OF THE
[_____SCHOOL DISTRICT]

In the Matter of the Expulsion of [student's name]	) NO.
	)
	) SUBPOENA
	)
	)
	)
_____	)

THE PEOPLE OF THE STATE OF CALIFORNIA TO: [Person being subpoenaed]

At the request of (name, address, and telephone): [Superintendent or superintendent's designee or pupil requesting subpoena]

You are hereby commanded to appear at: The District offices located at [District address] on [Date and Time]

And bring with you the following named books, documents, or other things now in your custody or under your control: [If applicable, documents being requested from this witness which are under his/her custody or control]

Disobedience of this subpoena is punishable as contempt in the manner prescribed by law. Upon service of this subpoena, you are entitled to witness fees and mileage actually traveled both ways, as provided by law, if you so request.

IF YOU HAVE ANY QUESTIONS ABOUT WITNESS FEES OR THE TIME OR DATE FOR YOU TO APPEAR, OR TO BE CERTAIN THAT YOUR PRESENCE IS REQUIRED, CONTACT THE PERSON REQUESTING THIS SUBPOENA, LISTED ABOVE, BEFORE THE DATE ON WHICH YOU ARE REQUIRED TO PRODUCE THE NAMED ITEMS.

   WITNESS my hand this _____ day of _____, 200___.

   [Signature of Issuing Board Member]

DECLARATION FOR SUBPOENA

The undersigned states that the books, papers, and documents or other things requested by this subpoena are material to the proper presentation of this case, and good cause exists for their production by reason of the following facts:

[Facts showing good cause for production of the matters and things described in the subpoena, specifying the exact things desired to be produced, setting forth in full detail the materiality of the things desired, and stating that the witness has the desired things in his or her possession].

I declare under penalty of perjury that the foregoing is true and correct. Executed at _____ -**, California.**

Date: _____   _____
                                [Signature of Requesting Party]

_____

THIS IS TO CERTIFY that I personally served the within subpoena by showing the original and delivering a true copy thereof personally to:

at the hour of _____ ___ **.m., on** _____**, 200__, at** _____ **by showing** _____**the original and leaving with** _____ **a true copy thereof.**

_____
[Signature of Person Serving Subpoena]

Release of Information Form **4.5**

AUTHORIZATION FOR RELEASE OF INFORMATION

I, the undersigned, do hereby authorize:

Name of School: _____

Address: _____

City, State, Zip: _____

To release documents related to:

Student's Name: _____
Date of Birth: _____

Summary of documents to be released:

_____
_____
_____
_____
_____

Person or organization records to be released to:

Name: _____

Address: _____

City, State, Zip: _____

Person authorized to release documents:

Signature: _____ Date: _____

Print Name: _____

Relationship to Student: _____

ADMINISTRATIVE PANEL FINDING OF FACTS (cont.)
[Date]
RE: [Student's name]
Page 1

[NAME] UNIFIED SCHOOL DISTRICT
ADMINISTRATIVE PANEL
FINDINGS OF FACT

In the Matter of the
Recommended Expulsion of

[STUDENTS NAME]
DOB: *****

This matter was heard before the [District] Unified School District Administrative Panel at [address of hearing location] on [day of week], [month/date], 2011. Present were the following Panel members: [**add name of panel members**].

[District] Unified School District was represented by [Name of representative]. The student was represented by [Name of Representative].

The District presented a packet of documents with [number] pages, to be included as part of the record. Student [did not] presented a packet of documents with [number] pages as documentary evidence.

The following witnesses testified during the hearing on behalf of [Name] School: [Name/Title of all witnesses]. The Student [Did or did not] testified during the hearing, but did not call any other witnesses to testify during the hearing [Or, list name s/titles of student's witnesses].

Having considered all evidence admitted at the hearing and the testimony presented, the Administrative Panel makes the following findings and recommendations.

FINDINGS OF FACT

1. At the time of the incident that led to the recommendation for Student's expulsion from the [Name] Unified School District, [Student's name] was a [Grade] grader at [Name] School.

2. As to 48900[**]:

ADMINISTRATIVE PANEL FINDING OF FACTS (cont.)
[Date]
RE: [Student's name]
Page 2

_____

_____

_____

_____

3. As to 48900[**]:

_____

_____

_____

_____

_____

4. As to 48900[**]:

_____

_____

_____

_____

5. As to 48900[**]:

_____

_____

_____

_____

6. As to 48915[**]:

_____

_____

_____

_____

ADMINISTRATIVE PANEL FINDING OF FACTS (cont.)
[Date]
RE: [Student's name]
Page 3

7. Other means of correction are not feasible or have repeatedly failed to bring about proper conduct:

_____

_____

_____

_____

8. Due to the nature of the act, the presence of the pupil causes a continuing danger to the physical safety of the pupil or others:

_____

_____

_____

_____

CONCLUSIONS OF LAW

Based on the documentary and testimonial evidence presented at the hearing and the findings of fact above, the Administrative Panel finds that [Student's Name] conduct violated Education Code sections 48900[**],[Description of section]; [list all sections with description]; and 48915[**], [List description].

The Administrative Panel further finds that [due to the nature of the act, [Student's name] presence on campus causes a continuing danger to the physical safety of the pupil or others and/or other means of correction are not feasible or have repeatedly failed to bring about proper conduct].

ADMINISTRATIVE PANEL FINDING OF FACTS (cont.)
[Date]
RE: [STUDENT NAME]
Page 1

[NAME] SCHOOL DISTRICT
ADMINISTRATIVE PANEL
FINDINGS OF FACT

In the Matter of the
Recommended Expulsion of

[NAME STUDENT]
DOB:

This matter was heard before the [NAME] School District Administrative Panel at [ADDRESS OF EXPULSION HEARING] on Monday, [DATE]. Present were the following Panel members: NAME OF PANEL MEMBERS]. The Panel was represented by Attorney Dora Dome.

[NAME] School, in the [NAME] School District, was represented by Attorney [NAME], Principal [NAME] and Assistant Principal, [NAME]. The Student was represented by his parents [NAMES]. The Parents additionally had the support of two translators at the hearing until approximately 6:00 pm. From approximately 6:00 pm until the conclusion of the hearing at approximately 10:00 pm, there was only one interpreter present translating for the family.

[NAME] School presented a packet of documents with 76 pages, through Exhibit T, which was admitted as part of the record. Student presented 10 pages of documents, through Student Exhibit 10, which was admitted as part of the record. During his testimony, it was noticed that Principal [NAME] was referring to a document to refresh his memory, regarding dates and his actions, that was not part of the evidence that had been admitted, nor had it been shared with the student and his parents. Upon noticing PRINCIPAL'S reference to the document, Ms. Dome confirmed with PRINCIPAL that the document was his personal notes that he was referring to during his testimony.

California Evidence Code 771, states in relevant part,

> (a) Subject to subdivision (c), if a witness, either while testifying or prior thereto, uses a writing to refresh his memory with respect to any matter about which he testifies, such writing must be produced at the hearing at the request of an adverse party and, unless the writing is so produced, the testimony of the witness concerning such matter shall be stricken.

> (b) If the writing is produced at the hearing, the adverse party may, if he chooses, inspect the writing, cross-examine the witness concerning it, and introduce in evidence such portion of it as may be pertinent to the testimony of the witness.

Pursuant to California Evidence Code 771, Ms. Dome instructed PRINCIPAL to discontinue referring to his notes, to remove them from the witness stand, and to make redacted copies of his notes to provide to Student, his Parents and the Panel members. Because the Student and parents were not represented by legal counsel and, while

ADMINISTRATIVE PANEL FINDING OF FACTS (cont.)
[Date]
RE: [STUDENT NAME]
Page 2

acknowledging that technical rules of evidence do not apply to Administrative Expulsion Hearings, it was Ms. Dome's position that Due Process required the document to be produced to the Student and his Parents. This redacted document was admitted into evidence as Panel Exhibit 1.

During the hearing, SCHOOL ATTORNEY introduced two "fear declarations," pursuant to CA Education Code Section 48918(f)(2), to support the introduction of Exhibits Q and R as direct evidence. Exhibit Q was supported by Exhibits N and O and argument by SCHOOL ATTORNEY. Exhibit R was supported by Exhibit P and argument by SCHOOL ATTORNEY. The process and the implications of the process were explained to PARENTS and he was provided copies of all of the declarations, which were verbally translated at the hearing, and was given an opportunity to argue why the witnesses should testify at the hearing or, in the alternative, why their respective witness statements should be admitted as hearsay. After hearing arguments from both sides, the Panel deliberated and determined that there was good cause to find that the testimony of both witnesses at the hearing would subject the witnesses to an unreasonable risk of psychological or physical harm and allowed their respective testimonies to be presented at the hearing in the form of a sworn declaration.

Exhibits Q and R are entered into evidence as direct evidence, which may be relied upon to support an expulsion recommendation.

The following witnesses testified during the hearing on behalf of [NAME] School: [NAME], Assistant Principal; [NAME], Student; [NAME], Student; NAME], Student; [NAME], Student; [NAME], Student; [NAME], Principal. [NAME], Mother and [NAME], Student, testified during the hearing.

Having considered all evidence admitted at the hearing and the testimony presented, the Administrative Panel makes the following findings and recommendations.

FINDINGS OF FACT

1. At the time of the incident that led to the recommendation for Student's expulsion from the [NAME] School District, [STUDENT NAME] was an 8th grader at [NAME] School.

2. **As to 48900(i) – Committed and obscene act or engaged in habitual profanity or vulgarity:**
   a. On February 7, 2020, while in TEACHER'S class, Student entered the class and sat in a seat toward the back of the room (not his seat in the class), where he took out his penis, exposing about half of it to WITNESS and WITNESS. (Test. NAME; NAME)

ADMINISTRATIVE PANEL FINDING OF FACTS (cont.)
[Date]
RE: [STUDENT NAME]
Page 3

b. At the same time, Student stated "VICTIM sucked my d**k," and talked about VICTIM "jacking him off." (Test. NAME; NAME)

c. Both WITNESS and WITNESS thought the comments and the exposure of his penis was inappropriate. WITNESS stated that it was "gross." (*Id.*)

d. Student also wrote comments on VICTIM'S notebook, without her permission, that were interpreted by VICTIM to be offensive and sexual in nature. Specifically, the word "water," which VICTIM believes refers to a sexually explicit song. (Test. VICTIM; Ex. L)

e. WITNESS also interpreted the writing on VICTIM's notebook that said "you're next" to be sexual in nature, since Student was talking about a sexual act prior to writing on the notebook and he interpreted Student to be saying that VICTIM was next. (Test. NAME)

f. Student exposed his penis to anonymous witness Q in the copy room. (Ex. Q)

g. The Panel finds that Student's act of exposing his penis to students in class and in the copy room, making sexual comments about VICTIM, and writing sexually inappropriate content on VICTIM's notebook all constitute obscene acts in violation of subsection (i).

h. The Panel finds the Student's denial of engaging in these incidents not to be credible.

3. **As to 48900.2 – Sexual Harassment:**

Unwelcome Conduct Of A Sexual Nature

a. While there was a period of time when some students engaged in the game, "Slap Ass Friday," there was evidence that Student slapped the asses of multiple girls outside of playing the game. (Test. WITNESS, WITNESS; WITNESS)

b. During class, Student has come up behind VICTIM and grabbed her butt without permission and not as part of the game. (Test. VICTIM)

c. During class, Student grabbed VICTIM's waist from behind and began thrusting into her. She could feel his penis touch her butt. (*Id.*)

d. Student has offered VICTIM money to allow him to touch her butt and to "let me f**k you." (*Id.*)

e. Student has asked VICTIM to give him a "hand job" and a "blow job." (*Id.*)

f. VICTIM told Student following each of the incidents to stop. (*Id.*)

g. Student touched the breast and butt of VICTIM more than 10 times. (Test. VICTIM)

h. During class, Student grabbed VICTIM's breast from behind, without her consent. (*Id.*)

i. Student would also touch VICTIM's butt when she would get up to get her books in class. (*Id.*)

j. VICTIM admitted that she has slapped Student's butt several times because she was trying to defend herself and she wanted him to "see how it feels" to have that done to him. (*Id.*)

ADMINISTRATIVE PANEL FINDING OF FACTS (cont.)
[Date]
RE: [STUDENT NAME]
Page 4

    k. One day after school as VICTIM was walking to the restroom, Student guided her to a wall, and asked her to touch his "d**k." VICTIM told him "no," at which point Student pulled his penis out of his pants, grabbed her hand, and forced her to touch his penis. (*Id.*)

    l. Student exposed his penis to anonymous witness Q in the copy room. (Ex. Q)

    m. Student asked Witness Q to "suck" his penis and to "jerk" him off. (*Id.*)

    n. Student forced Witness Q to touch his exposed penis while in the Copy room. (*Id.*)

    o. Student then grabbed the waist of Witness Q from behind and thrust his pelvis against her butt while saying, "Damn, I never knew you had an ass." (*Id.*)

    p. Student spread rumors that Witness Q "sucked his d**k." (*Id.*)

    q. Student grabbed Witness R by the waist while in the volleyball equipment room and began humping her fast and hurt her. (Ex. R)

    r. During the same incident, Student tried to pull Witness R's pants down. (*Id.*)

    s. Student also "took out his d**k" and said "suck my d**k" and "let me f**k her." (*Id.*)

    t. Student pushed Witness R against the wall while telling her to "suck" his d**k and to let him "smash." (*Id.*)

Severe or Pervasive

    a. Student engaged in the unwelcome sexual conduct directed toward VICTIM from September 2016 through December 2016. (Test. VICTIM)

    b. The act of thrusting his penis into VICTIM's butt and grabbing her butt without her permission is "severe."

    c. Student sexually touching VICTIM more than 10 times, without her consent, is "pervasive."

    d. The act of Student grabbing VICTIM's hand and forcing her to touch his penis is "severe."

    e. Student's act of grabbing the waist of Witness Q from behind and thrust his pelvis against her butt while saying, "Damn, I never knew you had an ass, was "severe."

    f. Student's acts against Witness R were "severe."

Creating an Intimidation, Offensive or Hostile Educational Environment

    a. Student's actions made VICTIM feel uncomfortable, disrespected and afraid. (*Id.*)

    b. VICTIM felt Student's actions were "disgusting" and made her constantly concerned about where he was and whether he was near her. (*Id.*)

    c. Since Student has been suspended, VICTIM feels "calmer and doesn't have to be on alert as much." (*Id.*)

ADMINISTRATIVE PANEL FINDING OF FACTS (cont.)
[Date]
RE: [STUDENT NAME]
Page 5

    d.   VICTIM felt scared and uncomfortable with Student at school. VICTIM felt concerned that Student would continue to touch her inappropriately if he remained at the same school. (Test. VICTIM)

    e.   VICTIM feels "more safe" since Student has not been at school. (*Id.*)

    f.   Witness Q was "scared and in shock" after the incident in the copy room. (Ex. Q)

    g.   Witness R was scared and did not know what to do. (Ex. R)

    h.   Since Student has been out of school, Witness R feels she does not have to worry about Student "pulling out his d**k and stuff." (*Id.*)

    i.   The Panel finds that Student's conduct constituted sexual harassment in violation of 48900.2.

    j.   The Panel finds the Student's denial of engaging in these incidents not to be credible.

4. **As to 48915(c)(4) – Sexual Battery:**

    Touching an Intimate Part

      a.   During class, Student has come up behind VICTIM and grabbed her butt without permission and not as part of the game. (Test. VICTIM)

      b.   During class, Student grabbed VICTIM's waist from behind and thrusting into her. She could feel his penis touch her butt. (*Id.*)

      c.   Student touched the breast and butt of VICTIM more than 10 times. (Test. VICTIM)

      d.   During class, Student grabbed VICTIM's breast from behind, without her consent. (*Id.*)

      e.   Student would also touch VICTIM's butt when she would get up to get her books in class. (*Id.*)

      f.   One day after school as VICTIM was walking to the restroom, STUDENT guided her to a wall, and asked her to touch his "d**k." VICTIM told him "no," at which point Student pulled his penis out of his pants, grabbed her hand, and forced her to touch his penis. (*Id.*)

      g.   Student forced Witness Q to touch his exposed penis while in the Copy room. (Ex. Q)

      h.   Student then grabbed the waist of Witness Q from behind and thrust his pelvis against her butt while saying, "Damn, I never knew you had an ass." (*Id.*)

      i.   Student grabbed Witness R by the waist while in the volleyball equipment room and began humping her fast and hurt her. (Ex. R)

      j.   During the same incident, Student tried to pull Witness R's pants down. (*Id.*)

    Against the Will of the Person Touched

      a.   VICTIM told Student following each of the incidents to stop, but he continued. (Test. VICTIM)

      b.   VICTIM did not want Student to touch her sexually. (*Id.*)

      c.   VICTIM did not give consent for Student to touch her intimate parts or to thrust his penis against her butt. (*Id.*)

ADMINISTRATIVE PANEL FINDING OF FACTS (cont.)
[Date]
RE: [STUDENT NAME]
Page 6

    d. VICTIM told Student numerous times to stop touching her and he continued. (Test. VICTIM)

    e. VICTIM did not consent to Student grabbing her hand and forcing her to touch his bare penis. (*Id.*)

    f. Witness Q did not consent to Student touching her. (Ex. Q)

    g. Witness R did not consent to Student touching her. (Ex. R)

While the person was Unlawfully Restrained

    a. Student grabbing VICTIM by the waist, holding her in place and thrusting his clothed penis against her butt is "unlawful restraint."

    b. Student grabbing VICTIM's hand and making her touch his exposed penis is "unlawful restraint."

    c. Witness Q was unlawfully restrained when Student forced her to touch her exposed penis in the Copy room and when he grabbed her by the waist and began thrusting his pelvis against her butt.

    d. Witness R was unlawfully restrained when Student grabbed Witness R by the waist while in the volleyball equipment room and began humping her fast and hurt her.

(Specific Purpose) Sexual Arousal, Sexual Abuse or Sexual Gratification

    a. Student would grin or smile when he would touch VICTIM. (Test. VICTIM)

    b. Student made sexual comments and requests for sexual favors toward VICTIM. (*Id.*)

    c. Student thrust his penis against VICTIM's butt. (*Id.*)

    d. Student forced VICTIM to touch his exposed penis. (Test. VICTIM)

    e. Student forced Witness Q to touch his exposed penis. (Ex. Q)

    f. Student grabbed Witness Q by her by the waist and began thrusting his pelvis against her butt. (*Id.*)

    g. Student grabbed Witness R by her by the waist and began thrusting his pelvis against her butt. (Ex. R)

    h. The Panel finds that the above facts constitute evidence of the purpose, **and** the specific purpose, of sexual arousal, sexual abuse, and sexual gratification.

    i. The Panel finds that student's conduct toward VICTIM, VICTIM, Witness Q, and Witness R included "unlawful restraint" (as described above) and constitutes "felony" sexual battery, in violation of CA Penal Code 243.4(a).

    j. The Panel also finds that Student's conduct of grabbing their butts and breast constitutes "misdemeanor" sexual battery, in violation of CA Penal Code 243.4(e)(1).

    k. The Panel finds Student's version of the various incidents, suggesting that several of the female students initiated the contact, not to be credible.

5. **Due to the nature of the act, the presence of the pupil causes a continuing danger to the physical safety of the pupil or others:**

ADMINISTRATIVE PANEL FINDING OF FACTS (cont.)
[Date]
RE: [STUDENT NAME]
Page 7

a. Student has engaged in inappropriate sexual conduct over the course of several months directed toward 8-9 female students. (Test. PRINCIPAL; ASSISTANT PRINCIPAL)

b. The conduct is serious in nature, in that much of it constitutes sexual battery. (*Id.*)

c. The victims have emotional scars that will stay with them for many years. (*Id.*)

d. One female student transferred schools as a result of Student's conduct against her. (*Id.*)

e. Some of the female students expressed that they were unable to focus on their academics when Student was around since much of the touching occurred during class. (ASSISTANT PRINCIPAL)

f. All of the female students who testified in person and via sworn declaration expressed fear and that Student made them feel unsafe on campus.

g. The Panel Finds that due to the nature of Student's acts, Student's presence causes a continuing to the physical safety of the Student and others.

CONCLUSIONS OF LAW

Based on the documentary and testimonial evidence presented at the hearing and the findings of fact above, the Administrative Panel finds that there is substantial evidence that STUDENT's conduct violated Education Code sections 48900(i); 48900.2; and 48915(c)(4).

The Administrative Panel further finds that due to the nature of the act, STUDENT'S presence on campus causes a continuing danger to the physical safety of the pupil or others.

Recommendation:

The Panel recommends that STUDENT be expelled from the [NAME] School District for one calendar year, pursuant to CA Education Code Section 48916(a).

(Signatures on following page)

_____   _____

[NAME], Panel Member   Date

_____   _____

[NAME], Panel Member   Date

_____   _____

[NAME], Panel Member   Date

CHAPTER 5

Special Education Discipline

TOOLS FOR THE TRADE

Special Education Discipline – Generally

A student identified as an individual with disabilities pursuant to the Individuals with Disabilities Education Act (IDEA) is subject to the same grounds for suspension and expulsion that apply to students without disabilities. The basic difference between the discipline of a student with special needs and a general education student is that a student with special needs is entitled to certain procedural protections throughout the disciplinary process and when a change of placement is being contemplated. (See 5.1 - Special Education Expulsion Flow Chart at the end of this chapter)

A student with an Individual Education Plan ("IEP") is treated the same as a general education student during the first ten (10) cumulative days of suspension. This means that a student with special needs is not entitled to IDEA protections for short-term suspensions, until the eleventh (11th) school day of removal. An IEP team can decide to proactively hold an IEP meeting to examine the behavior leading to the short-term suspensions during the first ten days, but the IDEA does not require such a meeting as part of the disciplinary procedural protections.

Tracking Partial Days of Suspension

IDEA requires the principal or designee to monitor the number of days, **including portions of days**, that students with a valid IEP have been suspended during the school year to determine when the procedural protections are triggered and the students' right to services during suspension begins. Therefore, it is essential that school districts have established and articulated clear procedures for tracking partial days of suspension. The first question for a district to consider is "how are partial days of suspension calculated?" If a student is suspended mid-day, is that calculated as a half day, full day, or are the hours of missed instruction totaled? While there is no one "right" way to calculate partial days of suspension, it is recommended that whatever method is adopted, it be utilized consistently in all schools throughout the district. Additionally, while it may be tempting to simplify the process and calculate all partial days as "full days" of suspension, this process will lead to reaching the ten (10) day threshold faster and triggering the procedural protections sooner.

The second question for a district to consider is: "who is responsible for tracking partial days of suspension?" There is typically a lack of clarity about who has this responsibility, with administrators saying it is the responsibility of the case managers and case managers saying it is the responsibility of the site administrator. The law does not dictate who is responsible for tracking partial days, only that partial days are tracked. Therefore, the school district must clearly identify who is responsible for tracking partial days of suspension in order to ensure that the triggering of IDEA procedural protections are not missed and the rights of students with special needs are provided.

Whoever is responsible for tracking partial days of suspension must understand 1) once a student with special needs reaches ten (10) cumulative days of removal, the IDEA procedural protections identified below are triggered; and 2) what the protocol is to initiate the procedural protections.

Services During Short-Term Suspensions

When a student with special needs is suspended for more than ten (10) cumulative school days in a school year, that student is entitled to continue to receive services, during the periods of suspension beyond ten (10) days. For instance, a student with special needs has already been suspended for nine (9) cumulative days this school year and has engaged in a conduct violation for which she is going to be suspended for an additional five (5) days, the additional five (5) days will bring the student's cumulative suspensions for the year to fourteen (14) days. IDEA would require, starting on day eleven (11) through day fourteen (14), that the student receive services while suspended.

The services provided to the student during these four days must: 1) enable the student to participate in the general curriculum; and 2) allow the student to make progress toward meeting the goals in the student's IEP. The student is not entitled to identical services to what she would have received if she were in school. The more services the student receives in her IEP, the more services she might need while suspended to meet the standard articulated above. For example, if the student was receiving resource services one hour per day, she might only need two total hours of home instruction during the four days in order to meet the legal standard. However, if she were in a self-contained Special Day Class ("SDC") with many other supports and services, the services she might need during the four-day suspension to meet the legal standard may be one to two hours during each of the four days. What those services will be during the short term suspension will be determined by appropriate school personnel in consultation with the teacher, and should be documented in the IEP and sent home to the parents of the student.

Manifestation Determination Procedures

Another disciplinary procedural safeguard provided by the IDEA is the requirement to conduct a manifestation determination within ten (10) school days of any decision to **change the placement** of a student with a disability because of a violation of a code of student conduct. (See below for definition of change in placement) It is important to remember that the requirement to conduct a manifestation determination when there is a proposed change in placement also applies to students with Section 504 Plans.

It is the decision to change the student's placement that triggers the requirement to conduct a manifestation determination. Therefore, the administrator must understand what proposed actions constitute a "change in placement." IDEA defines a "change in placement" as either: 1) a removal for more than ten (10) consecutive school days; or 2) a series of removals that constitute a pattern.

Change in Placement - Removal for More than 10 Consecutive School Days

The only way there can be a change in placement, in California, of a student with special needs based on a removal for more than 10 **consecutive** school days in the school year, is if the student is being recommended for expulsion or the student is facing a 45-day removal pursuant to IDEA special circumstances. In both instances, once the decision has been made to change the student's placement, the requirement to conduct the manifestation determination is triggered.

Change in Placement - Series of Removals That Constitute A Pattern

For there to be a change of placement based on a series of removals that constitute a pattern, all of the following three (3) criteria must be met:

1. The student has been removed for more than 10 **cumulative** school days in the school year;
2. The removals are for behavior substantially similar; **and**
3. The removals are in close proximity to one another. (The length and total amount of time of the removals are not relevant given California's suspension limitations.)

It is the administrator's responsibility to examine the above criteria and determine, on a case-by-case basis, whether there is a pattern of removals that constitute a change in placement. The best way to go about making this determination is for the administrator to consider the ten (10) cumulative days as a trigger to begin the analysis.

Once a student with special needs has reached ten (10) cumulative days of suspension in the school year, the administrator should review the previous suspensions that make up the ten (10) cumulative days and determine whether the behaviors are substantially similar. If the behaviors are **not** substantially similar, the analysis stops there, there is no change of placement based on a pattern, and a manifestation determination IEP is not required.

However, if the administrator examines the previous suspensions and finds that the behaviors are substantially similar, the administrator must then examine the proximity of the removals to one another. For example, if the removals were spread out over the course of 6 months, it is likely the criteria is not met, it is not a change of placement, and a manifestation determination IEP is not required. However, if the removals all occurred within the course of a 6-week period, the proximity criteria would be met, and the administrator should determine that there has been a change in placement based on a pattern of removals, and a manifestation determination IEP would be required.

There is no clear rule in making a determination about proximity. However, a useful way of thinking about proximity of removals is to count the total number of instructional days since the beginning of school and the current incident, and compare that to the number of instructional days the student has been suspended during that same timeframe. If the student has been suspended ten (10) out of forty (40) instructional days, they would likely meet the proximity standard and trigger the requirement to conduct a manifestation determination based on a pattern of removals. However, if the student has been suspended ten (10) out of one-hundred-forty (140) instructional days, it would be reasonable to conclude that the proximity standard has not been met and there is NOT a pattern of removals, thus no requirement to conduct a manifestation determination. (See 5.2 - Sample Change in Placement – Series of Removals Assessment Form at the end of this chapter)

Manifestation Determination IEP

Once it has been determined that there is a proposed change in placement either because of an expulsion recommendation, 45-day removal, or a pattern of removals, a manifestation determination IEP must be held within ten (10) school days to determine whether the conduct is a manifestation of the student's disability.

The district, the parent, and relevant members of the IEP team must review all relevant information in the student's file including: the child's IEP, any teacher observations, and any relevant information provided by the parents. Once the above information has been reviewed, the IEP Team must discuss and answer the following questions:

- Whether the conduct in question was caused by, or had a direct and substantial relationship to, the child's disability; **or**

- Whether the conduct in question was the direct result of the District's failure to implement the IEP.

As these questions are being discussed by the IEP Team, it is important that the team clearly state the causal connection, or lack thereof, between the behavior and the disability, as manifested by the student, or the specific elements of the IEP that were not implemented, if applicable, and how that failure led to the student's behavior. The IEP Team should focus on the manifestations of the disability for the specific student, as evidenced by the needs, goals, and services in the student's IEP and NOT on the manifestations of a particular diagnosis. For instance, the diagnoses of Emotional Disturbance or ADHD have countless manifestations. However, the inquiry should not be on whether the behavior would be a manifestation of anyone with the diagnosis, but whether the conduct was a manifestation of the way the diagnosis manifests for this particular student.

If either question is answered in the affirmative, the behavior is a manifestation of the disability and the proposed change in placement cannot go forward.

If the IEP Team determines that the behavior **was** a manifestation of the disability, the team must:

- Conduct a functional behavioral assessment, and implement a Behavioral Support Plan (BSP or PBIP), provided the district had not previously conducted such assessment;

- Review the BSP or PBIP if the child already has such a plan, and modify it, as necessary, to address the behavior; and

- Except in special circumstances, return the child to the placement from which the child was removed, unless the parent and the district agree to a change of placement as part of the modification of the BSP or PBIP.

If the team determines that the behavior **was not** a manifestation of the disability, then the proposed change in placement may proceed as follows:

- General education discipline procedures apply.

- Student may be suspended pending expulsion if expulsion is being recommended.

- Services may be provided in an interim alternative educational setting.

- The student should receive, *as appropriate*, a functional behavioral assessment, behavior intervention services and modifications, that are designed to address the behavior violation so that it does not recur.

When there is a disciplinary change in placement following a determination that the student's behavior was not a manifestation of the disability or pursuant to a 45-day change in placement, the student is entitled to services beginning the 11th cumulative day of removal, as discussed in Services During Short-Term Suspensions above. However, the services to be provided during the change in placement must be determined by the IEP Team. (See 5.3 - Sample Expulsion Checklist – IDEA/Section 504 Form at the end of this chapter)

Special Circumstances – 45-Day Placements

IDEA allows school personnel to remove a student with special needs to an interim alternative educational setting (IAES) for not more than 45 school days **without regard** to whether the behavior was a manifestation of the disability, when the student engages in the following conduct:

- Carries or possesses a weapon **to or at** school, **on** school premises, or **to or at** a school function;

- Knowingly possesses or uses illegal drugs, or sells or solicits the sale of a controlled substance, while **at** school, **on** school premises, or **at** a school function; or

- Inflicted serious bodily injury upon another person while **at** school, **on** school premises, **or** at a school function.

There are a few important things to note about this provision. First, the district's ability to utilize this provision for conduct that violates any of these sections is limited mostly to conduct that occurs at school or school functions. If the conduct involves a weapon, the district may also utilize this provision if the possession of the weapon occurs on the way to school. Practically speaking, the administrator must be able to establish that the conduct occurred within the applicable jurisdiction in order to remove a student with special needs to a 45-day interim placement for violation of any of these sections.

For example, if a fight that resulted in serious bodily injury occurred after school or off school grounds, the district would not be able to utilize the 45-day removal provision, as the conduct occurred outside of the jurisdiction for this section. The school could still suspend the student for the conduct pursuant to 48900(a)(1) & (2), and potentially recommend expulsion based on 48900(a)(1) & (2) and secondary findings, which are subject to the broader jurisdictional statement contained at 48900(s). However, if the IEP Team determined that the conduct was a manifestation of the student's disability, the expulsion process would stop and the student would be able to return to the placement from which s/he was removed.

Second, the 45-day removal provision is significant in that it is essentially sanctioned discrimination, as it allows a student with special needs who has engaged in one of the listed behaviors to be removed to an IAES for behavior that is a manifestation of the disability, without the consent of the parent. Using the same example above, let's say the fight occurred after school but on school grounds. The IEP team finds that the behavior is a manifestation of the disability, which would normally require that the student be returned to the placement from which s/he was removed. However, because the conduct occurred on campus, the 45-day removal provision can be utilized and the student can be placed in an IAES for up to 45 days, even though the behavior was a manifestation of the student's disability and the expulsion recommendation could not go forward.

Third, the basic assumptions that support using this process are: 1) the behavior is a manifestation of the disability; and 2) there is disagreement between the school and the parents about where the student should be placed following the conduct. Therefore, when utilizing the 45-day removal provision, it is important for the administrator to think about it as a "time-out," an opportunity to have the student safely maintained in the IAES while the IEP Team explores alternative placement options that the parents can agree to. If it becomes apparent that the IEP Team cannot reach agreement about placement, the 45-day removal process allows the district and/or parents time to pursue an administrative placement determination, while the student is still safely maintained in the IAES.

Lastly, because placement in the IAES is a change of placement, the location of the IAES and the services to be provided in the IAES must be determined by the IEP team. Additionally, the student should receive, *as appropriate*, a functional behavioral assessment, behavior intervention services, and modifications that are designed to address the behavior violation so that it does not recur.

Special Education Disciplinary Appeals

Appeal Procedures

If the parents disagree with the IEP team's manifestation determination or disciplinary change in placement, they have a right to file a disciplinary appeal.

Similarly, if the district believes that maintaining the current placement of the student is substantially likely to result in injury to the student or others, the district has the right to file a disciplinary appeal.

The appeals are filed with the Office of Administrative Hearings ("OAH") and are presided over by an Administrative Law Judge ("ALJ"). IDEA requires that the appeal be expedited, such that the hearing must occur within 20 school days of the date that the hearing is requested and the hearing decision must be rendered within 10 school days after the hearing has concluded. The student remains in the IAES pending the decision of the ALJ or until the expiration of the 45-day placement, whichever occurs first, unless the parent and the district agree otherwise.

Authority of the Hearing Officer

The ALJ hearing the disciplinary appeal only has two options when rendering a decision.

1) The ALJ may order the return of the student to the placement from which the student was

removed. This would mean that the ALJ found that the IEP Team's manifestation determination or placement decision was not appropriate or, if the appeal was filed by the district, that the district did not establish that it had done all it could to maintain the student safely in the student's original placement.

2) The ALJ may order a change of placement to the appropriate IAES for not more than 45 school days. This would mean that the ALJ found that the determination of the IEP Team was appropriate or that the student could not be safely maintained in the original placement.

However, it is important to note that the authority of the ALJ to change a student's placement pursuant to a disciplinary appeal is limited to a maximum of 45 days. Therefore, this is not a permanent solution to an IEP Team placement disagreement, because if the IEP Team cannot reach an agreement regarding placement prior to the expiration of the 45 days, the student has a right to return to the original placement from which s/he was removed.

Protections for Children Not Yet Eligible for Special Education

There is a group of general education students, who have not been identified as eligible for special education, who engage in conduct violations that could potentially lead to a change in placement (i.e., expulsion recommendation) and who are entitled to the procedural safeguard provided by IDEA.

Whether or not a particular student is entitled to the IDEA procedural safeguards will depend on whether the district may be *deemed to have knowledge* that the student was, or may be, a student with a disability at the time the student engaged the conduct violation. The determination of whether the district may be *deemed to have knowledge* is typically made by the school site administrator.

Is the District Deemed to Have Knowledge?

Below are the three criteria for determining whether the district may be *deemed to have knowledge*. I will first explain the criteria, provide examples of each situation, then summarize the implications of what it means for a district to be *deemed to have knowledge*.

1. The parent of the student has expressed concern in writing, to supervisory or administrative personnel of the appropriate educational agency or to a teacher of the student, that the student is in need of special education. In this scenario, if the parent sent a letter, email, etc., to the student's teacher or a school administrator indicating that the parent believes that the

student may need special education services, prior to the student engaging in the conduct violation, the district would *be deemed to have knowledge*.

2. The parent of the student has <u>requested a special education evaluation</u>. In this scenario, the parent came into the office and asked the clerk what the process is for her to have her child assessed for special education. The clerk described the process and asked the parent to make her request in writing to start the process. Two (2) weeks have passed and the parent has not turned in her written request for an evaluation, but her daughter has engaged in a conduct violation during this time and is facing an expulsion recommendation. In this scenario, the district would be *deemed to have knowledge*.

3. The teacher of the student, or other personnel of the district, has <u>expressed specific concerns about a pattern of behavior</u> demonstrated by the student, directly to the director of special education or to other supervisory personnel. In this scenario, the school is holding an Student Study Team ("SST") meeting for the student. During the meeting the teacher expresses specific concerns about the student's behavior in his class that the SST team tries to address with modifications and supports. Shortly following the meeting, the student engages in a conduct violation and is facing an expulsion recommendation. In this scenario, the district would be *deemed to have knowledge*.

Once the school administrator has been informed that there may be a *basis of knowledge*, s/he would be expected to investigate the allegation and, if substantiated, determine that there is a *basis of knowledge* and proceed to the next steps.

When a Basis of Knowledge Exists

It is important to note that a district being *deemed to have knowledge* is not a bad thing. If there is a *basis of knowledge* that the student was, or may have been a student with a disability at the time the student engaged in the conduct violation, then the student is entitled to special education protections. Practically speaking, all this means is that the school will need to jump through a few hoops before it can determine whether it has the authority to discipline the student.

Once a *basis of knowledge* has been established, the District must follow the steps below:

- Conduct an expedited comprehensive assessment (ideally within 30 days);

- Hold an IEP to determine whether the student meets the IDEA eligibility criteria;

- If the student **is no**t eligible for special education, the IDEA process stops, the student is a general education student, and general education discipline procedures apply;

- If the student **is** eligible for special education, complete the development of the IEP and then conduct a manifestation determination based on the IEP just developed;

- If the behavior is found **to be a manifestation** of the student's disability, the general education disciplinary process stops and the student is placed in the FAPE placement identified in the newly developed IEP and a functional behavioral assessment should be conducted to address the behavior at issue;

- If the behavior is found **not to be a manifestation** of the student's disability, the general education discipline procedures apply and the student may be disciplined for the conduct violation, subject to receiving continued educational services in the alternative setting.

When conducting a manifestation determination for a student in this scenario, it should be noted that the analysis of the first question, "whether the conduct in question was caused by, or had a direct and substantial relationship to, the child's disability?" is the same as described above in the section on manifestation determinations. However, the analysis of the second question, "whether the conduct in question was the direct result of the District's failure to implement the IEP?" is slightly more complicated. The student was not identified as a student with special needs, nor did the student have an IEP, at the time the conduct violation was committed. Therefore, the school by definition failed to implement the IEP. Significant, however, is the fact that, in this scenario, the analysis requires that the failure to implement the IEP **caused** the conduct violation. Consequently, the team must review the newly developed IEP and determine whether the failure to implement the newly developed IEP caused the student to engage in the conduct violation.

For example, a student is being recommended for expulsion for selling Ecstasy (a drug) on campus. She is assessed for special education and found eligible under the category of Specific Learning Disability ("SLD"). The student's IEP reflects supports and services to address her learning disability. The manifestation determination analysis would examine the supports and services identified in the newly developed IEP and would then assess whether the failure to provide the SLD services caused the student to sell drugs on campus. In this scenario, the outcome is likely that the conduct **was not** a manifestation of the disability and the expulsion recommendation could proceed.

However, in a different scenario, a student is being recommended for expulsion for hitting a teacher. The student is assessed and found eligible under the category of Emotional Disturbance ("ED"). The student's newly developed IEP includes a BSP that indicated that when the student is showing signs of agitation and escalation, she should be given a break from tasks and provided with strategies to de-escalate. However, in the incident with the teacher, instead of being given a break and provided with strategies to de-escalate, the teacher began yelling at and criticizing the student in front of the class and when the student tried to leave the class, the teacher blocked her exit. In response, the student hit the teacher, pushed him out of the way and left the class. In this scenario, the outcome is likely that the conduct **was** a manifestation of the disability, as it is likely that had the teacher implemented the BSP, the student's conduct would not have escalated the way it did and the student would not have hit the teacher. In this case, the expulsion recommendation would have to be withdrawn.

Exceptions To There Being A Basis of Knowledge

There are three situations in which the district will not be deemed to have knowledge, regardless of whether any of the scenarios above have occurred. They are:

1. The parent has not allowed an evaluation of the child;
2. The parent has refused services; or
3. The child has been evaluated and determined not to be a child with a disability. (This evaluation should have occurred within the calendar year.)

These exceptions recognize that situations exist where the student has been identified and/or evaluated and the parents have not allowed the district to properly serve the student. In these instances, the student would not be entitled to the IDEA protections and would be treated as a general education student for disciplinary purposes.

When There is Not A Basis of Knowledge

If the administrator, following an investigation into the matter, is unable to substantiate the allegation that the district has a basis of knowledge, then the student is a general education student and general education disciplinary procedures apply. However, IDEA requires that if the parent makes a request for an evaluation during the time period in which the student is subjected to disciplinary action, the evaluation must be conducted in an expedited manner.

Pending the results of this evaluation, the child shall remain in the disciplinary educational placement determined by school authorities, and the outcome of the evaluation will not impact the previous discipline levied against the student. (See 5.4 – Code of Federal Regulations for rules governing special education discipline at the end of this chapter)

CHAPTER 5: SPECIAL EDUCATION DISCIPLINE

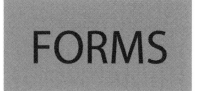

Special Education Expulsion Flow Chart **5.1**

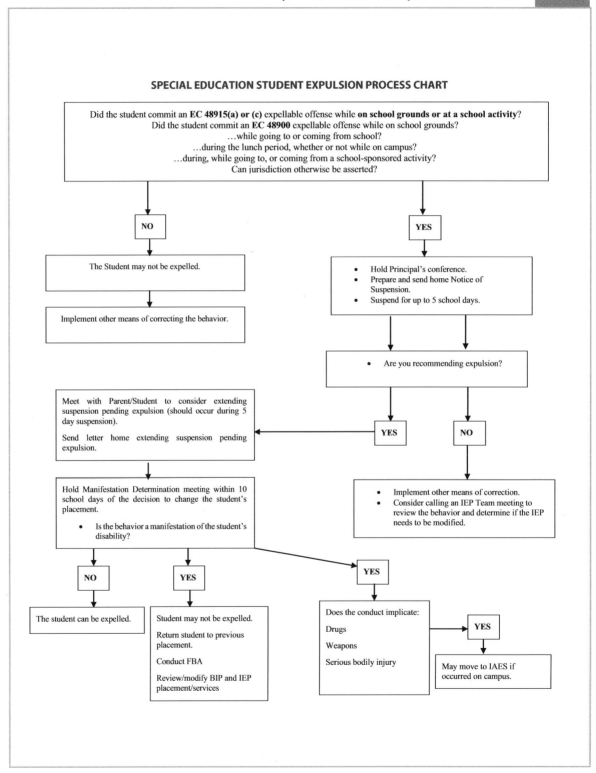

SPECIAL EDUCATION STUDENT EXPULSION PROCESS CHART

Did the student commit an **EC 48915(a) or (c)** expellable offense while **on school grounds or at a school activity**?
Did the student commit an **EC 48900** expellable offense while on school grounds?
…while going to or coming from school?
…during the lunch period, whether or not while on campus?
…during, while going to, or coming from a school-sponsored activity?
Can jurisdiction otherwise be asserted?

NO

The Student may not be expelled.

Implement other means of correcting the behavior.

YES

- Hold Principal's conference.
- Prepare and send home Notice of Suspension.
- Suspend for up to 5 school days.

- Are you recommending expulsion?

Meet with Parent/Student to consider extending suspension pending expulsion (should occur during 5 day suspension).

Send letter home extending suspension pending expulsion.

YES

NO

- Implement other means of correction.
- Consider calling an IEP Team meeting to review the behavior and determine if the IEP needs to be modified.

Hold Manifestation Determination meeting within 10 school days of the decision to change the student's placement.

- Is the behavior a manifestation of the student's disability?

NO

YES

YES

The student can be expelled.

Student may not be expelled.

Return student to previous placement.

Conduct FBA

Review/modify BIP and IEP placement/services

Does the conduct implicate:

Drugs

Weapons

Serious bodily injury

YES

May move to IAES if occurred on campus.

Change in Placement – Series of Removals Assessment Form **5.2**

INSERT DISTRICT LETTERHEAD AND/OR LOGO

Change in Placement – Series of Removals Assessment Form
Suspension Beyond 10 Cumulative School Days in a School Year
(To be completed by site administrator)

Date: _____ School: _____

Student: _____ DOB: _____

Grade: _____ CSIS: _____

Current Education Code 48900 violation: _____

Number of proposed suspension days for this offense: _____

Total cumulative suspension days this school year (including current suspension): _____

Is student entitled to IEP services during this suspension (Cumulative days of suspension exceeds 10 days)? _____

DETERMINATION OF EXTENT OF SERVICE NEEDS

1. School personnel under authority to remove determining extent of service to occur during suspension:

    _____   _____

    Title   Site Administrator

2. Special education teacher also involved in determining extent of service during suspension:

    _____

SUSPENSION HISTORY REVIEW

In considering this suspension, school personnel, _____ title
_____ reviewed the proposed suspension and history of suspensions and
determined this suspension does/does not constitute a pattern of removals that amount to a change in placement.

The following factors were considered (must meet all three for a pattern to exist):

_____ Cumulative days of removal exceeds 10 school days this school year;

_____ Behavior substantially similar; **AND**

_____ Proximity of removals;

_____ Manifest Determination not required (pattern does not constitute change in placement).

_____ Manifest Determination required (pattern does constitute change in placement).

Scheduled Manifest Determination IEP within 10 school days.

Date (if appropriate): _____.

INSERT DISTRICT LETTERHEAD AND/OR LOGO

Expulsion of Students with Special Needs – IDEA/Section 504
Checklist:

_____ Send copy of expulsion recommendation to superintendent/designee for violation of Ed Code(s) 48900 or 48915.

_____ Superintendent/designee schedules a meeting with the parent and the pupil to determine whether to extend the suspension within the first five days of the suspension.

_____ Superintendent/designee notifies the parent and the pupil of the decision to extend the suspension, their procedural rights, and of the expulsion hearing date, if known.

_____ Notify parent of suspension, procedural safeguards, and referral to Interim Alternative Education Setting (IAES), when appropriate.

_____ District provides written notice to parent of intent to conduct an IEP/Section 504 team meeting to make a manifestation determination.

_____ Hold IEP/Section 504 team meeting. Review all necessary components to make manifestation determination.

_____ IEP/Section 504 team determines if conduct was a manifestation of the student's disability and determines if the expulsion process can continue or makes recommendations for behavioral intervention and appropriate changes to the placement, instruction, and/or services as needed.

_____ If conduct is not a manifestation of the disability, Superintendent/designee arranges the expulsion hearing within thirty school days and the board meeting within forty school days (Education Code Section 48918 (a)).

_____ Superintendent/designee notifies the parent in writing of the date, time and place of the hearing, and the recommendation for expulsion and the procedural rights of the expulsion process.

_____ Site Administrator prepares packet for the hearing.

34 CFR §300.530 - 300.537

Code of Federal Regulations
Title 34. Education
Subtitle B. Regulations of the Offices of the Department of Education
Chapter III. Office of Special Education and Rehabilitative Services, Department of Education
Part 300. Assistance to States for the Education of Children with Disabilities (Refs & Annos)
Subpart E. Procedural Safeguards
Discipline Procedures

34 C.F.R. § 300.530

§ 300.530 Authority of school personnel.

Effective: October 13, 2006

Currentness

(a) Case-by-case determination. School personnel may consider any unique circumstances on a case-by-case basis when determining whether a change in placement, consistent with the other requirements of this section, is appropriate for a child with a disability who violates a code of student conduct.

(b) General.

(1) School personnel under this section may remove a child with a disability who violates a code of student conduct from his or her current placement to an appropriate interim alternative educational setting, another setting, or suspension, for not more than 10 consecutive school days (to the extent those alternatives are applied to children without disabilities), and for additional removals of not more than 10 consecutive school days in that same school year for separate incidents of misconduct (as long as those removals do not constitute a change of placement under § 300.536).

(2) After a child with a disability has been removed from his or her current placement for 10 school days in the same school year, during any subsequent days of removal the public agency must provide services to the extent required under paragraph (d) of this section.

(c) Additional authority. For disciplinary changes in placement that would exceed 10 consecutive school days, if the behavior that gave rise to the violation of the school code is determined not to be a manifestation of the child's disability pursuant to paragraph (e) of this section, school personnel may apply the relevant disciplinary procedures to children with disabilities in the same manner and for the same duration as the procedures would be applied to children without disabilities, except as provided in paragraph (d) of this section.

(d) Services.

(1) A child with a disability who is removed from the child's current placement pursuant to paragraphs (c), or (g) of this section must—

(i) Continue to receive educational services, as provided in § 300.101(a), so as to enable the child to continue to

Code of Federal Regulations
  Title 34. Education
    Subtitle B. Regulations of the Offices of the Department of Education
      Chapter III. Office of Special Education and Rehabilitative Services, Department of Education
        Part 300. Assistance to States for the Education of Children with Disabilities (Refs & Annos)
          Subpart E. Procedural Safeguards
          Discipline Procedures

34 C.F.R. § 300.531

§ 300.531 Determination of setting.

Effective: October 13, 2006

Currentness

The child's IEP Team determines the interim alternative educational setting for services under § 300.530(c), (d)(5), and (g).

(Authority: 20 U.S.C. 1415(k)(2))

SOURCE: 71 FR 46755, Aug. 14, 2006; 72 FR 17781, April 9, 2007; 80 FR 23666, April 28, 2015, unless otherwise noted.

AUTHORITY: 20 U.S.C. 1221e–3, 1406, 1411–1419, 3474, unless otherwise noted.

Notes of Decisions (1)

Current through March 24, 2016; 81 FR 16051.

End of Document	© 2016 Thomson Reuters. No claim to original U.S. Government Works.

Code of Federal Regulations
Title 34. Education
Subtitle B. Regulations of the Offices of the Department of Education
Chapter III. Office of Special Education and Rehabilitative Services, Department of Education
Part 300. Assistance to States for the Education of Children with Disabilities (Refs & Annos)
Subpart E. Procedural Safeguards
Discipline Procedures

34 C.F.R. § 300.532

§ 300.532 Appeal.

Effective: October 13, 2006

Currentness

(a) General. The parent of a child with a disability who disagrees with any decision regarding placement under §§ 300.530 and 300.531, or the manifestation determination under § 300.530(e), or an LEA that believes that maintaining the current placement of the child is substantially likely to result in injury to the child or others, may appeal the decision by requesting a hearing. The hearing is requested by filing a complaint pursuant to §§ 300.507 and 300.508(a) and (b).

(b) Authority of hearing officer.

(1) A hearing officer under § 300.511 hears, and makes a determination regarding an appeal under paragraph (a) of this section.

(2) In making the determination under paragraph (b)(1) of this section, the hearing officer may—

(i) Return the child with a disability to the placement from which the child was removed if the hearing officer determines that the removal was a violation of § 300.530 or that the child's behavior was a manifestation of the child's disability; or

(ii) Order a change of placement of the child with a disability to an appropriate interim alternative educational setting for not more than 45 school days if the hearing officer determines that maintaining the current placement of the child is substantially likely to result in injury to the child or to others.

(3) The procedures under paragraphs (a) and (b)(1) and (2) of this section may be repeated, if the LEA believes that returning the child to the original placement is substantially likely to result in injury to the child or to others.

(c) Expedited due process hearing.

(1) Whenever a hearing is requested under paragraph (a) of this section, the parents or the LEA involved in the dispute

Code of Federal Regulations
Title 34. Education
Subtitle B. Regulations of the Offices of the Department of Education
Chapter III. Office of Special Education and Rehabilitative Services, Department of Education
Part 300. Assistance to States for the Education of Children with Disabilities (Refs & Annos)
Subpart E. Procedural Safeguards
Discipline Procedures

34 C.F.R. § 300.533

§ 300.533 Placement during appeals.

Effective: October 30, 2007

Currentness

When an appeal under § 300.532 has been made by either the parent or the LEA, the child must remain in the interim alternative educational setting pending the decision of the hearing officer or until the expiration of the time period specified in § 300.530(c) or (g), whichever occurs first, unless the parent and the SEA or LEA agree otherwise.

(Authority: 20 U.S.C. 1415(k)(4)(A))

Credits

[72 FR 61307, Oct. 30, 2007]

SOURCE: 71 FR 46755, Aug. 14, 2006; 72 FR 17781, April 9, 2007; 80 FR 23666, April 28, 2015, unless otherwise noted.

AUTHORITY: 20 U.S.C. 1221e–3, 1406, 1411–1419, 3474, unless otherwise noted.

Notes of Decisions (2)

Current through March 24, 2016; 81 FR 16051.

End of Document	© 2016 Thomson Reuters. No claim to original U.S. Government Works.

Code of Federal Regulations
  Title 34. Education
    Subtitle B. Regulations of the Offices of the Department of Education
      Chapter III. Office of Special Education and Rehabilitative Services, Department of Education
        Part 300. Assistance to States for the Education of Children with Disabilities (Refs & Annos)
          Subpart E. Procedural Safeguards
            Discipline Procedures

34 C.F.R. § 300.534

§ 300.534 Protections for children not determined eligible for special education and related services.

Effective: October 13, 2006

Currentness

(a) General. A child who has not been determined to be eligible for special education and related services under this part and who has engaged in behavior that violated a code of student conduct, may assert any of the protections provided for in this part if the public agency had knowledge (as determined in accordance with paragraph (b) of this section) that the child was a child with a disability before the behavior that precipitated the disciplinary action occurred.

(b) Basis of knowledge. A public agency must be deemed to have knowledge that a child is a child with a disability if before the behavior that precipitated the disciplinary action occurred—

(1) The parent of the child expressed concern in writing to supervisory or administrative personnel of the appropriate educational agency, or a teacher of the child, that the child is in need of special education and related services;

(2) The parent of the child requested an evaluation of the child pursuant to §§ 300.300 through 300.311; or

(3) The teacher of the child, or other personnel of the LEA, expressed specific concerns about a pattern of behavior demonstrated by the child directly to the director of special education of the agency or to other supervisory personnel of the agency.

(c) Exception. A public agency would not be deemed to have knowledge under paragraph (b) of this section if—

(1) The parent of the child—

(i) Has not allowed an evaluation of the child pursuant to §§ 300.300 through 300.311; or

(ii) Has refused services under this part; or

Code of Federal Regulations
  Title 34. Education
    Subtitle B. Regulations of the Offices of the Department of Education
      Chapter III. Office of Special Education and Rehabilitative Services, Department of Education
        Part 300. Assistance to States for the Education of Children with Disabilities (Refs & Annos)
          Subpart E. Procedural Safeguards
          Discipline Procedures

34 C.F.R. § 300.535

§ 300.535 Referral to and action by law enforcement and judicial authorities.

Effective: October 13, 2006

Currentness

(a) Rule of construction. Nothing in this part prohibits an agency from reporting a crime committed by a child with a disability to appropriate authorities or prevents State law enforcement and judicial authorities from exercising their responsibilities with regard to the application of Federal and State law to crimes committed by a child with a disability.

(b) Transmittal of records.

(1) An agency reporting a crime committed by a child with a disability must ensure that copies of the special education and disciplinary records of the child are transmitted for consideration by the appropriate authorities to whom the agency reports the crime.

(2) An agency reporting a crime under this section may transmit copies of the child's special education and disciplinary records only to the extent that the transmission is permitted by the Family Educational Rights and Privacy Act.

(Authority: 20 U.S.C. 1415(k)(6))

SOURCE: 71 FR 46755, Aug. 14, 2006; 72 FR 17781, April 9, 2007; 80 FR 23666, April 28, 2015, unless otherwise noted.

AUTHORITY: 20 U.S.C. 1221e–3, 1406, 1411–1419, 3474, unless otherwise noted.

Notes of Decisions (1)

Current through March 24, 2016; 81 FR 16051.

| End of Document | © 2016 Thomson Reuters. No claim to original U.S. Government Works. |

Code of Federal Regulations
Title 34. Education
Subtitle B. Regulations of the Offices of the Department of Education
Chapter III. Office of Special Education and Rehabilitative Services, Department of Education
Part 300. Assistance to States for the Education of Children with Disabilities (Refs & Annos)
Subpart E. Procedural Safeguards
Discipline Procedures

34 C.F.R. § 300.536

§ 300.536 Change of placement because of disciplinary removals.

Effective: October 13, 2006

Currentness

(a) For purposes of removals of a child with a disability from the child's current educational placement under §§ 300.530 through 300.535, a change of placement occurs if—

(1) The removal is for more than 10 consecutive school days; or

(2) The child has been subjected to a series of removals that constitute a pattern—

(i) Because the series of removals total more than 10 school days in a school year;

(ii) Because the child's behavior is substantially similar to the child's behavior in previous incidents that resulted in the series of removals; and

(iii) Because of such additional factors as the length of each removal, the total amount of time the child has been removed, and the proximity of the removals to one another.

(b)(1) The public agency determines on a case-by-case basis whether a pattern of removals constitutes a change of placement.

(2) This determination is subject to review through due process and judicial proceedings.

(Authority: 20 U.S.C. 1415(k))

SOURCE: 71 FR 46755, Aug. 14, 2006; 72 FR 17781, April 9, 2007; 80 FR 23666, April 28, 2015, unless otherwise noted.

Code of Federal Regulations
  Title 34. Education
    Subtitle B. Regulations of the Offices of the Department of Education
      Chapter III. Office of Special Education and Rehabilitative Services, Department of Education
        Part 300. Assistance to States for the Education of Children with Disabilities (Refs & Annos)
          Subpart E. Procedural Safeguards
            Discipline Procedures

34 C.F.R. § 300.537

§ 300.537 State enforcement mechanisms.

Effective: October 13, 2006

Currentness

Notwithstanding §§ 300.506(b)(7) and 300.510(d)(2), which provide for judicial enforcement of a written agreement reached as a result of mediation or a resolution meeting, there is nothing in this part that would prevent the SEA from using other mechanisms to seek enforcement of that agreement, provided that use of those mechanisms is not mandatory and does not delay or deny a party the right to seek enforcement of the written agreement in a State court of competent jurisdiction or in a district court of the United States.

(Authority: 20 U.S.C. 1415(e)(2)(F), 1415(f)(1)(B))

SOURCE: 71 FR 46755, Aug. 14, 2006; 72 FR 17781, April 9, 2007; 80 FR 23666, April 28, 2015, unless otherwise noted.

AUTHORITY: 20 U.S.C. 1221e–3, 1406, 1411–1419, 3474, unless otherwise noted.

Current through March 24, 2016; 81 FR 16051.

End of Document	© 2016 Thomson Reuters. No claim to original U.S. Government Works.

CHAPTER 6

Foster and Homeless Students in the Disciplinary Process

TOOLS FOR THE TRADE

Foster and Homeless Students – Generally

Foster and homeless students are subject to the same disciplinary rules as every other student. However, similar to students with special needs, foster and homeless students are entitled to certain procedural protections when facing exclusionary discipline. Additionally, given the potential complexities of being in foster placement or homeless, school districts must ensure that these often marginalized students are provided the following rights and protections:

(a) All pupils have the right to participate fully in the educational process, free from discrimination and harassment.

(b) California's public schools have an affirmative obligation to combat racism, sexism, and other forms of bias, and a responsibility to provide equal educational opportunity.

(c) Harassment on school grounds directed at an individual on the basis of personal characteristics or status creates a hostile environment and jeopardizes equal educational opportunity as guaranteed by the California Constitution and the United States Constitution. (CA. Ed. Code 201)

CA Ed. Code 201 further requires schools to prevent a hostile environment and discrimination of any kind in the "educational process," which includes disciplinary proceedings. Students with the personal characteristics of homelessness or being in the foster care system are clearly entitled to these protections.

Homeless Students

The fundamental legal framework for schools to deal with student homelessness is contained in the McKinney-Vento Act at 42 U.S.C. § 11431. This statute is designed to ensure that children and youth experiencing homelessness have access to the same free, appropriate public education and services as their peers.

The McKinney-Vento Act specifically requires each school district to appoint "appropriate staff" as a liaison for students experiencing homelessness.

If a school district is recommending a "discretionary expulsion" pursuant to CA Ed. Code 48915(a) or 48900, and the pupil is a homeless child or youth, notice of the expulsion hearing must be provided to the district's liaison for homeless children and youth <u>at least 10 calendar days before the date of the hearing</u>. The notice may be made using the most cost-effective method possible, which may include, but is not limited to, electronic mail or a telephone call. If the student is being recommended for a mandatory expulsion pursuant to CA Ed. Code 48915(c), notice to the liaison is not required, but is highly recommended. (CA Ed. Code 48918.1)

It is imperative that the school site administrator is aware of this notice requirement and knows the identity of the homeless liaison for the district.

Foster Students

Similar to the provision for homeless students, CA Ed. Code 48853.5(c) requires each district to designate a liaison to deal with the needs of foster students. The educational liaison must notify a foster student's attorney **and** the appropriate representative of the county child welfare agency of the following:

1. Pending "discretionary expulsion" recommendation;
2. Pending proceedings to extend a suspension pending an expulsion decision, if the decision to recommend expulsion is a discretionary act; and,
3. If the foster child is an individual with exceptional needs, pending manifestation determination, if the district has proposed a change in placement due to an act for which the decision to recommend expulsion is discretionary.

The role of the educational liaison is advisory with respect to placement decisions and determination of the school of origin. It is imperative that the school site administrator is aware of this notice requirement and knows the identity of the educational liaison for the district.

In 2014, the federal Departments of Education and Justice issued guidelines for dealing with foster students to follow up on federal law that prohibits public school districts from discriminating in the administration of student discipline. These guidelines were to assist schools in developing and implementing policies and strategies that improve school climate and comply with federal law.

The guidelines observe that because of negative experiences, foster youth often have problems entering into trusting relationships with adults. A primary goal for schools is to develop trusting relationships. Steps to take include the following:

- Reduce the number of suspensions, expulsions, and arrests by providing targeted supports and interventions with a proven track record of success like restorative practices and Positive Behavioral Interventions and Supports ("PBIS").

- Provide students with enhanced/increased access to counselors, school psychologists, and school nurses.

- Establish clear parameters for school and local police; they should not be involved in "routine" school discipline matters.

- Designate a trained "single point of contact" staff member who can, among other things, identify preventive educational or behavioral health supports.

- Determine for each foster child if there is an engaged decision maker —a parent, a surrogate parent, or other legally authorized person to advocate for the child in the school discipline process and make sure students' rights are protected.

- Build school staff's capacity to support youth in care. School personnel need training and feedback to respond to student misconduct fairly, equitably and without regard to a student's personal characteristics such as race, color or ethnicity.

- Train staff about implicit or unconscious biases and harms associated with using or failing to counter stereotypes about children in the foster care system.

To support foster youth, especially when facing discipline, the school site should coordinate with the foster parent and assigned social worker. Steps to suggest to the parent and/or social worker include:

- Review the school's conduct and discipline code with the child and give concrete examples to make sure the child understands.

- Work with the school to find out what it does to promote positive behavior such as PBIS.

- Monitor the child's school progress and if there's a problem, do something.

- Share any strategies with the school that help address the child's behavior at home.

- Work with the school to create a plan that uses positive reinforcement, not punishment, to change the child's behavior.

- Within the constraints of confidentiality, tell the school if something upsetting happens to the child. This can help schools be more flexible and willing to problem-solve.

- If there's a pattern of misbehavior, consider whether the behavior is related to a disability. If this seems likely, refer the child for a special education assessment.

- If a student faces suspension or expulsion, balance the needs of individuals with the need to keep the school environment safe.

- Explain to school personnel any effects of abuse, neglect, and placement on children's behaviors and other traumas and disruptions the child has faced.

- Find out what the suspension is for, how long, and the circumstances surrounding the incident. Ask the student for his or her version.

- If the child has an IEP, make certain applicable procedures, such as a manifestation determination, occur as appropriate.

- If the youth is suspended, make sure the school provides an opportunity for the student to make up school work during the suspension.

- If a child faces expulsion, fully explore what avenues are open to allow the child to continue their education.

Many of the suggested approaches to discipline regarding homeless or foster students are also the same for guarding against disproportionate discipline of students of color. It is clear that the legislature is moving away from punitive responses to student misbehavior and encouraging school districts to think creatively about how to respond to student misbehavior in a way that helps the student understand the impact of her/his conduct and make better choices in the future. To that end, the legislature amended CA Ed. Code 48900(w) to state the following:

It is further the intent of the Legislature that the Multi-Tiered System of Supports, which includes restorative justice practices, trauma-informed practices, social and emotional learning, and school-wide positive behavior interventions and support, may be used to help pupils gain critical social and emotional skills, receive support to help transform trauma-related responses, understand the impact of their actions, and develop meaningful methods for repairing harm to the school community.

CHAPTER 7

Discriminatory Harassment And The Uniform Complaint Procedures (UCP)

UCP/Discipline Overlap

There are a number of federal anti-discrimination statutes that apply to public schools that are inextricably tied to certain CA Ed. Code violations. These federal anti-discrimination statutes codify the protections against "**discriminatory harassment**" and include Title VI of the Civil Rights Act of 1964 ("CRA"), Title IX of the Education Amendments of 1972 ("Title IX"), Section 504 of the Rehabilitation Act of 1973 ("Section 504"), and Title II of the Americans with Disabilities Act of 1990 ("ADA"). Violations of the specific Education Code sections, identified below, automatically trigger school districts to act consistent with federal law requirements, in addition to their state law obligations pursuant to CA Ed. Code 48900.

The CA Ed. Code section violations that automatically trigger corresponding obligations under federal law are the following:

- 48900(r) – Bullying based on sexual harassment

- 48900(r) – Bullying based on hate violence

- 48900(n) – Sexual Assault and Sexual Battery

- 48900.2 – Sexual Harassment

- 48900.3 – Hate Violence

In Chapter 1 – Suspensions, we reviewed an administrator's state law obligations when responding to violations of the above-referenced CA Ed. Code sections. This chapter examines an administrator's legal obligations to respond under federal and state anti-discrimination laws and focuses on discriminatory harassment perpetrated by a student. (See 7.1 - UCP Flow Chart at the end of this chapter)

Conduct that amounts to sexual harassment and sexual assault/sexual battery, whether as a subsection of bullying or as independent sections of the CA Ed. Code, by definition violates Title IX. Conduct that targets an individual or group based on their membership to a protected class (e.g., race or ethnicity, nationality, religion, gender, disability, sexual orientation, gender identity, gender expression) is by definition a violation of the relevant federal or state anti-discrimination statutes. It is important to note that while federal law may not clearly provide protections for all of the groups mentioned above, California state law does protect all of the groups mentioned, as such, utilization of and compliance with the UCP is required. (Board Policy/Administrative Regulations 1312.3)

A school district, once it has notice (see Notice section below), has the responsibility to respond promptly and effectively to discriminatory harassing conduct, whether physical, verbal, graphic, or written, that is sufficiently severe, pervasive, or persistent (i.e., that creates a hostile environment) that it denies or limits a student's ability to participate in or benefit from services, activities or opportunities offered by the district.

Additionally, the school district **must inform the harassed student and her family of their right to file a UCP complaint**. This notice should be in writing and a copy saved in the investigation file to document compliance. However, it is important to remember that the district is required to investigate allegations of discriminatory harassment and address the hostile educational environment when it has notice, even if there is not a formal complaint filed. (See 7.2 - Sample UCP Letter to Parent at the end of this chapter)

Notice

A school district's obligation to act is triggered when it has "notice" of the discriminatory harassment. Notice can be "actual" or "constructive." Actual notice occurs when the district is informed directly of allegations of harassment or a district employee directly observes the conduct. Constructive notice occurs when the district should have known that the harassment was occurring (e.g., a noose hanging in a tree on school grounds)

Prompt and Effective Response

Once a school district has notice of possible discriminatory harassment, it must take prompt and effective steps to <u>stop the harassment</u>, <u>eliminate the hostile environment</u>, and <u>prevent its recurrence</u>. School administrators must immediately initiate a thorough investigation to determine what happened. The investigation must be conducted by someone knowledgeable in the federal and state anti-discrimination laws being enforced and who understands the investigative and procedural requirements that must be followed. While conducting the investigation, it is important to make every effort to prevent disclosure of the names of the parties involved, except to the extent necessary to carry out an investigation. (See Chapter 2 – Disciplinary Investigation for best practice investigative strategies)

Interim Measures

While the investigation is pending, school administrators must ensure that anyone adversely impacted by the discriminatory harassment is safe and able to participate in and benefit from services, activities and opportunities offered by the school. As administrators consider appropriate interim measures to put into place, consideration should be given to minimizing the impact on the target of the harassment. For instance, if the harasser and the target are in the same class and it is determined that they should not remain in the same class, changing the placement of the harasser would be the preferred course of action. Other examples of interim measures include:

- Limit the interaction between the harasser and the harassed student.

- Create a "no contact" contract for the harasser.

- Provide the harassed student an additional opportunity to obtain a benefit that was denied. (e.g., retaking a test, changing unexcused absences to excused)

- Provide services to a student who was denied a benefit. (e.g., academic support services)

- Provide counseling to harassers or harassed students.

Interim measures should be put into place promptly, documented as part of the investigation, and shared with the student who has been harassed and her/his family. Parents need to know that the school is taking prompt and effective action. Additionally, to the extent any of the interim measures limit contact or interactions by the harasser, the student who was harassed and her family need to know what those limitations on the harasser are, so they can know if they have been violated and if an additional report is needed. Therefore, communication and documentation are critical to ensuring compliance.

Corrective Actions

Regardless of whether a school district's response to discriminatory harassment is self initiated or pursuant to a formal complaint, school administrators must always consider what corrective actions are necessary to address the hostile educational environment the conduct created. Below are examples of typical corrective actions:

- Interventions for the harassed student, accused, and/or witnesses, if applicable.

- Counseling, academic support, health services, increased supervision, restorative justice, etc.

- Separating the harassed student and the accused (avoid penalizing the victim/Complainant, but consider rights of accused).

- Follow-up inquires with the harassed student and witnesses to ensure harassment has stopped and that there is no retaliation.

- Age-appropriate training to students regarding harassment, including training on the district's procedures for addressing harassment.

- Staff training regarding identifying discriminatory harassment and appropriate responses.

- Clearly identify the offices or individuals with whom students can speak confidentially and identify the school's responsible employees.

- Conduct a school climate survey.

- Discipline the accused student.

Similar to interim measures, corrective actions must be documented and, to the extent appropriate, communicated with the complainant and the student who was harassed, if different.

Written Decision

If a formal UCP complaint is filed, there must be a written decision with the following components:

- Legal Standard

- Preponderance of the evidence – "More likely to be true than not"

- Factual determination as to each allegation

- Conclusions of law

- Disposition of the complaint

- Rationale for disposition

- Corrective/Remedial action

- Notice of right to appeal within fifteen (15) days

- Measures taken to eliminate hostile environment and prevent reoccurrence, if applicable

Depending on your district's UCP policy, the decision must be completed either within thirty (30) calendar days or sixty (60) calendar days. The complainant and the accused must be notified of the outcome of any investigation and any appeal. In allegations involving sexual harassment or sexual violence, the complainant must be provided information about remedies specific to the accused that directly impact the daily attendance of the complainant. For instance, if the accused student is being expelled from school, the district cannot tell the complainant that the accused student is being expelled, but must tell the complainant that the accused student will not be returning to school. Information about relevant portions of the decision should also be provided to the harassed student, if not the complainant, if applicable, and other parties involved in implementing the decision or affected by the complaint, while protecting the confidentiality and privacy of the parties. (See 7.3 - Sample UCP Written Decision at the end of this chapter)

Memo to File

There will be many incidents of discriminatory harassment that the school district must investigate even though a formal complaint has not been filed. In these instances, it is highly recommended that the administrator responsible for the investigation document the process and disposition with a "memo to file." The "memo to file" does not need to contain all of the components of the written decision described above. However, it should contain the following components:

- General summary of incident

- Summary on investigative process

- Summary of facts

- Summary of findings

- Summary of interim measures/corrective actions

The "memo to file," as well as all supporting documentation from the investigation, should be maintained by the district Compliance Officer in the event of an audit by the Office for Civil Rights ("OCR") or the California Department of Education ("CDE"). (See 7.4 - Sample UCP Memo to File at the end of this chapter)

School districts are required to maintain a log of UCP allegations received by the district in the academic school year. This log should be maintained by the district's compliance officer and kept up to date in the event of an OCR or CDE audit. It is imperative that site administrators understand their obligation to report all UCP allegations/incidents to the district compliance officer. (See 7.5 - Sample UCP Complaint Case Log at the end of this chapter)

CHAPTER 7: DISCRIMINATORY HARASSMENT

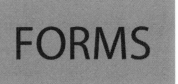

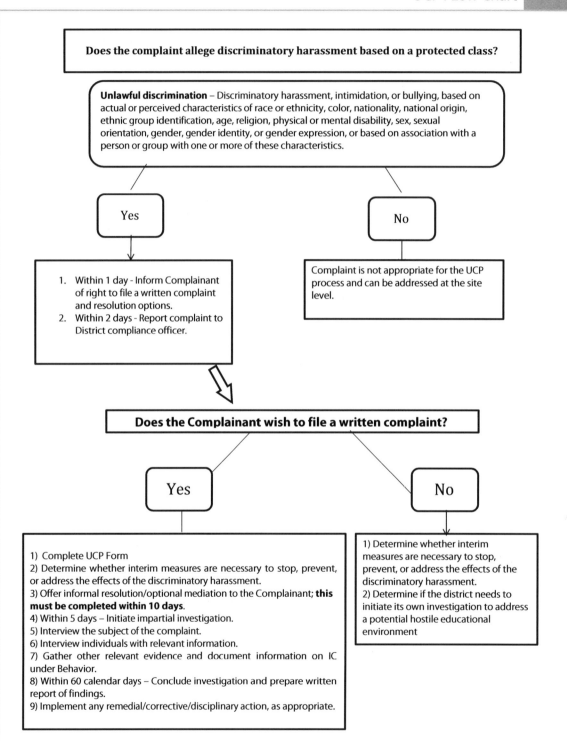

Does the complaint allege discriminatory harassment based on a protected class?

Unlawful discrimination – Discriminatory harassment, intimidation, or bullying, based on actual or perceived characteristics of race or ethnicity, color, nationality, national origin, ethnic group identification, age, religion, physical or mental disability, sex, sexual orientation, gender, gender identity, or gender expression, or based on association with a person or group with one or more of these characteristics.

Yes

No

1. Within 1 day - Inform Complainant of right to file a written complaint and resolution options.
2. Within 2 days - Report complaint to District compliance officer.

Complaint is not appropriate for the UCP process and can be addressed at the site level.

Does the Complainant wish to file a written complaint?

Yes

No

1) Complete UCP Form
2) Determine whether interim measures are necessary to stop, prevent, or address the effects of the discriminatory harassment.
3) Offer informal resolution/optional mediation to the Complainant; **this must be completed within 10 days**.
4) Within 5 days – Initiate impartial investigation.
5) Interview the subject of the complaint.
6) Interview individuals with relevant information.
7) Gather other relevant evidence and document information on IC under Behavior.
8) Within 60 calendar days – Conclude investigation and prepare written report of findings.
9) Implement any remedial/corrective/disciplinary action, as appropriate.

1) Determine whether interim measures are necessary to stop, prevent, or address the effects of the discriminatory harassment.
2) Determine if the district needs to initiate its own investigation to address a potential hostile educational environment

UCP Letter to Parent **7.2**

[Date]

[Address]

Re: [Student's Name]
        [Student's Birth Date]

Dear _____:

This letter is to inform you that during the investigation into the incident between your child and another student, we learned that the other student referred to your son using a racial slur. As a result, it is my obligation to inform you that you, on behalf of your son, have a right to file a Uniform Complaint against the student to determine if his conduct amounted to unlawful discrimination based on race. You are not required to file a complaint and the school will investigate the conduct regardless of whether you choose to file a formal complaint.

I have attached a copy of the [District] USD Uniform Complaint Procedures for your reference. If you have any questions, please do not hesitate to contact me.

Sincerely,

CONFIDENTIAL INVESTIGATION REPORT
Report of Investigation
Submitted by Dora J. Dome, Esq.
November 20, 2019

This report has been prepared in response to a request by NAME, Associate Superintendent, NAME Unified School District ("District"), that I conduct an independent investigation into the Complaint of former DISTRICT Parent NAME against DISTRICT, dated and received September 5, 2019 (hereinafter referred to as the "Complaint"), alleging, among other things, that NAME Middle School fosters an environment of rejection and racism that affected, her son, STUDENT'S, grades and his desire to attend school. The Complaint was filed pursuant to Board Policy and Administrative Regulations 1312.3 – Uniform Complaint Procedures.

BACKGROUND:

On June 12, 2019 PARENT sent an email to District Staff and Board members stating her concerns regarding STUDENT'S experiences as a student at NAME Middle School, specifically identifying alleged racism he experienced from other students as well as from some teachers. Following this email, PARENT met with several Board members and communicated with district staff regarding her concerns. In September, PARENT filed the instant Uniform Complaint, attaching the June 12, 2019 email as the basis for the complaint. I met with PARENT on October 8, 2019 to review her complaint, explain the process, and clarify her allegations. PARENT provided me with 70 pages of documentary evidence for my review. On October 19, 2019, I provided PARENT with a summary of her allegations, as I understood them, clarifying which were outside the statute of limitations and would not be investigated and those within the statute of limitations and would be investigated. On November 5, 2019, PARENT sent me a request to add an additional issue to her complaint. On November 11, 2019, PARENT clarified the additional issue she wanted to add to her complaint and the additional issue was added.

INVESTIGATION PROCESS:

I reviewed District Board Policy BP 1312.3 and AR 1312.3 – Uniform Complaint Procedures and Title VI of the Civil Rights Act of 1964. I reviewed 70 pages of documentary evidence provided by PARENT. I reviewed STUDENT's standardized test scores and SST reports and notes. I reviewed a list of various strategies utilized by MIDDLE SCHOOL to create a welcoming school environment. I reviewed the letter sent to 6th grade parents introducing the book Roll of Thunder, Hear My Cry, and inviting parents to participate in two MIDDLE SCHOOL sponsored book clubs. I reviewed the speech given by a student at MIDDLE SCHOOL's 2019 8th grade graduation. I conducted witness interviews of 14 witnesses, including PARENT and STUDENT, to gain an understanding of the general school climate at MIDDLE SCHOOL and the experiences of students of color, particularly those in the PROGRAM. There was one witness that I attempted to contact over the course of two weeks who initially did not respond to email messages or voice message. I eventually contacted this witness, who requested that I send my questions via email. As of the date of this report, I have not received a response from this witness.

ALLEGATIONS:

1. 8th grade – February 3, 2019

   - Two students said they learned about STUDENT today when they were learning about slaves. TEACHER made the boys apologize to STUDENT. SCHOOL'S response to this behavior was not sufficient to stop ongoing harassment of STUDENT.

2. 8th grade - Feb 2019

   - Someone threw a carrot at the TEACHER. The teacher immediately blamed STUDENT even though he did not see who threw it. They were able to determine it was not STUDENT. STUDENT was assumed to

CONFIDENTIAL INVESTIGATION REPORT

be the suspect by TEACHER because of his race.

3. 8th grade - February 12, 2019

   - TEACHER, Substitute teacher, reprimanded STUDENT for doing his work with another student, while several female students were in the back of the class talking and doing each other's hair. TEACHER did not reprimand the girls for their behavior and STUDENT believes he was singled out because of his race.

4. 8th grade – Spring 2019

   - Someone's phone was stolen in the after school program Homework center - Only PROGRAM students were searched. STUDENT was called in the next day about the phone that was stolen even though he was not in the homework center when it was stolen. STUDENT and the PROGRAM students were singled out and searched because of their race.

5. Continuing allegation

   - Middle School fostered an environment of rejection and racism that affected STUDENT's grades and his desire to attend school.

6. Enrollment in Math Rewind and Math Workshop – Added November 11, 2019

   - MIDDLE SCHOOL enrolls minorities in classes that serve no purpose.

FINDINGS:
Issues:

1. **Unsubstantiated**
   - In February 2019, TEACHER'S class was learning about slavery.
   - Two boys had a picture of a slave getting whipped on the back.
   - The boys showed the picture to STUDENT and said, "this looks like you."
   - PARENT reported the incident to PRINCIPAL.
   - PARENT indicated in our initial interview that PRINCIPAL spoke to the students about their behavior and had them apologize to STUDENT.
   - PRINCIPAL indicated that he spoke with the students about the inappropriateness of their behavior and had them apologize to STUDENT.
   - STUDENT indicated that the boys did not apologize.
   - In light of the fact that PARENT believed that the boys had apologized and PRINCIPAL'S certainty that he had the boys apologize for their behavior, I find that the boys in fact apologized to STUDENT.
   - STUDENT did not report any subsequent acts of harassment by these boys to PRINCIPAL.
   - There is no evidence that STUDENT continued to be harassed by these students.

2. **Unsubstantiated**
   - In February 2019, someone threw a carrot from the bus transporting students in the PROGRAM and it hit a teacher walking by the bus.
   - STUDENT's head was sticking out of the window close to where TEACHER believed the carrot originated.
   - TEACHER asked STUDENT if he had thrown the carrot at him, to which STUDENT responded "no."
   - TEACHER got PRINCIPAL to come to the bus to try to determine who had thrown the carrot.

CONFIDENTIAL INVESTIGATION REPORT

- PRINCIPAL investigated and was not able to determine who had thrown the carrot.
- STUDENT believes that he received a referral for the incident.
- PRINCIPAL indicated that because he was unable to determine who threw the carrot, no student received a consequence for this conduct.
- Based on STUDENT's statement that he was suspected of throwing the carrot because his head was out the window close to where the carrot originated, there is no evidence to suggest that TEACHER accused STUDENT of this act because of his race.

3. **Inconclusive**
   - STUDENT believes that TEACHER singled him out because of his race and allowed white students to talk and be off task without any consequence.
   - One witness who was in the class believes that TEACHER would make fun of the kids and single out the kids of color.
   - TEACHER occasionally substitute taught in ANOTHER TEACHER'S class. One day after TEACHER was a substitute, he left a note indicating that STUDENT had been sent to the office for talking off task and disruptive behavior.
   - While I find that TEACHER sent STUDENT out of class for talking and STUDENT and another witness believe that STUDENT was singled out because of his race, there is no conclusive evidence that race was the motivating factor for the behavioral referral.

4. **Partially Substantiated**
   - Sometime in the Spring of 2019, a student reported that a phone was stolen while in the Homework Center.
   - Students of different races attend Homework Center and many students of different races were present when this incident occurred.
   - The phone was stolen from a table area close to where the PROGRAM students sit.
   - Only the PROGRAM students, who were all students of color, were searched for the phone.
   - Although STUDENT was not present when the phone was stolen, he was searched the next day for the phone.
   - It is uncontested that only students of color were searched for the missing phone.
   - While a race neutral explanation has been offered explaining why only students of color were searched, it is problematic that only students of color were searched, adding to the perception that students of color are singled out and blamed when things go wrong.

5. **Partially Substantiated**
   - Some students of color, particularly students in the PROGRAM, feel that there are some students who make racially disparaging remarks to the African American students.
   - A couple of witnesses described instances where East Indian students refused to sit with them or play with them because they were Black.
   - Some witnesses described instances where they were excluded by white students from playing in their games.
   - Some students of color, particularly students in the PROGRAM, feel that there are some teachers who single out the African American students and blame them when things go wrong.
   - Three staff members were identified by a number of witnesses as the primary individuals that would treat students of color unfairly. None of the three staff members currently teach at MIDDLE SCHOOL.
   - Students and staff commonly hear students of all races using the "N" word when speaking with each other.
   - Witnesses indicated that comments were made by white parents to the effect of "not wanting their child in a class with 'those' kids," referring to students in the PROGRAM.
   - Witnesses indicated that comments were made by white parents to the effect of "the PROGRAM kids are bringing down our test scores."

CONFIDENTIAL INVESTIGATION REPORT

- Witnesses indicated that comments were made by white parents to the effect of "They don't pay taxes, we are paying for them to go to school here."
- Witnesses believe that there is a negative stigma associated with the PROGRAM and that the students are negatively stereotyped.
- Witnesses indicated that PROGRAM students are indirectly made to feel like outsiders.
- Witnesses indicated that PROGRAM parents are uncomfortable communicating with school staff.
- There appears to be an increase in racially inappropriate comments after the 6th grade students read Roll of Thunder, Hear My Cry.
- Historically the school has not done a good job preparing the students or their parents for the racial content covered in the book.
- There are sometimes only 2-3 African American students in a class reading the book and other students sometimes make teasing comments making the African American students feel uncomfortable.
- To the extent this allegation alleges that racial issues, including offensive racial language by all students, perceptions of students of color of being singled out by specific staff based on race, and the perception that there are white parents in the DISTRICT community that are racist and do not value the diversity that the PROGRAM brings to MIDDLE SCHOOL, they are **substantiated**.
- To the extent this allegation alleges that MIDDLE SCHOOL "fosters" an environment of rejection and racism it is **unsubstantiated**.
- Some witnesses indicated that they do not feel uncomfortable at MIDDLE SCHOOL or singled out because of their race.
- Witnesses indicated that when staff hear inappropriate racial comments, they intervene and try to educate the offender about the inappropriateness of the comment.
- In response to concerns about the impact of reading Roll of Thunder, Hear My Cry, the MIDDLE SCHOOL English Department moved the date the book is read to later in the semester and sent out a letter describing the book and inviting all 6th grade parents to participate in two book club events to help the parents understand the nature of the content, in order to better support the students around the complex racial issues that it raises.
- MIDDLE SCHOOL administration is implementing a number of strategies designed to create an accepting and welcoming school climate for the various groups that are represented in the school and that exist in our larger society.
- While the evidence supports a finding that STUDENT was at times exposed to inappropriate racial comments by students, the evidence also establishes that when adults on campus were made aware of the inappropriate behaviors, they intervened and addressed the behaviors.
- It is **inconclusive** whether STUDENT's academic challenges were impacted by attending a school where he and some students of color felt stigmatized and uncomfortable.

6. **Unsubstantiated**
   - STUDENT was enrolled in Math Rewind and Math Workshop during the 2018-19 academic school year.
   - STUDENT's standardized Math scores for 7th grade were in the below basic range.
   - STUDENT failed the second semester of Math during 7th grade.
   - MIDDLE SCHOOL provides academic remediation for any student, regardless of race, when their standardized test scores fall in the "below basic" or "far below basic" range.
   - There is no evidence that STUDENT was placed in a remedial Math class because of his race.

CONCLUSION AND DECISION:

Based on my review of the records and interviews with the various witnesses, it is apparent that Middle School is a microcosm of the society we live in. There are always going to be people who are indifferent, unkind and, in some instances, flat out racists. MIDDLE SCHOOL cannot control the values that any parent holds or the messages they

CONFIDENTIAL INVESTIGATION REPORT

share with their children. What MIDDLE SCHOOL can do is send a clear message to its student and parent community that it welcomes and values all of its students, in all of their diverse beauty.

There will inevitably be individuals who do not share these values and, I believe, that STUDENT experienced some of these individuals during his time at MIDDLE SCHOOL. However, I find that the MIDDLE SCHOOL staff, with one exception, appropriately addressed the issues that they were aware of. It is my finding that the search for the missing phone could have been handled in a way that did not single out the students of color as the only possible suspects and followed a racially neutral investigative protocol.

Remedies Requested:

1. DISTRICT, PRINCIPAL, ASSISTANT SUPERINTENDENT, SUPERINTENDEN, and TEACHER to apologize to STUDENT. **Denied**
   - I do not find that STUDENT's experiences at MIDDLE SCHOOL were the direct result of the actions or inactions of any of the individuals named. Therefore, requiring an apology from any of these individuals would be inappropriate.

2. DISTRICT to reimburse PARENT for STUDENT's educational expenses for high school and college. **Denied**
   - While I do not believe I have the authority to order compensatory damages as an investigator of a Uniform Complaint, I feel it is important to state that while the evidence supports a finding that STUDENT was at times exposed to inappropriate racial comments, there is no evidence that MIDDLE SCHOOL staff fostered, encouraged or supported the inappropriate behavior. The evidence suggests that when MIDDLE SCHOOL staff became aware of the inappropriate comments, they acted appropriately to address the behavior and minimize the likelihood that it would reoccur.

3. Damages for emotional distress. **Denied**
   - Similarly, while I do not believe I have the authority to order punitive damages as an investigator of a Uniform Complaint, I feel it is important to state that while the evidence supports a finding that STUDENT was at times exposed to inappropriate racial comments, there is no evidence that MIDDLE SCHOOL staff fostered, encouraged or supported the inappropriate behavior. The evidence suggests that when MIDDLE SCHOOL staff became aware of the inappropriate comments, they acted appropriately to address the behavior and minimize the likelihood that it would reoccur.

RECOMMENDED REMEDIAL ACTIONS

The PROGRAM creates unique challenges and opportunities for DISTRICT. By essentially bussing in many lower socio-economic students of color into a very affluent, primarily white school district, the District has created an opportunity for the PROGRAM students to access a quality of education not available in their community. However, the District has also combined communities with very different life experiences and, in doing so, has the obligation to create an educational environment where these different communities can not only coexist, but thrive together. To achieve this goal, DISTRICT will have to continually examine its practices to ensure that its staff, students, and parents are supported and educated on the various issues facing diverse school communities. The below list of recommended actions is not meant to be exhaustive, but illustrative of the types of activities MIDDLE SCHOOL should endeavor to engage in to continue to foster a school environment that welcomes and values racial and cultural diversity.

1. Staff professional development on cultural competence.
2. Ensure that parent meetings are held at times when working and/or single parents can attend and participate.
3. Educate the DISTRICT parent community about the PROGRAM and the value of the diversity it brings to the educational experiences of all students.
4. Educate PROGRAM parents about their educational rights and encourage them to communicate with school staff about the educational experiences of their children.

CONFIDENTIAL INVESTIGATION REPORT

5. Create opportunities for DISTRICT and PROGRAM parents to interact and engage around school activities and curriculum, similar to the book club for Roll of Thunder, Hear My Cry.

NO RETALIATION:

The District emphasizes that it takes allegations of harassment very seriously and will not tolerate it under any circumstances. The District encourages its students, parents, and employees to come forward when they are confronted with any instances of harassing, intimidating or bullying conduct. Please be advised that the District will not condone any retaliatory actions against any complainant for reporting what he or she perceives as inappropriate conduct or statements. Please keep the District informed about any additional instances that may occur so that it can investigate and remediate as needed in a timely manner.

Respectfully submitted,

DISTRICT INITIATED UCP
MEMO TO FILE
Submitted by Dora Dome, Attorney at Law
December 6, 2019

This report is in response to a District initiated investigation on behalf of the [SCHOOL DISTRICT] ("District"), in response to allegations made by High School ("HS") Student, VICTIM, that she had been sexually assaulted and sexually harassed by HS student HARASSER and that she was in a sexually coercive and abusive relationship with him. The allegations essentially allege that the school failed to properly investigate and respond to multiple allegations of sexual abuse. The purpose of the investigation is to assess the appropriateness of the HS and District response to VICTIM'S complaint of sexual harassment during the 2018-2019 school year and to make recommendations for additional responses, if appropriate. The Memo is submitted pursuant to Board Policy and Administrative Regulations 1312.3 – Uniform Complaint Procedures.

BACKGROUND:

In late November 2018, several students, who are friends of VICTIM, approached COUNSELOR, HS Guidance Counselor, indicating that they were concerned about VICTIM and described a sexually, physically and verbally abusive relationship VICTIM was having with HARRASER. COUNSELOR called VICTIM in to discuss the allegations. VICTIM confirmed the abusive relationship with HARRASER. In response, COUNSELOR made a CPS report and a police report. COUNSELOR contacted PRINCIPAL, ASSISTANT PRINCIPAL, and ASSISTANT SUPERINTENDENT/TITLE IX COMPLIANCE OFFICER, and provided them with the information she had obtained from VICTIM. The District and site administrators did a number of things in response to the allegations, which will be described below, and believed that they were being responsive to the needs of both VICTIM and HARRASER, consistent with the law.

INVESTIGATION PROCESS:

I reviewed District Board Policy BP 1312.3 and AR 1312.3 – Uniform Complaint Procedures, BP/AR 5145.7 – Sexual Harassment, and BP/AR 5145.3 – Nondiscrimination/harassment policies. The District provided voluminous documentation of its response to the incidents, which included two summaries of the various incidents provided by VICTIM, pictures of the text exchanges between VICTIM and HARRASER, email exchanges between staff, VICTIM and VICTIM's parents, multiple timelines created by various staff, Emergency Protective Order, attendance records for HARRASER, transcript of VICTIM's public comment to District School Board, and incident statements written by HARRASER. I later received copies of additional email correspondences between staff and with HARRASER's parents, and what appears to be witness statements or notes from PRINCIPAL. I interviewed COUNSELOR once. I interviewed District Guidance Coordinator, ASSISTANT SUPERINTENDENT/Student Services and Title IX Coordinator, HS Assistant Principal, and HS Principal twice. Lastly, I attempted to interview VICTIM, but was informed by her legal counsel that she would not be participating in an interview for this investigation.

FINDINGS OF FACTS:

- In late November 2018, three students approached COUNSELOR and informed her that they were concerned about a sexually, physically, and verbally abusive relationship VICTIM was having with HARRASER.
- COUNSELOR contacted VICTIM, who confirmed that she was in an abusive relationship with HARRASER. In response, COUNSELOR made a CPS report and a police report. COUNSELOR also

DISTRICT INITIATED UCP

contacted HS Principal, HS Assistant Principal, and District Title IX Coordinator, and provided them with the information she had obtained from VICTIM.

- VICTIM informed COUNSELOR that her parents did not believe her and that she was not feeling supported at home.
- COUNSELOR sent out a general email to VICTIM's teachers informing them that she was struggling, but did not say anything specific about what was going on.
- ASSISTANT SUPERINTENDET contacted DISTRICT GUIDANCE COUNSELOR and requested that she contact VICTIM, get more information about the allegations, and generally be an advocate for VICTIM.
- On December 1, 2018, DISTRICT GUIDANCE COUNSELOR contacted VICTIM to learn more about the allegations.
- DISTRICT GUIDANCE COUNSELOR learned that VICTIM had filed a police report against HARRASER for an alleged rape that occurred during the Thanksgiving break. HARRASER was arrested in response to this report.
- VICTIM indicated to DISTRICT GUIDANCE COUNSELOR that the police and her mother were making her feel like it was her fault that she was abused.
- VICTIM provided DISTRICT GUIDANCE COUNSELOR with a four page summary, listing multiple instances when HARRASER had had either sexually assaulted or sexually harassed her. In her summary, at least three of the incidents VICTIM alleges occurred during the school day. (Exhibit 1)
- On December 1, 2018, DISTRICT GUIDANCE COUNSELOR assessed VICTIM ' mental health (VICTIM already had an outside therapist), talked to VICTIM about how to speak to her parents about what was happening, spoke to the police about the allegations, and made a report to Officer.
- DISTRICT GUIDANCE COUNSELOR'S opinion was that the police were not taking VICTIM' allegations seriously. DISTRICT GUIDANCE COUNSELOR spoke with Officer twice over the weekend to provide more details with the hope that the police would take the allegations more seriously.
- In the screen shots of the text messages, there is a message from VICTIM to HARRASER indicating that they met at his home during lunch on a day that she had to return to school. While the message do not explicitly identify what they intended to do, HARRASER does say, "And be ready for punishment." (Exhibit 2)
- On December 3, 2018, DISTRICT GUIDANCE COUNSELOR sent an email summarizing what she told Officer to VICTIM, who provided edits to the details. DISTRICT GUIDANCE COUNSELOR sent the revised summary to Officer. (Exhibit 3)
- On December 3, 2018, DISTRICT GUIDANCE COUNSELOR forwarded an email from VICTIM to COUNSELOR, ASSISTANT SUPERINTENDENT, and ASSISTANT PRINCIPAL, in which VICTIM indicated her concerns that HARRASER had been released by the police, that VICTIM was concerned that HARRASER would be returning to school, and asking if there was a way for the administrators could make sure HARRASER stays away from her. (Exhibit 4)
- DISTRICT GUIDANCE COUNSELOR scheduled a meeting with VICTIM and ASSISTANT PRINCIPAL for Monday morning, December 4, 2018, to create a safety plan and obtain more details. At the meeting, DISTRICT GUIDANCE COUNSELOR informed VICTIM that HARRASER would not be at school that day, discussed obtaining a TRO, and identified a safe person on campus for VICTIM to contact if needed.
- During her meeting with DISTRICT GUIDANCE COUNSELOR and ASSISTANT PRINCIPAL, VICTIM wrote a statement listing eight things HARRASER did to her. The eight items were incorporated into the timeline that was created and being added to by the various administrators. There are at least two items, numbers 3 and 7, which happened during lunch and over which the school may have had jurisdiction. (Exhibit 5)
- On December 4, 2018, DISTRICT GUIDANCE COUNSELOR provided ASSISTANT PRINCIPAL with a summary of what VICTIM reported HARRASER had done to her. (Exhibit 6)

DISTRICT INITIATED UCP

- On December 4, 2018, VICTIM'S mother, sent COUNSELOR an email with the subject, "Formal Request for Complaint." In this email, VICTIM'S mother requests that COUNSELOR pass the email along to PRINCIPAL "as my formal request for action." (Exhibit 7)
- COUNSELOR forwarded the email to PRINCIPAL and ASSISTANT PRINCIPAL within 36 minutes. PRINCIPAL forwarded the email to ASSISTANT SUPERINTENDENT 41 minutes later and requested a call to discuss the response. (Exhibit 8)
- PRINCIPAL responded to VICTIM'S mother "Formal Complaint" email on the evening of December 4, 2018, reassuring her that the school will continue to make sure VICTIM is safe on campus, informing her that the police are taking the lead in the investigation, and that he would update the family as things continue to develop. (Exhibit 9)
- From December 4, 2018 through December 8, 2018, HARRASER's parents did not allow him to attend school while there was still a restraining order in place.
- HARRASER attended school from December 11, 2017 through December 18, 2017.
- On December 11, 2018, ASSISTANT PRINCIPAL counseled HARRASER to act as if the restraining order was still in place and to have no contact with VICTIM. HARRASER agreed. ASSISTANT PRINCIPAL also compared VICTIM and HARRASER's class schedules and determined that they did not have any classes together and that there was only one time that their paths might cross between second and third period. ASSISTANT PRINCIPAL met with VICTIM about where she and HARRASER may pass each other and discussed how she could avoid it.
- On December 11, 2018, after checking-in with VICTIM, who told her that she was feeling anxious about seeing HARRASER since he was arrested, COUNSELOR called VICTIM' mother to check–in and to suggest that VICTIM be allowed to spend time with her friends as a way to deal with her anxiety.
- On December 11, 2018, DISTRICT GUIDANCE COUNSELOR and ASSISTANT PRINCIPAL met with VICTIM to discuss additional safety planning in response to concerns VICTIM had raised. They changed her schedule, allowed her to leave campus early, and identified safe places on campus where she could go if needed.
- On December 13, 2018, DISTRICT GUIDANCE COUNSELOR accompanied VICTIM for an interview with a Social Worker, the District Attorney and Detective, and observed the interview through the glass.
- VICTIM felt that Detective was accusing her of making things up and twisting her words. DISTRICT GUIDANCE COUNSELOR's impressions were that Detective was trying to dissuade VICTIM from continuing with her complaint.
- Around December 14th or 15th, 2018, VICTIM informed ASSISTANT PRINCIPAL that she saw HARRASER everywhere and that she felt his friends were following her in the halls.
- On December 15, 2018, DISTRICT GUIDANCE COUNSELOR spoke with VICTIM to discuss additional safety planning in the event HARRASER was at school during the week of December 18, 2018.
- On December 17, 2018, VICTIM sent an email to PRINCIPAL, ASSISTANT PRINCIPAL, COUNSELOR, and DISTRICT GUIDANCE COUNSELOR, indicating that she did not feel safe on campus if HARRASER was going to be there and that the previous week "was incredibly traumatic…" She also indicated that she spoke to a Detective on Friday and that he told her there was no reason the school was unable to start its investigation. (Exhibit 10)
- On December 18, 2018, site administrators questioned students who might have been able to observe any harassment by HARRASER and his friends during the previous week. While all of the students questioned seemed to know about the case, no student observed HARRASSER near VICTIM during the previous week.
- On December 19, 2018, VICTIM contacted DISTRICT GUIDANCE COUNSELOR asking for a status update, and DISTRICT GUIDANCE COUNSELOR told her that the case was still being investigated and strategized ways to avoid HARRASER.

DISTRICT INITIATED UCP

- ASSISTANT SUPERINTENDENT arranged for HARRASER to take his finals at the District Office in response to the concerns articulated by VICTIM about her experiences the previous week.
- On December 19, 2018, DISTRICT GUIDANCE COUNSELOR informed VICTIM, via text message, that the investigation was still pending and that HARRASER would be taking his finals at the district office and would not be on campus for the rest of the week.
- On December 19, 2018, PRINCIPAL and ASSISTANT PRINCIPAL interviewed HARRASER for the first time. HARRASER wrote two statements. PRINCIPAL and ASSISTANT PRINCIPAL created a summary of their interview with HARRASER. PRINCIPAL indicated that although he met with HARRASER and his parents on December 4, 2018, he was directed by ASSISTANT SUPERINTENDENT not to take a statement since there was an ongoing police investigation. (Exhibit 11 & 12)
- Between December 1, 2018 through December 22, 2018, the beginning of winter break, DISTRICT GUIDANCE COUNSELOR checked in with VICTIM regarding her mental health six times in person and two times over the phone.
- On December 20, 2018, ex-girlfriend of HARRASER, wrote a statement indicating that she dated HARRASER for approximately 1.5 years and that "one time he threatened to post pictures of me on social media if I did not send him more." The statement is not signed and it is not clear what type of pictures she was referring to in her statement. However, during my interview with PRINCIPAL, he referred to the pictures as "nudes." It is not clear where he obtained the additional information about the nature of the photos. (Exhibit 13)
- Sometime in December 2018, PRINCIPAL, ASSISTANT PRINCIPAL, and ASSISTANT SUPERINTENDENT, met to discuss the allegations and determine if there was a nexus to school activity. No one recalls who made it or how the decision that there was no nexus was made.
- On January 5, 2019, at the end of winter break, VICTIM sent an email to ASSISTANT PRINCIPAL asking for an update and indicating that she did not feel safe continuing to be at school with HARRASER. (Exhibit 14)
- On January 5, 2019, VICTIM also sent text messages to DISTRICT GUIDANCE COUNSELOR asking for a status update. DISTRICT GUIDANCE COUNSELOR forwarded this information to ASSISTANT SUPERINTENDENT, ASSISTANT PRINCIPAL, and PRINCIPAL. (Exhibit 15)
- On January 8, 2019, ASSISTANT SUPERINTENDENT and DISTRICT GUIDANCE COUNSELOR met with VICTIM and ASSISTANT SUPERINTENDENT informed VICTIM that the school was still investigating but did not want to interfere with the police investigation. He also informed her that she would have warning prior to HARRASER's return to campus. He asked her to stop speaking about the incident, as it was interfering with the investigation.
- On January 11, 2019, VICTIM sent an email with numerous attachments of information she found on HARRASER's Reddit page. (Exhibit 16)
- On January 18, 2019, VICTIM' father, sent PRINCIPAL, ASSISTANT SUPERINTENDENT and ASSISTANT PRINCIPAL an email asking for resolution in the case, indicating that the police had informed him that a school investigation would not interfere with the police investigation, and asking that HARRASER be expelled. (Exhibit 17)
- On January 19, 2019, DISTRICT GUIDANCE COUNSELOR helped VICTIM identify the incidents that occurred during school hours. On the timeline, there is a section titled "Possible Nexus," which lists three incidents that VICTIM alleges occurred during school hours. (Exhibit 18)
- On January 22, 2019, PRINCIPAL responded to VICTIM'S FATHER email acknowledging his concern and indicating that the school was continuing to investigate the matter.
- On January 26, 2019, VICTIM'S FATHER sent PRINCIPAL, ASSISTANT SUPERINTENDENT, and ASSISTANT PRINCIPAL an email expressing his frustration with the school's lack of consequences for HARRASER, referenced that school must follow Title IX, and threatened litigation if the matter was not resolved.

DISTRICT INITIATED UCP

- On January 24, 2019, VICTIM sent an email to SUPERINTENDENT, PRINCIPAL, ASSISTANT SUPERINTENDENT, and ASSISTANT PRINCIPAL asking that they not allow HARRASER to return to HS. VICTIM references legal pressure the school may be under from HARRASER's attorney and provides citations to support the schools decision to involuntarily transfer him from HS. VICTIM also states, that other girls are afraid of HARRASER on campus and that she is "genuinely scared" of HARRASER. (Exhibit 19)
- On January 24, 2019, DISTRICT GUIDANCE COUNSELOR met with VICTIM, who said she was suicidal and afraid HARRASER would return to campus. DISTRICT GUIDANCE COUNSELOR conducted a threat assessment and determined that VICTIM was not actively suicidal.
- On January 26, 2019, ASSISTANT SUPERINTENDENT facilitated a meeting with HARRASER, HARRASER'S PARENTS, HARRASER's attorney, and PRINCIPAL. A summary of the meeting was created. In the summary, it is noted that HARRASER admitted that he and VICTIM agreed to meet at lunch to engage in sex on an "A" day. On "A" days, both VICTIM and HARRASER have classes and must return to school after lunch. HARRASER also admitted to hitting VICTIM in the breasts. There are at least two instances where he gave inconsistent statements documented in the summary. It was determined that the school did not have jurisdiction to discipline HARRASER for his conduct. It was agreed that HARRASER would be put on Independent Study and attend a different school site. (Exhibit 20)
- On January 31, 2019, DISTRICT GUIDANCE COUNSELOR, PRINCIPAL, ASSISTANT SUPERINTENDENT and ASSISTANT PRINCIPAL meet and DISTRICT GUIDANCE COUNSELOR shared the three incidents that she and VICTIM identified that may have a nexus to school activity. This meeting occurred after the administrators had already met with HARRASER, his parents and his attorney, and determined that there was no nexus.
- On February 1, 2019, VICTIM did not come to school because she was afraid she would see HARRASER on campus. VICTIM came to school at noon to meet with DISTRICT GUIDANCE COUNSELOR, but DISTRICT GUIDANCE COUNSELOR still did not know what had been determined about HARRASER returning to school.
- On February 5, 2019, ASSISTANT SUPERINTENDENT, PRINCIPAL, ASSISTANT PRINCIPAL, and DISTRICT GUIDANCE COUNSELOR met with VICTIM and VICTIM'S FATHER, where they informed them that HARRASER would not be returning to campus and that HARRASER was not going to be expelled.
- DISTRICT GUIDANCE COUNSELOR continued to check-in with VICTIM at least weekly for the remainder of the school year. DISTRICT GUIDANCE COUNSELOR made two CPS reports during that time in response to VICTIM contacting her about verbal and emotional abuse by her parents.
- DISTRICT GUIDANCE COUNSELOR'S last meeting with VICTIM was May 23, 2019, to conduct a final check-in, wherein VICTIM indicated that she appreciated DISTRICT GUIDANCE COUNSELOR'S support.
- On May 28, 2019, VICTIM sent ASSISTANT PRINCIPAL an email asking if HARRASER would be at graduation and informing her that after prom in the lobby of a hotel, HARRASER was there and yelled mean words at her, which caused her to have a panic attack. (Exhibit 21)
- On May 30, 2019, VICTIM'S FATHER sent PRINCIPAL and ASSISTANT PRINCIPAL an email informing them that VICTIM "was aggressively accosted by HARRASER" and stating his belief that it was during a school function. (Exhibit 22)
- PRINCIPAL responded to VICTIM'S FATHER email later the same day indicating that he and ASSISTANT PRINCIPAL had met with VICTIM, interviewed the one student she was able to identify and that the student did not corroborate her claim. He also informed VICTIM'S FATHER that HARRASER did not attend the prom and that the incident occurred after prom ended, at a hotel and that it was not a school event. (Exhibit 22)

CONCLUSIONS OF LAW:

DISTRICT INITIATED UCP

Title IX Obligations:

- District Administrative Regulation 5145.7 – Sexual Harassment, requires a school employee to forward a report of sexual harassment to the Principal or district compliance officer within one school day of receiving the report. COUNSELOR complied with this legal requirement when she forwarded VICTIM' report to both PRINCIPAL and ASSISTANT SUPERINTENDENT.
- AR 5145.7 requires the Principal or designee, in consultation with the compliance officer to determine whether interim measures are necessary pending the results of the investigation. DISTRICT GUIDANCE COUNSELOR'S ongoing support of VICTIM, both at school and during aspects of the police investigation, complied with this legal requirement.
- AR 5145.7 requires the principal or compliance officer to inform the student/parent of the right to file a formal written complaint in accordance with the district's UCP. The District failed to inform VICTIM and her parents of their right to file a UCP once they were on notice of VICTIM' allegation.
- AR 5145.7 requires the compliance officer to contact the complainant and investigate the complaint in accordance with AR 1312.3 – Uniform Complaint Procedures. The District failed to investigate VICTIM' allegations in accordance with the procedures set forth in the UCP.
- The District additionally failed to initiate the UCP process when it received VICTIM'S mother's email of December 4, 2018 making a formal complaint.
- AR 1312.3 requires that the person assigned to investigate and resolve complaints receive training and are knowledgeable about the laws and programs at issue in the complaints in which they are assigned. ASSISTANT SUPERINTENDENT was not knowledgeable of his obligations as the Title IX Compliance officer for the District. ASSISTANT SUPERINTENDENT was not aware that he was required to maintain a record of each complaint and subsequent related actions, including steps taken during the investigation. ASSISTANT SUPERINTENDENT was not aware of the procedural requirements of Title IX and his obligation to implement them as the District Compliance Officer.
- Title IX requires that the District address the hostile educational environment that resulted from the alleged conduct. While the District put in place a number of interim measures to address the hostile educational environment for VICTIM, it failed to communicate timely and effectively to VICTIM about when HARRASER would be on campus. On three different occasions, December 3rd (after the initial report), December 17th (after VICTIM complained that she felt unsafe with HARRASER on campus the previous week), and January 5th (at the end of winter break), VICTIM initiated communication with site administrators and staff about her feelings of being unsafe and wanting to know whether HARRASER would be on campus. The site administrators had an obligation to proactively keep VICTIM informed of the status of HARRASER on campus.
- Title IX required that the District investigate VICTIM' complaint that HARRASER called her mean names while in the hotel lobby following Prom, as a form of possible retaliation, even though the incident did not happen at a school sponsored event. While the site administrators did interview a witness in response to the allegation, they were unaware that the incident implicated Title IX and that it would have been appropriate to contact HARRASER about the allegation and reinforce the prohibition against retaliation.

Education Code Obligations

- California Education Code 48900, et seq., sets forth the district's obligations to respond to student misconduct. Section 48900(s) establishes when a district has jurisdiction over the misconduct. Specifically, 48900(s)(3) states that the district has jurisdiction to discipline a student for conduct

DISTRICT INITIATED UCP

related to school activity or school attendance that occur… "During the lunch period whether on or off campus."

- VICTIM' timeline, which she provided to DISTRICT GUIDANCE COUNSELOR on December 1, 2018, lists three different incidents that she alleges occurred at lunch, during school hours, that if substantiated, amount to sexual assault (forced oral copulation and rape) and sexual battery, in violation of 48900(n). VICTIM additionally alleged that HARRASER demanded nude photos during AP Psyche and that the photos were taken in the girls bathroom, which, if substantiated that VICTIM's sending of the photos were a form of sexual coercion, would violate 48900.2 – Sexual Harassment.

- The site administrators failed to adequately investigate whether there was a nexus to school activity or attendance to determine whether it was appropriate to assert jurisdiction over the conduct. Specifically, the site administration failed to adequately question VICTIM to gain sufficient details regarding her allegations, to determine if there was a nexus to school activity or attendance.

- The site administration improperly delayed its investigation into the allegation in deference to the police investigation. Specifically, the site administration failed to question HARRASER until December 19, 2018, 18 days after learning of the allegations, in deference to allowing the police to conduct their investigation.

- The site administration failed to adequately investigate the alleged conduct to determine if there was a preponderance of the evidence to support a suspension or if there was substantial evidence to support an expulsion recommendation of HARRASER. Specifically, the site administration was in possession of factual information that suggested that some of the alleged conduct occurred under the schools jurisdiction and failed to investigate. The site administration became aware that HARRASER had admitted to some of the conduct, but they never investigated whether the conduct had a nexus to school activity or attendance. They were also aware that HARRASER had lied on at least two occasions about his relationship with VICTIM and whether he had threatened to share nude photos of a different girl on social media. HARRASER's inconsistencies should have at least caused the site administration to question his veracity and investigate further. The site was also in possession of HARRASER's ex-girlfriend's statement indicating that HARRASER had threatened to share pictures of her as a form of coercion to make her share additional pictures against her will. This information should have at least triggered the site administration to investigate further. The site administrators indicated that they interviewed a number of student witnesses, however, they failed to properly document their interviews or obtain witness statements. Site staff created a "google document" that each of them were regularly editing. As a result, individuals are unsure who added what information and when it was added, making it very difficult to accurately track the progression of the process and when information was obtained.

DECISION:

Based on my interviews with witnesses and my review of the documentary evidence provided to me, the District's response to VICTIM' allegations was reasonable, timely and mostly effective, in that they immediately put interim measure in place. The response was reasonably calculated to end the harassment and prevent the harassment from recurring in that VICTIM was immediately provided counseling, a safety plan was created and she was provided with names of safe people to speak to and safe locations to be on campus. HARRASER did not attend school for the first week following her allegations and, when he did return, the administration assessed their respective class schedules, made appropriate adjustments, and directed HARRASER not to contact VICTIM. While HARRASER did attend school for seven days, when that did not address VICTIM' concerns, he was not allowed to return to campus for finals. HARRASER was ultimately transferred to another

DISTRICT INITIATED UCP

school setting and did not attend HS after December 19, 2018. DISTRICT GUIDANCE COUNSELOR also checked in with VICTIM regularly and provided emotional support both during the school process and the police process.

However, the District's failure to timely and effectively communicate with VICTIM about whether and when HARRASER would be on campus resulted in her feeling unsafe and did not eliminate VICTIM' perception of a hostile educational environment. Furthermore, the site administrations response to VICTIM' complaint about the Prom night incident did not adequately address their obligation to prevent retaliation against the target. Other than interim measures, the District's response failed to provide any of the procedural protections required under Title IX and described in its sexual harassment and UCP policies.

By deferring their investigation pending the police investigation, failing to investigate whether their was a nexus to school activity or attendance, and failing to conduct and document witness interviews, the site administrations response to VICTIM' allegations, failed to comply with the California Education Code requirements. It is clear that even though the district transferred HARRASER to another school setting, VICTIM and her parents wanted HARRASER expelled from school. Parents do not get to dictate district disciplinary action. However, they do have a right to expect the site and district administrators understand the laws they are charged with enforcing. It is likely that had the site administrators conducted a thorough investigation, regardless of the outcome, and had been able to timely and clearly respond to VICTIM and her family about the status of the case and whether HARRASER would be returning to HS, the situation may not have escalated as it did. This decision does not address the sufficiency of the evidence to support disciplinary action against HARRASER.

CORRECTIVE ACTIONS:

- Update District Board Policy BP 1312.3 and AR 1312.3 – Uniform Complaint Procedures, BP/AR 5145.7 – Sexual Harassment, and BP/AR 5145.3 – Nondiscrimination/harassment policies to reflect the current state of the law and procedural requirements.
- Create a Title IX log, as required by law.
- Training to District Compliance Officer on Title IX and his obligations as a compliance officer for the district.
- Training to site administrators and the District compliance officer on the Uniform Complaint Procedures process (UCP) and their corresponding obligation to report and respond to complaints of discriminatory harassment.
- Training to site administrators and the District compliance officer on proper investigation strategies and techniques, including interviewing witnesses, gathering evidence, and documenting the investigative process.
- Update Incident report forms to make them sworn declarations.
- Training to site administrators and relevant district personnel on California Education Code discipline requirements, including the impact of concurrent police investigations on district processes.

Respectfully submitted,

List of attachments

Uniform Complaint Procedures (UCP), Online Self-Certification Process

SAMPLE COMPLAINT CASE LOG FOR UCP 3

School Year: _____ 2016 - 2017 _____

Thomas Jefferson Unified School District
Name of LEA

12345 Main Street, Springfield, CA 99876
Address

123-234-4567
Phone number of Contact Person

Evidence of proper implementation of the investigation process*

Case #	Complainant(s) Initials	Title	Allegation	School	Date Rec'd	Due Date- 60 days	Date Closed	Appeal
UCP 001	ND	Student	Discrimination, Aggressive and unprofessional behavior of teacher	ML King, Jr ES	11/1/2015	12/31/2015	1/31/2016	No
UCP 002	EH	Parent	Not a UCP – Parent request retaining teacher at Smith ES	C Chavez HS	12/15/2015	2/13/2016	3/13/2016	No
UCP 003	MA	Community member	Multiple allegations regarding ELAC meeting held on 04/06/16	F Korematsu HS	2/8/2016	4/9/2016	5/9/2016	Appeal to CDE 5/23/2016 Appeal denied
UCP 004	ZD	Parent	Charged fee for band equipment	A Lincoln MS	5/18/2016	7/17/2016	n/a	n/a

*Complaints in accordance with CCR, Title 5, Section 4610(b). Upload a completed log in CMT, at any time during the upload period and prior to the last day of the review. Districts are not required to upload complaint documents in CMT, as part of the self-certification. LEAs are not required to use this sample.

Please see additional instructions for this process on the "LEA Self-Certification Form and Instructions for Completion of an Online Review for UCP 3."

June 2016 (2)

CHAPTER 8

Student Records

TOOLS FOR THE TRADE

Definitions

"Parent" means a natural parent, an adopted parent, or legal guardian. If the parents are divorced or legally separated, only a parent having **legal custody** of the pupil may challenge the content of a record, offer a written response to a record, or consent to release records to others. A Parent with only "**physical custody**" or "**visitation rights**," may access the student records, but s/he cannot make educational decisions. Either parent may grant consent if both parents have notified, in writing, the school or school district that an agreement has been made. If a pupil has attained the age of 18 years or is attending an institution of postsecondary education, education rights transfer to her/him and the pupil shall thereafter have the authority to consent to a release of her/his records.

"Pupil record" means any item of information directly related to an identifiable pupil, other than directory information, that is maintained by a school district or required to be maintained by an employee in the performance of his or her duties whether recorded by handwriting, print, tapes, film, microfilm, or other means. "Pupil record" does not include informal notes related to a pupil compiled by a school officer or employee that remain in the sole possession of the maker and are not accessible or revealed to any other person except a substitute. For purposes of this subdivision, "substitute" means a person who performs the duties of the individual who made the notes on a temporary basis, and does not refer to a person who permanently succeeds the maker of the notes in his or her position.

"Directory information" means one or more of the following items: pupil's name, address, telephone number, date of birth, email address, major field of study, participation in officially recognized activities and sports, weight and height of members of athletic teams, dates of attendance, degrees and awards received, and the most recent previous public or private school attended by the pupil. However, the school district must identify each year which items it considers directory information **and** the entities that the information may be released to.

"Access" means a personal inspection and review of a record or an accurate copy of a record, or receipt of an accurate copy of a record, an oral description or communication of a record or an accurate copy of a record, and a request to release a copy of any record.

"County placing agency" means the county social service department or county probation department. (CA Ed. Code 49061)

Access to Student Records - Generally

The District must release Student Records to a parent who signs a written request or to a third party when accompanying the request is a signed and dated consent by the parent or by the student if over 18 years of age or under the age of 18 years but attending a postsecondary institution. In this case the student has the sole authority to release his or her records.

A school district may permit access to pupil records to any person for whom a parent of the pupil has executed written consent specifying the records to be released and identifying the party or class of parties to whom the records may be released. The recipient must be notified that the transmission of the information to others without the written consent of the parent is prohibited. The consent notice shall be permanently kept with the record file.

Release of records with consent is subject to the following conditions:

a. To give consent, a parent must have the student's educational rights. If both parents have educational rights, only one needs to sign the consent.

b. If capable of authentication, consent may be by electronic means.

c. The consent form should have a specific list of the records to be disclosed, the purpose of the disclosure, and the name of the party or class of parties to whom disclosure will be made.

d. If requested, the parent shall receive a copy of the records disclosed.

Access – Legitimate Educational Interest

In addition to when a parent provides written consent, access to student records may be permitted when there is a legitimate educational interest, as defined in section 49076. Below is a list of recipients who may access student records. The list is not exhaustive, but illustrative of the most common situations that site administrators may encounter.

- The parent of a dependent child (e.g., claimed as a dependent on the parent's income tax return) over 18 years of age.

- A student who has reached 16 years of age or has completed the 10th grade.

- To members of a school attendance review board (SARB) and any volunteer aide age 18 or older who has been investigated, selected, and trained by the SARB to provide follow-up services to a referred student.

- A district attorney who is participating in or conducting a truancy mediation program pursuant to Section 48263.5 of this code or Section 601.3 of the Welfare and Institutions Code, or participating in the presentation of evidence in a truancy petition pursuant to Section 681 of the Welfare and Institutions Code.

- A district attorney's office for consideration against a parent or guardian for failure to comply with the Compulsory Education Law or with Compulsory Continuation Education.

- A probation officer, district attorney, or counsel of record for a minor for purposes of conducting a criminal investigation or an investigation in regards to declaring a person a ward of the court or involving a violation of a condition of probation.

    ◦ For purposes of this subparagraph, a probation officer, district attorney, and counsel of record for a minor shall be deemed to be local officials for purposes of Section 99.31(a)(5)(i) of Title 34 of the Code of Federal Regulations. ***NOTE: Law enforcement officers are NOT authorized to obtain student records using this exception.**

- A judge or probation officer for the purpose of conducting a truancy mediation program for a pupil, or for purposes of presenting evidence in a truancy petition pursuant to Section 681 of the Welfare and Institutions Code. The judge or probation officer shall certify in writing to the school district that the information will be used only for truancy purposes. **A school district releasing pupil information to a judge or probation officer pursuant to this subparagraph shall inform, or provide written notification to, the parent or guardian of the pupil within 24 hours of the release of the information.**

- A pupil 14 years of age or older who meets both of the following criteria:

  ○ The pupil is a homeless child or youth, as defined in paragraph (2) of Section 725 of the federal McKinney-Vento Homeless Assistance Act (42 U.S.C. Sec. 11434a(2)).

  ○ The pupil is an unaccompanied youth, as defined in paragraph (6) of Section 725 of the federal McKinney-Vento Homeless Assistance Act (42 U.S.C. Sec. 11434a(6)).

- An individual who completes items 1 to 4, inclusive, of the Caregiver's Authorization Affidavit, as provided in Section 6552 of the Family Code, and signs the affidavit for the purpose of enrolling a minor in school.

- An agency caseworker or other representative of a state or local child welfare agency, or tribal organization, as defined in Section 450b of Title 25 of the United States Code, that has legal responsibility for the care and protection of the pupil.

- A foster family agency with jurisdiction over a currently enrolled or former pupil, a short-term residential treatment program staff responsible for the education or case management of a pupil, and a caregiver who has direct responsibility for the care of the pupil, including a certified or licensed foster parent, an approved relative or nonrelated extended family member, or a resource family, as defined in Section 1517 of the Health and Safety Code and Section 16519.5 of the Welfare and Institutions Code, pursuant to Section 49069.3 of this code.

- Appropriate persons in connection with an emergency if the knowledge of the information is necessary to protect the health or safety of a pupil or other persons. Schools or school districts releasing information pursuant to this subparagraph **shall record the following information**, as set forth in Section 99.32(a)(5) of Title 34 of the Code of Federal Regulations:

  ○ (i) The articulable and significant threat to the health or safety of a student or other individuals that formed the basis for the disclosure; and

- ◦ (ii) The parties to whom the agency or institution disclosed the information.

- A contractor or consultant with a legitimate educational interest who has a formal written agreement or contract with the school district regarding the provision of outsourced institutional services or functions by the contractor or consultant.

- To District employees, contractors, consultants, volunteers, or others whose duties and responsibilities, whether routine or because of a special circumstance, require access, provided that there is a legitimate educational interest to access the records as part of these duties and responsibilities.

- Information concerning a pupil shall be furnished in compliance with a court order or a lawfully issued subpoena. The school district shall make a reasonable effort to notify the pupil's parent or legal guardian and the pupil **in advance of compliance** with a lawfully issued subpoena so that the parent may seek protective action and, in the case of compliance with a court order, if lawfully possible within the requirements of the order.

  - ◦ Once a court order or lawfully issued subpoena is issued to obtain a pupil's contact information, the school district shall make a reasonable effort to enter into an agreement with the entity that obtained the court order or subpoena requiring that the pupil contact information be maintained in a confidential manner.

- The service of a lawfully issued subpoena or a court order upon a public school employee solely for the purpose of causing him or her to produce a school record pertaining to any pupil may be complied with by that employee, in lieu of the personal appearance as a witness in the proceeding, by submitting to the court, or other agency, or person designated in the subpoena, at the time and place required by the subpoena or court order, a copy of that record, accompanied by an affidavit certifying that the copy is a true copy of the original record on file in the school or school office.

- Each school district shall release the information it has specific to a particular pupil's **identity and location** that relates to the transfer of that pupil's records to another school district within this state or any other state or to a private school in this state to a designated peace officer, upon his or her request, **when a proper police purpose exists** for the use of that information. As permitted by Part 99 (commencing with Section 99.1) of Title 34 of the Code of Federal Regulations, the designated <u>peace officer or law enforcement agency</u> **shall** <u>show the school district</u> that the peace officer or law enforcement agency has <u>obtained prior written consent from one parent,</u> **or** <u>provide information indicating that there is an emergency</u> in which the information is necessary to protect the health or safety of the pupil or other individuals, or that the peace officer or law enforcement agency has <u>obtained a lawfully issued subpoena or a court order.</u>

- ○ In order to protect the privacy interests of the pupil, a request to a school district for pupil record information pursuant to this section shall meet the following requirements:

  - ▪ For purposes of this section, "proper police purpose" means that <u>probable cause exists that the pupil has been kidnapped</u> and that his or her abductor may have enrolled the pupil in a school and that the agency has begun an active investigation.

  - ▪ Only designated peace officers and federal criminal investigators and federal law enforcement officers, as defined in Section 830.1 of the Penal Code, <u>whose names have been submitted to the school district in writing by a law enforcement agency,</u> may request and receive the information specified in subdivision (a). Each law enforcement agency shall ensure that each school district has at all times a current list of the names of designated peace officers authorized to request pupil record information.

  - ▪ This section <u>does **not** authorize</u> designated peace officers to obtain any pupil record information other than that authorized by this section.

  - ▪ Whenever the designated peace officer requesting information authorized for release by this section does so in person, by telephone, or by some means <u>other than in writing,</u> the officer **shall** provide the <u>school district with a letter confirming the request for pupil record information</u> **before any release of information**.

- • To appropriate law enforcement authorities in circumstances where CA Ed. Code

48902 requires that the district provide special education and disciplinary records of a student with disabilities who is suspended or expelled for committing an act violating Penal Code 245 (assault with a deadly weapon).

- When disclosing records for these purposes, the school district shall obtain written certification from the recipient of the record(s) that the information will not be disclosed to another party without prior written consent of the student's parent or guardian or the holder of the student's educational rights, unless specifically authorized by state or federal law

Disclosure of Student Records to Law Enforcement

All disclosures of confidential student records must comply with the requirements of the specific exception being relied upon to release the records. This is particularly relevant when responding to requests for student information from law enforcement officers. School administrators interact with law enforcement officers on a regular basis and are often requested to provide them with confidential student information in conjunction with a criminal investigation. School administrators must understand that law enforcement officers are not allowed to access student records unless it is for a health and safety emergency or in response to a suspected kidnapping, both of which are described above. School administrators will often get push back from the officers for failing to disclose the student information, but it is important that you stand your ground and ask the officer to provide you with the legal authority that allows the disclosure. If the officer is unable to provide legal authority to support the disclosure, the student records must not be disclosed. Keep in mind that a law enforcement officer would never give a school administrator confidential police records without proper legal authority.

However, when school administrators and law enforcement officers are simultaneously investigating an active school discipline case (that is also potentially a criminal case), any evidence gathered during this collaborative investigation can be shared between the parties. It is best practice to make copies of all evidence gathered and ensure that when the officers leaves the school site, both the officer and the school have identical copies of all the evidence gathered. This practice allows both the officer and the school to gather and maintain the evidence and avoids the legal complication of trying to share confidential or protected information after the fact.

If your school district utilizes the services of School Resource Officers ("SRO"), school administrators need to understand the limitations that apply to the SRO. While the SRO is considered a school official and has a legitimate educational interest in accessing confidential student records, this access is not unlimited. An SRO may only access the records of students that the SRO actually has a legitimate interest in accessing. For instance, if a student engages in a conduct violation and the SRO is part of the team responding to the incident, similar to an administrator, the SRO would have a legitimate educational interest in accessing records of that student that are relevant to the SRO's investigation. However, an SRO would be prohibited from accessing the records of a student for conduct that occurred off-campus and is unrelated to school activity or attendance. Similarly, an SRO is prohibited from accessing confidential student records for the purpose of providing them to a law enforcement agency in circumvention of the statutory exceptions.

School administrators are recommended to direct all questions about release of student records to the Department of Student Services at the District Office.

Protocol For Accessing Student Records

It is imperative that school districts have a clear protocol for releasing student records. Below are guidelines that should be followed when responding to requests for student records.

A request for access to inspect, review, copy, or have an oral description or communication of student records should be handled by the District's Custodian of Records or staff members designated for this purpose who shall do the following when receiving a request:

1. Verify the requester's identity.
2. Ensure that the requester has a right to access the student records.
3. Ensure that within <u>five school days</u> following the date of request, an authorized person shall be granted access to inspect, review, and obtain copies of student records during regular school hours.
4. Arrange for a qualified certificated staff member to interpret records when requested.
5. Take steps to prevent the alteration, damage, or loss of records during inspection.
6. Maintain an access log for each student's record which lists all persons, agencies, or organizations requesting or receiving information from the records and, for educational staff or contractors, the legitimate educational interest of the requester.
7. In instances of inspection by persons who do not have assigned educational

responsibility, make an entry in the log indicating the record inspected, the name of the person granted access, the reason access was granted, and the time and circumstances of inspection.

8. Provide copies of any student record at a reasonable fee not to exceed the actual cost of furnishing the copies. No charge shall be made for providing up to two transcripts or up to two verifications of various records for any former student. No charge shall be made to locate or retrieve any student record. Copying costs may be waived for a parent who states he or she cannot afford the expense.

Protocol For Responding to Subpoenas For Student Records

> **The following is a general overall discussion of subpoenas and how to deal with them. Because there are many additional variations and potential issues, this discussion is not exhaustive. In specific cases, contacting the District's attorney may be necessary in order to ensure District compliance.**

1. What is a subpoena?

A subpoena is document issued by one of the attorneys representing a party in a pending court or administrative proceeding commanding a designated individual to be present at a specific time or place. The majority of subpoenas the District receives are a type called a "subpoena duces tecum" which will direct a "custodian of the records" to bring to a court or administrative proceeding specified documents. A subpoena's format can vary greatly from one to another, but a subpoena always should contain the name of the proceeding, the court or administrative agency in which the proceeding is pending, the name and telephone number of the issuing attorney, and a case number.

2. How must a subpoena arrive at the District?

To be valid, a subpoena must be handed by an adult to the District staff member named on the subpoena or left at a District school site or office with an employee. This is called "service of the subpoena." Under most circumstances, a subpoena that arrives by fax, mail, or email attachment does not create a legal obligation on the part of the District to comply, because there is insufficient legal "service."

3. What if a subpoena arrives by fax, mail, or email attachment?

If a subpoena does arrive by means other than personal delivery, the District should contact the lawyer whose name appears on the document and indicate that although copy of subpoena made its way to the District, there was no personal delivery so no documents will be produced. Although there is no duty to respond to a subpoena that is not personally delivered, the prudent course is to check with the lawyer who issued the subpoena to confirm the District's understanding of how the subpoena arrived and prevent any enforcement proceedings against the District in court based on inaccurate or false statements. The District should also expect that an attorney who tried to serve a subpoena by some "short cut," thinking the District would simply provide the requested documents, will re-serve the subpoena correctly.

4. What should be done with a subpoena?

The District should develop a procedure, distributed to all employees who are in positions with public access, whether at a school site or the District Office, to have one designated administrator in the District, and in each department involved, notified if a subpoena shows up, either properly served personally or otherwise, to ensure no District default regarding subpoenas. As part of whatever policy the District develops, the subpoena should be <u>date and time stamped upon receipt</u> and a copy should go also to the District employee whose name appears on the document. Most often, however, the subpoena will not name a particular person, but require a particular department head or a "custodian of the records" of a specific category of documents, to produce the documents. This person should receive a copy of the subpoena and promptly prepare the response by gathering the documents listed. Whether the documents requested are financial information, staff records, cumulative files, student discipline records, attendance data, special education files, or other records, the subpoena should go to the appropriate department administrator. Note that in some cases with multiple categories of records, more that one District administrator should receive a copy. This is a sound reason for having a District-wide policy in effect to keep track of District compliance with subpoenas.

5. What if there is not enough time to assemble all of the documents by the date required in the subpoena?

Often, there is a very short time within which to provide subpoenaed documents. Therefore, it is important to begin immediate efforts to respond to a subpoena when it arrives. Sometimes, however, there will not be enough time to locate and assemble requested documents. Just as in the situation where the subpoena arrives by means other than personal delivery, the lawyer who issued the subpoena should be contacted if enough time is not available to comply. The issuing attorney can agree with the District to alter the terms of the subpoena. Make certain that the attorney confirms any agreement in writing. If the lawyer refuses to be reasonable, the administrator who is the "custodian of the records," should state, with particulars, what the problem is and submit a declaration as part of a Motion for In Camera Review and for Protective Order, as discussed below. In the case of insufficient time, the District should at least have this Motion on file with the court to prevent any adverse legal consequences.

6. What documents should be assembled to comply with a subpoena?

All documents reasonably included in the category of records identified in a subpoena should be located and gathered together. Documents may be in paper files, in photographs, audio recordings, or maintained on electronic media. This may require going to several sources, plus downloading emails or data in computer files. If there are no District records reasonably included in a category listed in a subpoena, that fact should be noted also.

7. Once the documents are assembled, what happens to them?

Once gathered, the assembled documents are copied. The District should have one set to keep with its files to show exactly what was produced. The other copy should go into a large envelope bearing the District's name, the proceeding, and the case number that appears on the subpoena.

8. Must the District administrator deliver the documents personally?

Unless a subpoena expressly requires testimony from a District administrator or employee, the documents may be sent to the location noted on the subpoena accompanied by a declaration signed by the administrator who oversaw the assembly of the documents as the "custodian of the records." This declaration is the equivalent of sworn testimony stating that the documents are from the District's files and were prepared by District staff as part of the regular and customary process of making such records. A form for this declaration often accompanies a subpoena. The District's counsel can assist in preparing the declaration. This signed declaration is attached to the documents placed in the envelope containing the assembled documents. Seal the envelope and attach another copy of the declaration to the outside. The entire package is then most often combined with a Motion, as described below, and sent or delivered to the location on the subpoena (**NOT to the lawyer who issued the subpoena**) far enough in advance to arrive on time.

9. How does the District protect confidential information?

Most often, District files required to comply with a subpoena are pupil records or human resources information pertaining to a particular staff member. The District has a clear legal duty to prevent disclosure of these records to unauthorized individuals. The law, however, also obligates the District to produce documents listed in a lawful subpoena. To resolve this legal conflict and meet each of these legal duties, the District may refer the issue to the District's attorney to prepare a "Motion for In Camera Review and Protective Order." This is a request from the District to the judge presiding over the proceeding to keep the District's records from disclosure until the judge has reviewed them privately. The Motion asks the judge to keep the documents under seal, and to release only those records the judge deems necessary to the case, and then require whoever sees the released records to be bound by a court order to keep them confidential or otherwise be in contempt of court and subject to punishment.

10. What must the District do if pupil records are sought?

As soon as a subpoena is received asking for pupil records, the **District must send a letter** to the parents or guardians of the pupils involved disclosing the receipt of the subpoena, and the District's intention to comply with the law and turn over the documents. Additionally, a telephone call to the parent/guardian is good practice to be certain the parent/guardian is aware of the subpoena. In the letter, the parent/guardian is to be informed of the time and place the records will be turned over and that they can seek legal counsel to object to the release of the records. The District should exercise care to be certain that the parent/guardian of *all* pupils whose identifiable information is in a subpoena request receive this notice. Often, the requested records of one student will include references to other District students.

11. If a motion is warranted, what must the District do?

When the District prepares confidential documents in answer to a subpoena and the District's counsel drafts a Motion, at the time and location on the subpoena for bringing in the documents, the District's attorney will be present to file the motion and state the District's position. Alternatively, the District can have an administrator appear or leave the matter for the judge to decide based on the package of documents with the declaration and written Motion and with no District representative present. In any case, the Motion with a copy of the Declaration (without the documents) must be sent to the lawyer who issued the subpoena as well as any other lawyers in the case. The attorney who issued the subpoena should be able to provide the names and addresses of the other lawyers involved. Often, a subpoena is issued by a deputy public defender. In this instance, the opposing counsel is most likely in the district attorney's office.

Destruction or Retention of Student Records

The classification of pupil records determines their retention or destruction requirements. There are three classifications of pupil records:

1. <u>Permanent Pupil Records</u>—5 C.C.R. § 430(d)(1), § 432(b)(1) - Defined as records which are maintained in perpetuity-<u>they are never destroyed</u>

They include:

- Legal name and sex of pupil

- Date and place of birth

- Method of verifying date of birth

- Verification of mandatory immunizations or exemption from immunizations

- Name and address of pupil's parent or minor pupil's address if different

- Entering and leaving date for every school year, summer session, or extra session

- Subjects taken during each session

- The mark or number of credits toward graduation allowed for work taken

- Date of high school graduation or equivalent

2. <u>Mandatory Interim Pupil Records</u>—5 C.C.R. § 430(d)(2), § 432(b)(2), 437, 438 - Defined as records schools are directed to compile and maintain for a stipulated period of time and then destroy when the student leaves the school, "or when their usefulness ceases." They may be transferred in the cumulative file to a new district but must be transferred if the new district requests them. <u>Otherwise, they may be destroyed the third school year after the school year in which they originated.</u>

They include:

- A log or record identifying those persons or organizations requesting or receiving pupil record information

- Health information including Child Health Developmental Disabilities Prevention Report verification of waiver

- Language training record

- Participation in special education programs

- Progress slips and/or notices

- Parental restrictions regarding access to directory information

- Results of standardized tests

- Expulsion records

3. <u>Permitted Pupil Records</u>—5 C.C.R. § 430(b)(2), § 432 (d)(3), 437, 438 - Defined as records which have clear importance only to the current educational process of the student. <u>They may be destroyed when their usefulness ceases or six months following a student's withdrawal or graduation.</u>

They include:

- Objective counselor and/or teacher ratings

- Standardized tests results older than 3 years

- Routine discipline data

- Verified reports of relevant behavioral patterns

- All disciplinary notices

- Attendance records

The method the district utilizes to destroy pupil records must ensure that the records are not available for public inspection during or following their destruction. (CA Ed. Code 49062; 5 C.C.R. § 437)

For printed documents or photographic prints, this means a shredding process that guarantees complete obliteration to the point that piecing the shreds together is impossible such as with a cross-cut or confetti machine. Complete burning also can satisfy this requirement, but this could be impractical or potentially violate air quality laws.

For electronic media, this means that data is deleted in a manner that precludes any recovery. This could also include complete destruction of hard drives or other physical repositories of electronic data. Don't be the school district that dumps boxes of student records in the trash bin for trash pick-up only to find that someone has gone through the schools trash bin, found the documents, and published them online!

Counseling Records And Confidentiality

Educational counseling is a specialized service provided by a school counselor possessing a valid credential with a specialization in pupil personnel services who is assigned specific times to directly counsel pupils. (CA Ed. Code 49600(a)).

CA. Ed. Code 49600 codifies that educational counseling includes, but is not limited to: academic counseling, career and vocational counseling, and personal and social counseling. In providing academic counseling, a school counselor should discuss, at minimum: "establishment and implementation with parental involvement of the pupil's immediate and long-range educational plans;" "optimizing progress towards achievement of proficiency standards;" completion of the required curriculum in accordance with the pupil's needs, abilities, interests, and aptitudes;" and "Academic planning for access and success in higher education programs including advisement on courses needed for admission to public colleges and universities, standardized admissions tests, and financial aid." (CA Ed. Code 49600(b)(1)(A)-(D)).

In providing career and vocational counseling, a school counselor should assist the student in: "planning for the future;" "becoming aware of their career potential;" "developing realistic perceptions of work;" and "relating to the work world." (CA Ed. Code 49600(b)(2)(A)-(D)). Finally, personal and social counseling should focus on fostering interpersonal relationships to promote "development of their academic abilities, careers and vocations, personalities, and social skills." (CA Ed. Code 49600(c)).

Confidentiality of Information Received During Counseling

California law strictly protects the confidentiality of personal information shared by a student while receiving counseling from a school counselor. Any information of a personal nature disclosed by a pupil 12 years of age or older in the process of receiving counseling from a school counselor, and any information of a personal nature disclosed to a school counselor by the pupil's parent or guardian, is confidential. (CA Ed. Code 49602). In other words, not all information is confidential, only such information that is "of a personal nature," disclosed by a student 12 years of age or older, or a student's parents, "in the process of receiving counseling from a school counselor." While this section does not define "information of a personal nature," it does codify that such information does not "include routine objective information related to academic and career counseling."

Therefore, when responding the requests to access student records, administrators must keep in mind that student counseling records have additional protections and limits on who may access them and be careful not to inadvertently disclose these records without proper legal authority.

The information may not be revealed, released, discussed, or referred to by the school counselor except that such information may be shared: with psychotherapists, other health care providers, or the school nurse solely for purposes of referring the student for treatment; with local child protective agencies to report of child abuse or neglect; with the principal or parents when the school counselor has reasonable cause to believe that disclosure is necessary to avert a clear and present danger to the health, safety, or welfare of the pupil, administrators, teachers, school staff, parents, pupils, and other school community members; with the principal or other school personal, and, as necessary, the parents and other persons outside the school, when the pupil indicates that a crime, involving the likelihood of personal injury or significant or substantial property losses, will be or has been committed; and, with persons specified in a written waiver of confidentiality after this written waiver of confidence is read and signed by the student and maintained in the pupil record file. (CA Ed. Code 49602(a)-(e)).

School counselors must be careful not to disclose confidential information without consent or pursuant to a statutory exception. While the issue has not been addressed in California, several other jurisdictions have found that school counselors were personally liable for damages pursuant to a 42 USC §1983 claim or common law tort claim, for disclosing confidential information.

The remaining paragraphs of CA Ed. Code 49602 further codify the purpose and extent of such confidentiality. While school counselors do not enjoy any doctor-patient privilege between themselves and the students they counsel, the Legislature created a "privilege of confidentiality under this section to assist the pupil whenever possible to communicate more effectively with parents, school staff, and others." Furthermore, CA Ed. Code 49602 specifically disallows disclosure of confidential information shared during a counseling session to the student's parents "when the school counselor has reasonable cause to believe that the disclosure would result in a clear and present danger to the health, safety, or welfare of the pupil." On the other hand, CA Ed. Code 49602 requires a school counselor to "disclose information deemed to be confidential pursuant to this section to law enforcement agencies when ordered to do so by order of a court of law, to aid in the investigation of a crime, or when ordered to testify in any administrative or judicial proceeding." Such confidentiality also does not "limit the counselor from conferring with other school staff, as appropriate, regarding modification of the pupil's academic program."

Most importantly, the remaining paragraphs of CA Ed. Code 49602 codify: "No person required by this section to keep information discussed during counseling confidential shall incur any civil or criminal liability as a result of keeping that information confidential." However, a school counselor could potentially face liability for failing to disclose such confidential information when there is a mandatory reporting requirement.

Confidential Medical Appointments

CA Ed. Code 46010.1 requires the school to excuse a student to obtain confidential medical services without parental consent. This section also makes it mandatory to provide annual notice to pupils and parents of the availability of confidential medical appointments. The school *must* excuse the pupil who requests to leave school for a confidential appointment.

"Confidential Medical Services" are not defined in the CA Ed. Code, but the Family Code does list the reasons a minor may go to a doctor without the otherwise required parental consent for medical care or treatment. Family Code sections 6920-6929 allow minors to seek medical advice without their parents' consent or knowledge for prevention or treatment of <u>pregnancy, sexually transmitted diseases, rape, sexual assault, and drug- or alcohol-related problems</u>. The school should not ask the student the reason for the confidential appointment. It is the responsibility of the physician to determine if the reason for the office visit is one for which the minor can be treated without parental consent. The Health and Safety Code sections also provide in cases of sexual abuse or drug or alcohol treatment for the health care professional to attempt parental contact under specified circumstances. This is in stark contrast to the absolute prohibition against school contact with the parents regarding these appointments.

The school, however, must document the absence for a confidential medical appointment. To have a pupil counted in the ADA, CA Ed. Code 48205 lists illness and several other grounds for an excused absence including subdivision (1)(3), "For the purpose of having medical, dental, optometrical, or chiropractic services rendered." To protect against any liability claims for a student absent from the campus, the school must have a record that the student was excused from the site.

The school may not ask the pupil the reason for the confidential medical appointment, but the school may verify that the student was at the doctor's office. (*See* 66 Ops. Cal. Atty.Gen. 244, 246-47, n.5 (1983)). The verification, however, can only extend to confirming the student showed up for the appointment, not why. Some schools will accept the statement of the pupil if that pupil has a reputation for honesty, but that is a policy consideration for each school district.

Accordingly, the school must have documentation in its files that the pupil's absence was excused to comply with attendance requirements and the calculation of the school's ADA for funding purposes. The record should simply show a generic excused absence without further explanation to keep the reason confidential.

Parents have an unrestricted right to review their child's pupil records under CA Ed. Code 49061(b). The parent may learn of the excused absence, but the school, albeit most uncomfortably, may be forced to leave it to the parent to turn to the student for further explanation. The school cannot disclose this information. Additionally, the school should take precautions to prevent automatic parental notifications when pupils are absent when the reason is a confidential medical appointment. (87 Ops. Cal.Atty.Gen.168, 172 (2004)). This Attorney General's opinion emphasizes that the Legislative intent in Health and Safety Code section 132115(a)(1) is to keep these medical services confidential even from parents. Some California school districts have established procedures for pupils who want to go to a confidential medical appointment to work through the school nurse or counselor. Any reference for the reason the pupil had a confidential medical appointment in a credentialed school counselor's file is not a disclosable pupil record. CA Ed. Code 49602 protects disclosure of "counseling records" for a student 12 years of age or older regarding matters "of a personal nature" from classification as pupil records without the student's consent. This protection extends to further consultation with the school nurse to refer the pupil for treatment. (CA Ed.

Code 49602(a)). Additionally, any notes a counselor or school nurse makes solely for his or her own use is not a pupil record reachable by parents. (5 C.C.R §430(d)).

School administrators may find themselves in the difficult situation of telling the parent they can say nothing more than the pupil's absence is excused if asked. This suggests that established procedures for confidential medical appointments and accounting for excused absences be set up to avoid automatic notification to parents of a student absence, be assured of maximum state funding, and a means to make it relatively safe and easy for the students to use this option.

APPENDIX

2020 version of the CA Ed Code 48900 et seq

State of California

EDUCATION CODE

Section 48900

48900. A pupil shall not be suspended from school or recommended for expulsion, unless the superintendent of the school district or the principal of the school in which the pupil is enrolled determines that the pupil has committed an act as defined pursuant to any of subdivisions (a) to (r), inclusive:

(a) (1) Caused, attempted to cause, or threatened to cause physical injury to another person.

(2) Willfully used force or violence upon the person of another, except in self-defense.

(b) Possessed, sold, or otherwise furnished a firearm, knife, explosive, or other dangerous object, unless, in the case of possession of an object of this type, the pupil had obtained written permission to possess the item from a certificated school employee, which is concurred in by the principal or the designee of the principal.

(c) Unlawfully possessed, used, sold, or otherwise furnished, or been under the influence of, a controlled substance listed in Chapter 2 (commencing with Section 11053) of Division 10 of the Health and Safety Code, an alcoholic beverage, or an intoxicant of any kind.

(d) Unlawfully offered, arranged, or negotiated to sell a controlled substance listed in Chapter 2 (commencing with Section 11053) of Division 10 of the Health and Safety Code, an alcoholic beverage, or an intoxicant of any kind, and either sold, delivered, or otherwise furnished to a person another liquid, substance, or material and represented the liquid, substance, or material as a controlled substance, alcoholic beverage, or intoxicant.

(e) Committed or attempted to commit robbery or extortion.

(f) Caused or attempted to cause damage to school property or private property.

(g) Stole or attempted to steal school property or private property.

(h) Possessed or used tobacco, or products containing tobacco or nicotine products, including, but not limited to, cigarettes, cigars, miniature cigars, clove cigarettes, smokeless tobacco, snuff, chew packets, and betel. However, this section does not prohibit the use or possession by a pupil of the pupil's own prescription products.

(i) Committed an obscene act or engaged in habitual profanity or vulgarity.

(j) Unlawfully possessed or unlawfully offered, arranged, or negotiated to sell drug paraphernalia, as defined in Section 11014.5 of the Health and Safety Code.

(k) (1) Disrupted school activities or otherwise willfully defied the valid authority of supervisors, teachers, administrators, school officials, or other school personnel engaged in the performance of their duties.

State of California

EDUCATION CODE

Section 48900

48900. A pupil shall not be suspended from school or recommended for expulsion, unless the superintendent of the school district or the principal of the school in which the pupil is enrolled determines that the pupil has committed an act as defined pursuant to any of subdivisions (a) to (r), inclusive:

(a) (1) Caused, attempted to cause, or threatened to cause physical injury to another person.

(2) Willfully used force or violence upon the person of another, except in self-defense.

(b) Possessed, sold, or otherwise furnished a firearm, knife, explosive, or other dangerous object, unless, in the case of possession of an object of this type, the pupil had obtained written permission to possess the item from a certificated school employee, which is concurred in by the principal or the designee of the principal.

(c) Unlawfully possessed, used, sold, or otherwise furnished, or been under the influence of, a controlled substance listed in Chapter 2 (commencing with Section 11053) of Division 10 of the Health and Safety Code, an alcoholic beverage, or an intoxicant of any kind.

(d) Unlawfully offered, arranged, or negotiated to sell a controlled substance listed in Chapter 2 (commencing with Section 11053) of Division 10 of the Health and Safety Code, an alcoholic beverage, or an intoxicant of any kind, and either sold, delivered, or otherwise furnished to a person another liquid, substance, or material and represented the liquid, substance, or material as a controlled substance, alcoholic beverage, or intoxicant.

(e) Committed or attempted to commit robbery or extortion.

(f) Caused or attempted to cause damage to school property or private property.

(g) Stole or attempted to steal school property or private property.

(h) Possessed or used tobacco, or products containing tobacco or nicotine products, including, but not limited to, cigarettes, cigars, miniature cigars, clove cigarettes, smokeless tobacco, snuff, chew packets, and betel. However, this section does not prohibit the use or possession by a pupil of the pupil's own prescription products.

(i) Committed an obscene act or engaged in habitual profanity or vulgarity.

(j) Unlawfully possessed or unlawfully offered, arranged, or negotiated to sell drug paraphernalia, as defined in Section 11014.5 of the Health and Safety Code.

(k) (1) Disrupted school activities or otherwise willfully defied the valid authority of supervisors, teachers, administrators, school officials, or other school personnel engaged in the performance of their duties.

State of California

EDUCATION CODE

Section 48900.1

48900.1. (a) The governing board of each school district may adopt a policy authorizing teachers to require the parent or guardian of a pupil who has been suspended by a teacher pursuant to Section 48910 for reasons specified in subdivision (i) or (k) of Section 48900, to attend a portion of a schoolday in the classroom of his or her child or ward. The policy shall take into account reasonable factors that may prevent compliance with a notice to attend. The attendance of the parent or guardian shall be limited to the class from which the pupil was suspended.

(b) The policy shall be adopted pursuant to the procedures set forth in Sections 35291 and 35291.5. Parents and guardians shall be notified of this policy prior to its implementation. A teacher shall apply any policy adopted pursuant to this section uniformly to all pupils within the classroom.

The adopted policy shall include the procedures that the district will follow to accomplish the following:

(1) Ensure that parents or guardians who attend school for the purposes of this section meet with the school administrator or his or her designee after completing the classroom visitation and before leaving the schoolsite.

(2) Contact parents or guardians who do not respond to the request to attend school pursuant to this section.

(c) If a teacher imposes the procedure pursuant to subdivision (a), the principal shall send a written notice to the parent or guardian stating that attendance by the parent or guardian is pursuant to law. This section shall apply only to a parent or guardian who is actually living with the pupil.

(d) A parent or guardian who has received a written notice pursuant to subdivision (c) shall attend class as specified in the written notice. The notice may specify that the attendance of the parent or guardian be on the day the pupil is scheduled to return to class, or within a reasonable period of time thereafter, as established by the policy of the board adopted pursuant to subdivision (a).

(Amended by Stats. 2004, Ch. 895, Sec. 9. Effective January 1, 2005.)

STATE OF CALIFORNIA
AUTHENTICATED
ELECTRONIC LEGAL MATERIAL

State of California

EDUCATION CODE

Section 48900.2

48900.2. In addition to the reasons specified in Section 48900, a pupil may be suspended from school or recommended for expulsion if the superintendent or the principal of the school in which the pupil is enrolled determines that the pupil has committed sexual harassment as defined in Section 212.5.

For the purposes of this chapter, the conduct described in Section 212.5 must be considered by a reasonable person of the same gender as the victim to be sufficiently severe or pervasive to have a negative impact upon the individual's academic performance or to create an intimidating, hostile, or offensive educational environment. This section shall not apply to pupils enrolled in kindergarten and grades 1 to 3, inclusive.

(Added by Stats. 1992, Ch. 909, Sec. 2. Effective January 1, 1993.)

State of California

EDUCATION CODE

Section 48900.3

48900.3. In addition to the reasons set forth in Sections 48900 and 48900.2, a pupil in any of grades 4 to 12, inclusive, may be suspended from school or recommended for expulsion if the superintendent or the principal of the school in which the pupil is enrolled determines that the pupil has caused, attempted to cause, threatened to cause, or participated in an act of, hate violence, as defined in subdivision (e) of Section 233.

(Amended by Stats. 1999, Ch. 646, Sec. 25. Effective January 1, 2000.)

State of California

EDUCATION CODE

Section 48900.4

48900.4. In addition to the grounds specified in Sections 48900 and 48900.2, a pupil enrolled in any of grades 4 to 12, inclusive, may be suspended from school or recommended for expulsion if the superintendent or the principal of the school in which the pupil is enrolled determines that the pupil has intentionally engaged in harassment, threats, or intimidation, directed against school district personnel or pupils, that is sufficiently severe or pervasive to have the actual and reasonably expected effect of materially disrupting classwork, creating substantial disorder, and invading the rights of either school personnel or pupils by creating an intimidating or hostile educational environment.

(Amended by Stats. 2002, Ch. 643, Sec. 2. Effective January 1, 2003.)

State of California

EDUCATION CODE

Section 48900.5

48900.5. (a) Suspension, including supervised suspension as described in Section 48911.1, shall be imposed only when other means of correction fail to bring about proper conduct. A school district may document the other means of correction used and place that documentation in the pupil's record, which may be accessed pursuant to Section 49069.7. However, a pupil, including an individual with exceptional needs, as defined in Section 56026, may be suspended, subject to Section 1415 of Title 20 of the United States Code, for any of the reasons enumerated in Section 48900 upon a first offense, if the principal or superintendent of schools determines that the pupil violated subdivision (a), (b), (c), (d), or (e) of Section 48900 or that the pupil's presence causes a danger to persons.

(b) Other means of correction include, but are not limited to, the following:

(1) A conference between school personnel, the pupil's parent or guardian, and the pupil.

(2) Referrals to the school counselor, psychologist, social worker, child welfare attendance personnel, or other school support service personnel for case management and counseling.

(3) Study teams, guidance teams, resource panel teams, or other intervention-related teams that assess the behavior, and develop and implement individualized plans to address the behavior in partnership with the pupil and the pupil's parents.

(4) Referral for a comprehensive psychosocial or psychoeducational assessment, including for purposes of creating an individualized education program, or a plan adopted pursuant to Section 504 of the federal Rehabilitation Act of 1973 (29 U.S.C. Sec. 794(a)).

(5) Enrollment in a program for teaching prosocial behavior or anger management.

(6) Participation in a restorative justice program.

(7) A positive behavior support approach with tiered interventions that occur during the schoolday on campus.

(8) After school programs that address specific behavioral issues or expose pupils to positive activities and behaviors, including, but not limited to, those operated in collaboration with local parent and community groups.

(9) Any of the alternatives described in Section 48900.6.

(Amended by Stats. 2019, Ch. 497, Sec. 61. (AB 991) Effective January 1, 2020.)

State of California

EDUCATION CODE

Section 48900.6

48900.6. As part of or instead of disciplinary action prescribed by this article, the principal of a school, the principal's designee, the superintendent of schools, or the governing board may require a pupil to perform community service on school grounds or, with written permission of the parent or guardian of the pupil, off school grounds, during the pupil's nonschool hours. For the purposes of this section, "community service" may include, but is not limited to, work performed in the community or on school grounds in the areas of outdoor beautification, community or campus betterment, and teacher, peer, or youth assistance programs. This section does not apply if a pupil has been suspended, pending expulsion, pursuant to Section 48915. However, this section applies if the recommended expulsion is not implemented or is, itself, suspended by stipulation or other administrative action.

(Amended (as amended by Stats. 1995, Ch. 972) by Stats. 2000, Ch. 225, Sec. 1. Effective January 1, 2001.)

State of California

EDUCATION CODE

Section 48900.7

48900.7. (a) In addition to the reasons specified in Sections 48900, 48900.2, 48900.3, and 48900.4, a pupil may be suspended from school or recommended for expulsion if the superintendent or the principal of the school in which the pupil is enrolled determines that the pupil has made terroristic threats against school officials or school property, or both.

  (b) For the purposes of this section, "terroristic threat" shall include any statement, whether written or oral, by a person who willfully threatens to commit a crime which will result in death, great bodily injury to another person, or property damage in excess of one thousand dollars ($1,000), with the specific intent that the statement is to be taken as a threat, even if there is no intent of actually carrying it out, which, on its face and under the circumstances in which it is made, is so unequivocal, unconditional, immediate, and specific as to convey to the person threatened, a gravity of purpose and an immediate prospect of execution of the threat, and thereby causes that person reasonably to be in sustained fear for his or her own safety or for his or her immediate family's safety, or for the protection of school district property, or the personal property of the person threatened or his or her immediate family.

  (Added by Stats. 1997, Ch. 405, Sec. 1. Effective January 1, 1998.)

State of California

EDUCATION CODE

Section 48900.8

48900.8. For purposes of notification to parents, and for the reporting of expulsion or suspension offenses to the department, each school district shall specifically identify, by offense committed, in all appropriate official records of a pupil each suspension or expulsion of that pupil for the commission of any of the offenses set forth in Section 48900, 48900.2, 48900.3, 48900.4, 48900.7, or 48915.

(Amended by Stats. 2005, Ch. 677, Sec. 33. Effective October 7, 2005.)

State of California

EDUCATION CODE

Section 48900.9

48900.9. (a) The superintendent of a school district, the principal of a school, or the principal's designee may refer a victim of, witness to, or other pupil affected by, an act of bullying, as defined in paragraph (1) of subdivision (r) of Section 48900, committed on or after January 1, 2015, to the school counselor, school psychologist, social worker, child welfare attendance personnel, school nurse, or other school support service personnel for case management, counseling, and participation in a restorative justice program, as appropriate.

(b) A pupil who has engaged in an act of bullying, as defined in paragraph (1) of subdivision (r) of Section 48900, may also be referred to the school counselor, school psychologist, social worker, child welfare attendance personnel, or other school support service personnel for case management and counseling, or for participation in a restorative justice program, pursuant to Section 48900.5.

(Amended by Stats. 2015, Ch. 303, Sec. 104. (AB 731) Effective January 1, 2016.)

STATE OF CALIFORNIA
AUTHENTICATED
ELECTRONIC LEGAL MATERIAL

State of California

EDUCATION CODE

Section 48901

48901. (a) No school shall permit the smoking or use of a tobacco product by pupils of the school while the pupils are on campus, or while attending school-sponsored activities or while under the supervision and control of school district employees.

(b) The governing board of any school district maintaining a high school shall take all steps it deems practical to discourage high school students from smoking.

(c) For purposes of this section, "smoking" has the same meaning as in subdivision (c) of Section 22950.5 of the Business and Professions Code.

(d) For purposes of this section, "tobacco product" means a product or device as defined in subdivision (d) of Section 22950.5 of the Business and Professions Code.

(Amended by Stats. 2016, 2nd Ex. Sess., Ch. 7, Sec. 9. (SB 5 2x) Effective June 9, 2016.)

State of California

EDUCATION CODE

Section 48901.1

48901.1. Notwithstanding Section 47610 or any other law, commencing July 1, 2020, the following provisions apply to charter schools:

(a) A pupil enrolled in a charter school in kindergarten or any of grades 1 to 5, inclusive, shall not be suspended on the basis of having disrupted school activities or otherwise willfully defied the valid authority of supervisors, teachers, administrators, school officials, or other school personnel engaged in the performance of their duties, and those acts shall not constitute grounds for a pupil enrolled in a charter school in kindergarten or any of grades 1 to 12, inclusive, to be recommended for expulsion.

(b) A pupil enrolled in a charter school in any of grades 6 to 8, inclusive, shall not be suspended on the basis of having disrupted school activities or otherwise willfully defied the valid authority of supervisors, teachers, administrators, school officials, or other school personnel engaged in the performance of their duties. This subdivision is inoperative on July 1, 2025.

(Added by Stats. 2019, Ch. 279, Sec. 3. (SB 419) Effective January 1, 2020.)

State of California

EDUCATION CODE

Section 48901.5

48901.5. (a) The governing board of each school district, or its designee, may regulate the possession or use of any electronic signaling device that operates through the transmission or receipt of radio waves, including, but not limited to, paging and signaling equipment, by pupils of the school district while the pupils are on campus, while attending school-sponsored activities, or while under the supervision and control of school district employees.

(b) No pupil shall be prohibited from possessing or using an electronic signaling device that is determined by a licensed physician and surgeon to be essential for the health of the pupil and use of which is limited to purposes related to the health of the pupil.

(Amended by Stats. 2002, Ch. 253, Sec. 2. Effective January 1, 2003.)

STATE OF CALIFORNIA
AUTHENTICATED
ELECTRONIC LEGAL MATERIAL

State of California

EDUCATION CODE

Section 48901.7

48901.7. (a) The governing body of a school district, a county office of education, or a charter school may adopt a policy to limit or prohibit the use by its pupils of smartphones while the pupils are at a schoolsite or while the pupils are under the supervision and control of an employee or employees of that school district, county office of education, or charter school.

(b) Notwithstanding subdivision (a), a pupil shall not be prohibited from possessing or using a smartphone under any of the following circumstances:

(1) In the case of an emergency, or in response to a perceived threat of danger.

(2) When a teacher or administrator of the school district, county office of education, or charter school grants permission to a pupil to possess or use a smartphone, subject to any reasonable limitation imposed by that teacher or administrator.

(3) When a licensed physician and surgeon determines that the possession or use of a smartphone is necessary for the health or well-being of the pupil.

(4) When the possession or use of a smartphone is required in a pupil's individualized education program.

(Added by Stats. 2019, Ch. 42, Sec. 2. (AB 272) Effective January 1, 2020.)

State of California

EDUCATION CODE

Section 48902

48902. (a) The principal of a school or the principal's designee shall, before the suspension or expulsion of any pupil, notify the appropriate law enforcement authorities of the county or city in which the school is situated, of any acts of the pupil that may violate Section 245 of the Penal Code.

(b) The principal of a school or the principal's designee shall, within one schoolday after suspension or expulsion of any pupil, notify, by telephone or any other appropriate method chosen by the school, the appropriate law enforcement authorities of the county or the school district in which the school is situated of any acts of the pupil that may violate subdivision (c) or (d) of Section 48900.

(c) Notwithstanding subdivision (b), the principal of a school or the principal's designee shall notify the appropriate law enforcement authorities of the county or city in which the school is located of any acts of a pupil that may involve the possession or sale of narcotics or of a controlled substance or a violation of Section 626.9 or 626.10 of the Penal Code. The principal of a school or the principal's designee shall report any act specified in paragraph (1) or (5) of subdivision (c) of Section 48915 committed by a pupil or nonpupil on a schoolsite to the city police or county sheriff with jurisdiction over the school and the school security department or the school police department, as applicable.

(d) A principal, the principal's designee, or any other person reporting a known or suspected act described in subdivision (a) or (b) is not civilly or criminally liable as a result of making any report authorized by this article unless it can be proven that a false report was made and that the person knew the report was false or the report was made with reckless disregard for the truth or falsity of the report.

(e) The principal of a school or the principal's designee reporting a criminal act committed by a schoolage individual with exceptional needs, as defined in Section 56026, shall ensure that copies of the special education and disciplinary records of the pupil are transmitted, as described in Section 1415(k)(6) of Title 20 of the United States Code, for consideration by the appropriate authorities to whom he or she reports the criminal act. Any copies of the pupil's special education and disciplinary records may be transmitted only to the extent permissible under the federal Family Educational Rights and Privacy Act of 1974 (20 U.S.C. Sec. 1232g et seq.).

(Amended by Stats. 2013, Ch. 76, Sec. 41. (AB 383) Effective January 1, 2014.)

State of California

EDUCATION CODE

Section 48903

48903. (a) Except as provided in subdivision (g) of Section 48911 and in Section 48912, the total number of days for which a pupil may be suspended from school shall not exceed 20 schooldays in any school year, unless for purposes of adjustment, a pupil enrolls in or is transferred to another regular school, an opportunity school or class, or a continuation education school or class, in which case the total number of schooldays for which the pupil may be suspended shall not exceed 30 days in any school year.

(b) For the purposes of this section, a school district may count suspensions that occur while a pupil is enrolled in another school district toward the maximum number of days for which a pupil may be suspended in any school year.

(Amended by Stats. 1998, Ch. 527, Sec. 1. Effective January 1, 1999.)

STATE OF CALIFORNIA
AUTHENTICATED
ELECTRONIC LEGAL MATERIAL

State of California

EDUCATION CODE

Section 48904

48904. (a) (1) Notwithstanding Section 1714.1 of the Civil Code, the parent or guardian of any minor whose willful misconduct results in injury or death to any pupil or any person employed by, or performing volunteer services for, a school district or private school or who willfully cuts, defaces, or otherwise injures in any way any property, real or personal, belonging to a school district or private school, or personal property of any school employee, shall be liable for all damages so caused by the minor. The liability of the parent or guardian shall not exceed ten thousand dollars ($10,000), adjusted annually for inflation. The parent or guardian shall be liable also for the amount of any reward not exceeding ten thousand dollars ($10,000), adjusted annually for inflation, paid pursuant to Section 53069.5 of the Government Code. The parent or guardian of a minor shall be liable to a school district or private school for all property belonging to the school district or private school loaned to the minor and not returned upon demand of an employee of the school district or private school authorized to make the demand.

(2) The Superintendent annually shall compute an adjustment of the liability limits prescribed by this subdivision to reflect the percentage change in the average annual value of the Implicit Price Deflator for State and Local Government Purchases of Goods and Services for the United States, as published by the United States Department of Commerce for the 12-month period ending in the prior fiscal year. The annual adjustment shall be rounded to the nearest one hundred dollars ($100).

(b) (1) Any school district or private school whose real or personal property has been willfully cut, defaced, or otherwise injured, or whose property is loaned to a pupil and willfully not returned upon demand of an employee of the school district or private school authorized to make the demand may, after affording the pupil his or her due process rights, withhold the grades, diploma, and transcripts of the pupil responsible for the damage until the pupil or the pupil's parent or guardian has paid for the damages thereto, as provided in subdivision (a).

(2) The school district or private school shall notify the parent or guardian of the pupil in writing of the pupil's alleged misconduct before withholding the pupil's grades, diploma, or transcripts pursuant to this subdivision. When the minor and parent are unable to pay for the damages, or to return the property, the school district or private school shall provide a program of voluntary work for the minor in lieu of the payment of monetary damages. Upon completion of the voluntary work, the grades, diploma, and transcripts of the pupil shall be released.

(3) The governing board of each school district or governing body of each private school shall establish rules and regulations governing procedures for the

State of California

EDUCATION CODE

Section 48904.3

48904.3. (a) Upon receiving notice that a school district has withheld the grades, diploma, or transcripts of any pupil pursuant to Section 48904, any school district to which the pupil has transferred shall likewise withhold the grades, diploma, or transcripts of the pupil as authorized by that section, until the time that it receives notice, from the district that initiated the decision to withhold, that the decision has been rescinded under the terms of that section.

(b) Any school district that has decided to withhold a pupil's grades, diploma, or transcripts pursuant to Section 48904 shall, upon receiving notice that the pupil has transferred to any school district in this state, notify the parent or guardian of the pupil in writing that the decision to withhold will be enforced as specified in subdivision (a).

(c) For purposes of this section and Section 48904, "school district" is defined to include any county superintendent of schools.

(d) This section and Section 48904 shall also apply to the state special schools, as described in subdivision (a) of Section 48927.

(Amended by Stats. 2002, Ch. 492, Sec. 2. Effective January 1, 2003.)

State of California

EDUCATION CODE

Section 48905

48905. An employee of a school district whose person or property is injured or damaged by the willful misconduct of a pupil who attends school in such district, when the employee or the employee's property is (1) located on property owned by the district, (2) being transported to or from an activity sponsored by the district or a school within the district, (3) present at an activity sponsored by such district or school, or (4) otherwise injured or damaged in retaliation for acts lawfully undertaken by the employee in execution of the employee's duties, may request the school district to pursue legal action against the pupil who caused the injury or damage, or the pupil's parent or guardian pursuant to Section 48904.

(Repealed and added by Stats. 1983, Ch. 498, Sec. 91. Effective July 28, 1983.)

State of California

EDUCATION CODE

Section 48906

48906. When a principal or other school official releases a minor pupil to a peace officer for the purpose of removing the minor from the school premises, the school official shall take immediate steps to notify the parent, guardian, or responsible relative of the minor regarding the release of the minor to the officer, and regarding the place to which the minor is reportedly being taken, except when a minor has been taken into custody as a victim of suspected child abuse, as defined in Section 11165.6 of the Penal Code, or pursuant to Section 305 of the Welfare and Institutions Code. In those cases, the school official shall provide the peace officer with the address and telephone number of the minor's parent or guardian. The peace officer shall take immediate steps to notify the parent, guardian, or responsible relative of the minor that the minor is in custody and the place where he or she is being held. If the officer has a reasonable belief that the minor would be endangered by a disclosure of the place where the minor is being held, or that the disclosure would cause the custody of the minor to be disturbed, the officer may refuse to disclose the place where the minor is being held for a period not to exceed 24 hours. The officer shall, however, inform the parent, guardian, or responsible relative whether the child requires and is receiving medical or other treatment. The juvenile court shall review any decision not to disclose the place where the minor is being held at a subsequent detention hearing.

(Amended by Stats. 2005, Ch. 279, Sec. 1. Effective January 1, 2006.)

State of California

EDUCATION CODE

Section 48907

48907. (a) Pupils of the public schools, including charter schools, shall have the right to exercise freedom of speech and of the press including, but not limited to, the use of bulletin boards, the distribution of printed materials or petitions, the wearing of buttons, badges, and other insignia, and the right of expression in official publications, whether or not the publications or other means of expression are supported financially by the school or by use of school facilities, except that expression shall be prohibited which is obscene, libelous, or slanderous. Also prohibited shall be material that so incites pupils as to create a clear and present danger of the commission of unlawful acts on school premises or the violation of lawful school regulations, or the substantial disruption of the orderly operation of the school.

(b) The governing board or body of each school district or charter school and each county board of education shall adopt rules and regulations in the form of a written publications code, which shall include reasonable provisions for the time, place, and manner of conducting such activities within its respective jurisdiction.

(c) Pupil editors of official school publications shall be responsible for assigning and editing the news, editorial, and feature content of their publications subject to the limitations of this section. However, it shall be the responsibility of a journalism adviser or advisers of pupil publications within each school to supervise the production of the pupil staff, to maintain professional standards of English and journalism, and to maintain the provisions of this section.

(d) There shall be no prior restraint of material prepared for official school publications except insofar as it violates this section. School officials shall have the burden of showing justification without undue delay prior to a limitation of pupil expression under this section.

(e) "Official school publications" refers to material produced by pupils in the journalism, newspaper, yearbook, or writing classes and distributed to the student body either free or for a fee.

(f) This section does not prohibit or prevent the governing board or body of a school district or charter school from adopting otherwise valid rules and regulations relating to oral communication by pupils upon the premises of each school.

(g) An employee shall not be dismissed, suspended, disciplined, reassigned, transferred, or otherwise retaliated against solely for acting to protect a pupil engaged in the conduct authorized under this section, or refusing to infringe upon conduct that is protected by this section, the First Amendment to the United States Constitution, or Section 2 of Article I of the California Constitution.

(Amended by Stats. 2010, Ch. 142, Sec. 2. (SB 438) Effective January 1, 2011.)

State of California

EDUCATION CODE

Section 48908

48908. All pupils shall comply with the regulations, pursue the required course of study, and submit to the authority of the teachers of the schools.

(Repealed and added by Stats. 1983, Ch. 498, Sec. 91. Effective July 28, 1983.)

STATE OF CALIFORNIA
AUTHENTICATED
ELECTRONIC LEGAL MATERIAL

State of California

EDUCATION CODE

Section 48909

48909.   When a petition is requested in juvenile court or a complaint is filed in any court alleging that a minor of compulsory school attendance age or any pupil currently enrolled in a public school in a grade to and including grade 12 is a person who (a) has used, sold, or possessed narcotics or other hallucinogenic drugs or substances; (b) has inhaled or breathed the fumes of, or ingested any poison classified as such in Section 4160 of the Business and Professions Code; or (c) has committed felonious assault, homicide, or rape the district attorney may, within 48 hours, provide written notice to the superintendent of the school district of attendance, notwithstanding the provisions of Section 827 of the Welfare and Institutions Code, and to the pupil's parent or guardian.

(Amended by Stats. 1991, Ch. 1202, Sec. 1.)

State of California

EDUCATION CODE

Section 48910

48910.   (a) A teacher may suspend any pupil from class, for any of the acts enumerated in Section 48900, for the day of the suspension and the day following. The teacher shall immediately report the suspension to the principal of the school and send the pupil to the principal or the designee of the principal for appropriate action. If that action requires the continued presence of the pupil at the schoolsite, the pupil shall be under appropriate supervision, as defined in policies and related regulations adopted by the governing board of the school district. As soon as possible, the teacher shall ask the parent or guardian of the pupil to attend a parent-teacher conference regarding the suspension. If practicable, a school counselor or a school psychologist may attend the conference. A school administrator shall attend the conference if the teacher or the parent or guardian so requests. The pupil shall not be returned to the class from which he or she was suspended, during the period of the suspension, without the concurrence of the teacher of the class and the principal.

(b) A pupil suspended from a class shall not be placed in another regular class during the period of suspension. However, if the pupil is assigned to more than one class per day this subdivision shall apply only to other regular classes scheduled at the same time as the class from which the pupil was suspended.

(c) A teacher may also refer a pupil, for any of the acts enumerated in Section 48900, to the principal or the designee of the principal for consideration of a suspension from the school.

(Amended by Stats. 2004, Ch. 895, Sec. 10. Effective January 1, 2005.)

State of California

EDUCATION CODE

Section 48911

48911. (a) The principal of the school, the principal's designee, or the district superintendent of schools may suspend a pupil from the school for any of the reasons enumerated in Section 48900, and pursuant to Section 48900.5, for no more than five consecutive schooldays.

(b) Suspension by the principal, the principal's designee, or the district superintendent of schools shall be preceded by an informal conference conducted by the principal, the principal's designee, or the district superintendent of schools between the pupil and, whenever practicable, the teacher, supervisor, or school employee who referred the pupil to the principal, the principal's designee, or the district superintendent of schools. At the conference, the pupil shall be informed of the reason for the disciplinary action, including the other means of correction that were attempted before the suspension as required under Section 48900.5, and the evidence against him or her, and shall be given the opportunity to present his or her version and evidence in his or her defense.

(c) A principal, the principal's designee, or the district superintendent of schools may suspend a pupil without affording the pupil an opportunity for a conference only if the principal, the principal's designee, or the district superintendent of schools determines that an emergency situation exists. "Emergency situation," as used in this article, means a situation determined by the principal, the principal's designee, or the district superintendent of schools to constitute a clear and present danger to the life, safety, or health of pupils or school personnel. If a pupil is suspended without a conference before suspension, both the parent and the pupil shall be notified of the pupil's right to a conference and the pupil's right to return to school for the purpose of a conference. The conference shall be held within two schooldays, unless the pupil waives this right or is physically unable to attend for any reason, including, but not limited to, incarceration or hospitalization. The conference shall then be held as soon as the pupil is physically able to return to school for the conference.

(d) At the time of suspension, a school employee shall make a reasonable effort to contact the pupil's parent or guardian in person or by telephone. If a pupil is suspended from school, the parent or guardian shall be notified in writing of the suspension.

(e) A school employee shall report the suspension of the pupil, including the cause for the suspension, to the governing board of the school district or to the district superintendent of schools in accordance with the regulations of the governing board of the school district.

State of California

EDUCATION CODE

Section 48911.1

48911.1. (a) A pupil suspended from a school for any of the reasons enumerated in Sections 48900 and 48900.2 may be assigned, by the principal or the principal's designee, to a supervised suspension classroom for the entire period of suspension if the pupil poses no imminent danger or threat to the campus, pupils, or staff, or if an action to expel the pupil has not been initiated.

(b) Pupils assigned to a supervised suspension classroom shall be separated from other pupils at the schoolsite for the period of suspension in a separate classroom, building, or site for pupils under suspension.

(c) School districts may continue to claim apportionments for each pupil assigned to and attending a supervised suspension classroom provided as follows:

(1) The supervised suspension classroom is staffed as otherwise provided by law.

(2) Each pupil has access to appropriate counseling services.

(3) The supervised suspension classroom promotes completion of schoolwork and tests missed by the pupil during the suspension.

(4) Each pupil is responsible for contacting his or her teacher or teachers to receive assignments to be completed while the pupil is assigned to the supervised suspension classroom. The teacher shall provide all assignments and tests that the pupil will miss while suspended. If no classroom work is assigned, the person supervising the suspension classroom shall assign schoolwork.

(d) At the time a pupil is assigned to a supervised suspension classroom, a school employee shall notify, in person or by telephone, the pupil's parent or guardian. Whenever a pupil is assigned to a supervised suspension classroom for longer than one class period, a school employee shall notify, in writing, the pupil's parent or guardian.

(e) This section does not place any limitation on a school district's ability to transfer a pupil to an opportunity school or class or a continuation education school or class.

(f) Apportionments claimed by a school district for pupils assigned to supervised suspension shall be used specifically to mitigate the cost of implementing this section.

(Added by Stats. 1994, Ch. 1016, Sec. 2. Effective January 1, 1995.)

STATE OF CALIFORNIA
AUTHENTICATED
ELECTRONIC LEGAL MATERIAL

State of California

EDUCATION CODE

Section 48911.2

48911.2. (a) If the number of pupils suspended from school during the prior school year exceeded 30 percent of the school's enrollment, the school should consider doing at least one of the following:

(1) Implement the supervised suspension program described in Section 48911.1.

(2) Implement an alternative to the school's off-campus suspension program, which involves a progressive discipline approach that occurs during the schoolday on campus, using any of the following activities:

(A) Conferences between the school staff, parents, and pupils.

(B) Referral to the school counselor, psychologist, child welfare attendance personnel, or other school support service staff.

(C) Detention.

(D) Study teams, guidance teams, resource panel teams, or other assessment-related teams.

(b) At the end of the academic year, the school may report to the district superintendent in charge of school support services, or other comparable administrator if that position does not exist, on the rate of reduction in the school's off-campus suspensions and the plan or activities used to comply with subdivision (a).

(c) It is the intent of the Legislature to encourage schools that choose to implement this section to examine alternatives to off-campus suspensions that lead to resolution of pupil misconduct without sending pupils off campus. Schools that use this section should not be precluded from suspending pupils to an off-campus site.

(Added by Stats. 1994, Ch. 1016, Sec. 3. Effective January 1, 1995.)

STATE OF CALIFORNIA
AUTHENTICATED
ELECTRONIC LEGAL MATERIAL

State of California

EDUCATION CODE

Section 48911.5

48911.5. The site principal of a contracting nonpublic, nonsectarian school providing services to individuals with exceptional needs under Sections 56365 and 56366, shall have the same duties and responsibilities with respect to the suspension of pupils with previously identified exceptional needs prescribed for the suspension of pupils under Section 48911.

(Added by Stats. 1985, Ch. 907, Sec. 3. Effective September 23, 1985.)

State of California

EDUCATION CODE

Section 48912

48912. (a) The governing board may suspend a pupil from school for any of the acts enumerated in Section 48900 for any number of schooldays within the limits prescribed by Section 48903.

(b) Notwithstanding the provisions of Section 35145 of this code and Section 54950 of the Government Code, the governing board of a school district shall, unless a request has been made to the contrary, hold closed sessions if the board is considering the suspension of, disciplinary action against, or any other action against, except expulsion, any pupil, if a public hearing upon that question would lead to the giving out of information concerning a school pupil which would be in violation of Article 5 (commencing with Section 49073) of Chapter 6.5.

(c) Before calling a closed session to consider these matters, the governing board shall, in writing, by registered or certified mail or by personal service, notify the pupil and the pupil's parent or guardian, or the pupil if the pupil is an adult, of the intent of the governing board to call and hold a closed session. Unless the pupil or the pupil's parent or guardian shall, in writing, within 48 hours after receipt of the written notice of the board's intention, request that the hearing be held as a public meeting, the hearing to consider these matters shall be conducted by the governing board in closed session. In the event that a written request is served upon the clerk or secretary of the governing board, the meeting shall be public, except that any discussion at that meeting which may be in conflict with the right to privacy of any pupil other than the pupil requesting the public meeting, shall be in closed session.

(Amended by Stats. 1992, Ch. 1360, Sec. 4. Effective January 1, 1993.)

State of California

EDUCATION CODE

Section 48912.5

48912.5. The governing board of a school district may suspend a pupil enrolled in a continuation school or class for a period not longer than the remainder of the semester if any of the acts enumerated in Section 48900 occurred. The suspension shall meet the requirements of Section 48915.

(Added by Stats. 1983, Ch. 498, Sec. 91. Effective July 28, 1983.)

State of California

EDUCATION CODE

Section 48913

48913. The teacher of any class from which a pupil is suspended may require the suspended pupil to complete any assignments and tests missed during the suspension.

(Repealed and added by Stats. 1983, Ch. 498, Sec. 91. Effective July 28, 1983.)

State of California

EDUCATION CODE

Section 48913.5

48913.5. (a) Upon the request of a parent, a legal guardian or other person holding the right to make educational decisions for the pupil, or the affected pupil, a teacher shall provide to a pupil in any of grades 1 to 12, inclusive, who has been suspended from school for two or more schooldays the homework that the pupil would otherwise have been assigned.

(b) If a homework assignment that is requested pursuant to subdivision (a) and turned into the teacher by the pupil either upon the pupil's return to school from suspension or within the timeframe originally prescribed by the teacher, whichever is later, is not graded before the end of the academic term, that assignment shall not be included in the calculation of the pupil's overall grade in the class.

(Added by Stats. 2019, Ch. 779, Sec. 3. (AB 982) Effective January 1, 2020.)

STATE OF CALIFORNIA
AUTHENTICATED
ELECTRONIC LEGAL MATERIAL

State of California

EDUCATION CODE

Section 48914

48914. Each school district is authorized to establish a policy that permits school officials to conduct a meeting with the parent or guardian of a suspended pupil to discuss the causes, the duration, the school policy involved, and other matters pertinent to the suspension.

(Amended by Stats. 1987, Ch. 134, Sec. 6. Effective July 7, 1987.)

State of California

EDUCATION CODE

Section 48915

48915. (a) (1) Except as provided in subdivisions (c) and (e), the principal or the superintendent of schools shall recommend the expulsion of a pupil for any of the following acts committed at school or at a school activity off school grounds, unless the principal or superintendent determines that expulsion should not be recommended under the circumstances or that an alternative means of correction would address the conduct:

(A) Causing serious physical injury to another person, except in self-defense.

(B) Possession of any knife or other dangerous object of no reasonable use to the pupil.

(C) Unlawful possession of any controlled substance listed in Chapter 2 (commencing with Section 11053) of Division 10 of the Health and Safety Code, except for either of the following:

(i) The first offense for the possession of not more than one avoirdupois ounce of marijuana, other than concentrated cannabis.

(ii) The possession of over-the-counter medication for use by the pupil for medical purposes or medication prescribed for the pupil by a physician.

(D) Robbery or extortion.

(E) Assault or battery, as defined in Sections 240 and 242 of the Penal Code, upon any school employee.

(2) If the principal or the superintendent of schools makes a determination as described in paragraph (1), he or she is encouraged to do so as quickly as possible to ensure that the pupil does not lose instructional time.

(b) Upon recommendation by the principal or the superintendent of schools, or by a hearing officer or administrative panel appointed pursuant to subdivision (d) of Section 48918, the governing board of a school district may order a pupil expelled upon finding that the pupil committed an act listed in paragraph (1) of subdivision (a) or in subdivision (a), (b), (c), (d), or (e) of Section 48900. A decision to expel a pupil for any of those acts shall be based on a finding of one or both of the following:

(1) Other means of correction are not feasible or have repeatedly failed to bring about proper conduct.

(2) Due to the nature of the act, the presence of the pupil causes a continuing danger to the physical safety of the pupil or others.

(c) The principal or superintendent of schools shall immediately suspend, pursuant to Section 48911, and shall recommend expulsion of a pupil that he or she determines has committed any of the following acts at school or at a school activity off school grounds:

STATE OF CALIFORNIA
AUTHENTICATED
ELECTRONIC LEGAL MATERIAL

State of California

EDUCATION CODE

Section 48915.1

48915.1. (a) If the governing board of a school district receives a request from an individual who has been expelled from another school district for an act other than those described in subdivision (a) or (c) of Section 48915, for enrollment in a school maintained by the school district, the board shall hold a hearing to determine whether that individual poses a continuing danger either to the pupils or employees of the school district. The hearing and notice shall be conducted in accordance with the rules and regulations governing procedures for the expulsion of pupils as described in Section 48918. A school district may request information from another school district regarding a recommendation for expulsion or the expulsion of an applicant for enrollment. The school district receiving the request shall respond to the request with all deliberate speed but shall respond no later than five working days from the date of the receipt of the request.

(b) If a pupil has been expelled from his or her previous school for an act other than those listed in subdivision (a) or (c) of Section 48915, the parent, guardian, or pupil, if the pupil is emancipated or otherwise legally of age, shall, upon enrollment, inform the receiving school district of his or her status with the previous school district. If this information is not provided to the school district and the school district later determines the pupil was expelled from the previous school, the lack of compliance shall be recorded and discussed in the hearing required pursuant to subdivision (a).

(c) The governing board of a school district may make a determination to deny enrollment to an individual who has been expelled from another school district for an act other than those described in subdivision (a) or (c) of Section 48915, for the remainder of the expulsion period after a determination has been made, pursuant to a hearing, that the individual poses a potential danger to either the pupils or employees of the school district.

(d) The governing board of a school district, when making its determination whether to enroll an individual who has been expelled from another school district for these acts, may consider the following options:

(1) Deny enrollment.

(2) Permit enrollment.

(3) Permit conditional enrollment in a regular school program or another educational program.

(e) Notwithstanding any other provision of law, the governing board of a school district, after a determination has been made, pursuant to a hearing, that an individual expelled from another school district for an act other than those described in subdivision (a) or (c) of Section 48915 does not pose a danger to either the pupils or

State of California

EDUCATION CODE

Section 48915.01

48915.01. If the governing board of a school district has established a community day school pursuant to Section 48661 on the same site as a comprehensive middle, junior, or senior high school, or at any elementary school, the governing board does not have to meet the condition in paragraph (2) of subdivision (d) of Section 48915 when the board, pursuant to subdivision (f) of Section 48915, refers a pupil to a program of study and that program of study is at the community day school. All the other conditions of subdivision (d) of Section 48915 are applicable to the referral as required by subdivision (f) of Section 48915.

(Added by Stats. 1996, Ch. 937, Sec. 3. Effective September 26, 1996.)

State of California

EDUCATION CODE

Section 48915.2

48915.2. (a) A pupil expelled from school for any of the offenses listed in subdivision (a) or (c) of Section 48915, shall not be permitted to enroll in any other school or school district during the period of expulsion unless it is a county community school pursuant to subdivision (c) of Section 1981, or a juvenile court school, as described in Section 48645.1, or a community day school pursuant to Article 3 (commencing with Section 48660) of Chapter 4 of Part 27.

(b) After a determination has been made, pursuant to a hearing under Section 48918, that an individual expelled from another school district for any act described in subdivision (a) or (c) of Section 48915 does not pose a danger to either the pupils or employees of the school district, the governing board of a school district may permit the individual to enroll in the school district after the term of expulsion, subject to one of the following conditions:

(1) He or she has established legal residence in the school district, pursuant to Section 48200.

(2) He or she is enrolled in the school pursuant to an interdistrict agreement executed between the affected school districts pursuant to Chapter 5 (commencing with Section 46600) of Part 26.

(Amended by Stats. 1995, Ch. 974, Sec. 3. Effective January 1, 1996. Operative July 1, 1996, by Sec. 9 of Ch. 974, which was amended by Stats. 1996, Ch. 937.)

State of California

EDUCATION CODE

Section 48915.5

48915.5. (a) An individual with exceptional needs, as defined in Section 56026, may be suspended or expelled from school in accordance with Section 1415(k) of Title 20 of the United States Code, the discipline provisions contained in Sections 300.530 to 300.537, inclusive, of Title 34 of the Code of Federal Regulations, and other provisions of this part that do not conflict with federal law and regulations.

(b) A free appropriate public education for individuals with exceptional needs suspended or expelled from school shall be in accordance with Section 1412(a)(1) of Title 20 of the United States Code and Section 300.530(d) of Title 34 of the Code of Federal Regulations.

(c) If an individual with exceptional needs is excluded from schoolbus transportation, the pupil is entitled to be provided with an alternative form of transportation at no cost to the pupil or parent or guardian provided that transportation is specified in the pupil's individualized education program.

(d) If the individual with exceptional needs is a foster child, as defined in Section 48853.5, and the local educational agency has proposed a change of placement due to an act for which a decision to recommend expulsion is at the discretion of the principal or the district superintendent of schools, the attorney for the individual with exceptional needs and an appropriate representative of the county child welfare agency shall be invited to participate in the individualized education program team meeting that makes a manifestation determination pursuant to Section 1415(k) of Title 20 of the United States Code. The invitation may be made using the most cost-effective method possible, which may include, but is not limited to, electronic mail or a telephone call.

(e) If the individual with exceptional needs is a homeless child or youth, as defined in Section 11434a(2) of Title 42 of the United States Code, and the local educational agency has proposed a change of placement due to an act for which a decision to recommend expulsion is at the discretion of the principal or the district superintendent of schools, the local educational agency liaison for homeless children and youth designated pursuant to Section 11432(g)(1)(J)(ii) of Title 42 of the United States Code shall be invited to participate in the individualized education program team meeting that makes a manifestation determination pursuant to Section 1415(k) of Title 20 of the United States Code. The invitation may be made using the most cost-effective method possible, which may include, but is not limited to, electronic mail or a telephone call.

(Amended by Stats. 2014, Ch. 767, Sec. 1. (AB 1806) Effective January 1, 2015.)

State of California

EDUCATION CODE

Section 48916

48916. (a) An expulsion order shall remain in effect until the governing board, in the manner prescribed in this article, orders the readmission of a pupil. At the time an expulsion of a pupil is ordered for an act other than those described in subdivision (c) of Section 48915, the governing board shall set a date, not later than the last day of the semester following the semester in which the expulsion occurred, when the pupil shall be reviewed for readmission to a school maintained by the district or to the school the pupil last attended. If an expulsion is ordered during summer session or the intersession period of a year-round program the governing board shall set a date, not later than the last day of the semester following the summer session or intersession period in which the expulsion occurred, when the pupil shall be reviewed for readmission to a school maintained by the district or to the school the pupil last attended. For a pupil who has been expelled pursuant to subdivision (c) of Section 48915, the governing board shall set a date of one year from the date the expulsion occurred, when the pupil shall be reviewed for readmission to a school maintained by the district, except that the governing board may set an earlier date for readmission on a case-by-case basis.

(b) The governing board shall recommend a plan of rehabilitation for the pupil at the time of the expulsion order, which may include, but not be limited to, periodic review as well as assessment at the time of review for readmission. The plan may also include recommendations for improved academic performance, tutoring, special education assessments, job training, counseling, employment, community service, or other rehabilitative programs.

(c) The governing board of each school district shall adopt rules and regulations establishing a procedure for the filing and processing of requests for readmission and the process for the required review of all expelled pupils for readmission. Upon completion of the readmission process, the governing board shall readmit the pupil, unless the governing board makes a finding that the pupil has not met the conditions of the rehabilitation plan or continues to pose a danger to campus safety or to other pupils or employees of the school district. A description of the procedure shall be made available to the pupil and the pupil's parent or guardian at the time the expulsion order is entered.

(d) If the governing board denies the readmission of an expelled pupil pursuant to subdivision (c), the governing board shall make a determination either to continue the placement of the pupil in the alternative educational program initially selected for the pupil during the period of the expulsion order or to place the pupil in another

State of California

EDUCATION CODE

Section 48916.1

48916.1. (a) At the time an expulsion of a pupil is ordered, the governing board of the school district shall ensure that an educational program is provided to the pupil who is subject to the expulsion order for the period of the expulsion. Except for pupils expelled pursuant to subdivision (d) of Section 48915, the governing board of a school district is required to implement the provisions of this section only to the extent funds are appropriated for this purpose in the annual Budget Act or other legislation, or both.

(b) Notwithstanding any other provision of law, any educational program provided pursuant to subdivision (a) may be operated by the school district, the county superintendent of schools, or a consortium of districts or in joint agreement with the county superintendent of schools.

(c) Any educational program provided pursuant to subdivision (b) may not be situated within or on the grounds of the school from which the pupil was expelled.

(d) If the pupil who is subject to the expulsion order was expelled from any of kindergarten or grades 1 to 6, inclusive, the educational program provided pursuant to subdivision (b) may not be combined or merged with educational programs offered to pupils in any of grades 7 to 12, inclusive. The district or county program is the only program required to be provided to expelled pupils as determined by the governing board of the school district. This subdivision, as it relates to the separation of pupils by grade levels, does not apply to community day schools offering instruction in any of kindergarten and grades 1 to 8, inclusive, and established in accordance with Section 48660.

(e) (1) Each school district shall maintain the following data:

(A) The number of pupils recommended for expulsion.

(B) The grounds for each recommended expulsion.

(C) Whether the pupil was subsequently expelled.

(D) Whether the expulsion order was suspended.

(E) The type of referral made after the expulsion.

(F) The disposition of the pupil after the end of the period of expulsion.

(2) The Superintendent may require a school district to report this data as part of the coordinated compliance review. If a school district does not report outcome data as required by this subdivision, the Superintendent may not apportion any further money to the school district pursuant to Section 48664 until the school district is in compliance with this subdivision. Before withholding the apportionment of funds to a school district pursuant to this subdivision, the Superintendent shall give written notice to the governing board of the school district that the school district has failed

State of California

EDUCATION CODE

Section 48916.5

48916.5. The governing board may require a pupil who is expelled from school for reasons relating to controlled substances, as defined in Sections 11054 to 11058, inclusive, of the Health and Safety Code, or alcohol, prior to returning to school to enroll in a county-supported drug rehabilitation program. No pupil shall be required to enroll in a rehabilitation program pursuant to this section without the consent of his or her parent or guardian.

(Added by Stats. 1988, Ch. 50, Sec. 1.)

STATE OF CALIFORNIA
AUTHENTICATED
ELECTRONIC LEGAL MATERIAL

State of California

EDUCATION CODE

Section 48917

48917. (a) The governing board, upon voting to expel a pupil, may suspend the enforcement of the expulsion order for a period of not more than one calendar year and may, as a condition of the suspension of enforcement, assign the pupil to a school, class, or program that is deemed appropriate for the rehabilitation of the pupil. The rehabilitation program to which the pupil is assigned may provide for the involvement of the pupil's parent or guardian in his or her child's education in ways that are specified in the rehabilitation program. A parent or guardian's refusal to participate in the rehabilitation program shall not be considered in the governing board's determination as to whether the pupil has satisfactorily completed the rehabilitation program.

(b) The governing board shall apply the criteria for suspending the enforcement of the expulsion order equally to all pupils, including individuals with exceptional needs as defined in Section 56026.

(c) During the period of the suspension of the expulsion order, the pupil is deemed to be on probationary status.

(d) The governing board may revoke the suspension of an expulsion order under this section if the pupil commits any of the acts enumerated in Section 48900 or violates any of the district's rules and regulations governing pupil conduct. When the governing board revokes the suspension of an expulsion order, a pupil may be expelled under the terms of the original expulsion order.

(e) Upon satisfactory completion of the rehabilitation assignment of a pupil, the governing board shall reinstate the pupil in a school of the district and may also order the expungement of any or all records of the expulsion proceedings.

(f) A decision of the governing board to suspend an expulsion order does not affect the time period and requirements for the filing of an appeal of the expulsion order with the county board of education required under Section 48919. Any appeal shall be filed within 30 days of the original vote of the governing board.

(Amended by Stats. 1995, Ch. 95, Sec. 1. Effective January 1, 1996.)

STATE OF CALIFORNIA
AUTHENTICATED
ELECTRONIC LEGAL MATERIAL

State of California

EDUCATION CODE

Section 48918

48918.   The governing board of each school district shall establish rules and regulations governing procedures for the expulsion of pupils. These procedures shall include, but are not necessarily limited to, all of the following:

(a) (1) The pupil shall be entitled to a hearing to determine whether the pupil should be expelled. An expulsion hearing shall be held within 30 schooldays after the date the principal or the superintendent of schools determines that the pupil has committed any of the acts enumerated in Section 48900, unless the pupil requests, in writing, that the hearing be postponed. The adopted rules and regulations shall specify that the pupil is entitled to at least one postponement of an expulsion hearing, for a period of not more than 30 calendar days. Any additional postponement may be granted at the discretion of the governing board of the school district.

(2) Within 10 schooldays after the conclusion of the hearing, the governing board of the school district shall decide whether to expel the pupil, unless the pupil requests in writing that the decision be postponed. If the hearing is held by a hearing officer or an administrative panel, or if the governing board of the school district does not meet on a weekly basis, the governing board of the school district shall decide whether to expel the pupil within 40 schooldays after the date of the pupil's removal from his or her school of attendance for the incident for which the recommendation for expulsion is made by the principal or the superintendent of schools, unless the pupil requests in writing that the decision be postponed.

(3) If compliance by the governing board of the school district with the time requirements for the conducting of an expulsion hearing under this subdivision is impracticable during the regular school year, the superintendent of schools or the superintendent's designee may, for good cause, extend the time period for the holding of the expulsion hearing for an additional five schooldays. If compliance by the governing board of the school district with the time requirements for the conducting of an expulsion hearing under this subdivision is impractical due to a summer recess of governing board meetings of more than two weeks, the days during the recess period shall not be counted as schooldays in meeting the time requirements. The days not counted as schooldays in meeting the time requirements for an expulsion hearing because of a summer recess of governing board meetings shall not exceed 20 schooldays, as defined in subdivision (c) of Section 48925, and unless the pupil requests in writing that the expulsion hearing be postponed, the hearing shall be held not later than 20 calendar days before the first day of school for the school year. Reasons for the extension of the time for the hearing shall be included as a part of the record at the time the expulsion hearing is conducted. Upon the commencement of

STATE OF CALIFORNIA
AUTHENTICATED
ELECTRONIC LEGAL MATERIAL

State of California

EDUCATION CODE

Section 48918.1

48918.1. (a) (1) If the decision to recommend expulsion is a discretionary act and the pupil is a foster child, as defined in Section 48853.5, the governing board of the school district shall provide notice of the expulsion hearing to the pupil's attorney and an appropriate representative of the county child welfare agency at least 10 calendar days before the date of the hearing. The notice may be made using the most cost-effective method possible, which may include, but is not limited to, electronic mail or a telephone call.

(2) If a recommendation of expulsion is required and the pupil is a foster child, as defined in Section 48853.5, the governing board of the school district may provide notice of the expulsion hearing to the pupil's attorney and an appropriate representative of the county child welfare agency at least 10 calendar days before the date of the hearing. The notice may be made using the most cost-effective method possible, which may include, but is not limited to, electronic mail or a telephone call.

(b) (1) If the decision to recommend expulsion is a discretionary act and the pupil is a homeless child or youth, as defined in Section 11434a(2) of Title 42 of the United States Code, the governing board of the school district shall provide notice of the expulsion hearing to the local educational agency liaison for homeless children and youth designated pursuant to Section 11432(g)(1)(J)(ii) of Title 42 of the United States Code at least 10 calendar days before the date of the hearing. The notice may be made using the most cost-effective method possible, which may include, but is not limited to, electronic mail or a telephone call.

(2) If a recommendation of expulsion is required and the pupil is a homeless child or youth, as defined in Section 11434a(2) of Title 42 of the United States Code, the governing board of the school district may provide notice of the expulsion hearing to the local educational agency liaison for homeless children and youth designated pursuant to Section 11432(g)(1)(J)(ii) of Title 42 of the United States Code at least 10 calendar days before the date of the hearing. The notice may be made using the most cost-effective method possible, which may include, but is not limited to, electronic mail or a telephone call.

(Amended by Stats. 2014, Ch. 767, Sec. 2. (AB 1806) Effective January 1, 2015.)

State of California

EDUCATION CODE

Section 48918.5

48918.5. In expulsion hearings involving allegations brought pursuant to subdivision (n) of Section 48900, the governing board of each school district shall establish rules and regulations governing procedures. The procedures shall include, but are not limited to, all of the following:

(a) At the time that the expulsion hearing is recommended, the complaining witness shall be provided with a copy of the applicable disciplinary rules and advised of his or her right to: (1) receive five days' notice of the complaining witness's scheduled testimony at the hearing, (2) have up to two adult support persons of his or her choosing, present in the hearing at the time he or she testifies; and (3) to have the hearing closed during the time they testify pursuant to subdivision (c) of Section 48918.

(b) An expulsion hearing may be postponed for one schoolday in order to accommodate the special physical, mental, or emotional needs of a pupil who is the complaining witness where the allegations arise under subdivision (n) of Section 48900.

(c) The district shall provide a nonthreatening environment for a complaining witness in order to better enable them to speak freely and accurately of the experiences that are the subject of the expulsion hearing, and to prevent discouragement of complaints. Each school district shall provide a room separate from the hearing room for the use of the complaining witness prior to and during breaks in testimony. In the discretion of the person conducting the hearing, the complaining witness shall be allowed reasonable periods of relief from examination and cross-examination during which he or she may leave the hearing room. The person conducting the hearing may arrange the seating within the hearing room of those present in order to facilitate a less intimidating environment for the complaining witness. The person conducting the hearing may limit the time for taking the testimony of a complaining witness to the hours he or she is normally in school, if there is no good cause to take the testimony during other hours. The person conducting the hearing may permit one of the complaining witness's support persons to accompany him or her to the witness stand.

(d) Whenever any allegation is made of conduct violative of subdivision (n) of Section 48900, complaining witnesses and accused pupils are to be advised immediately to refrain from personal or telephonic contact with each other during the pendency of any expulsion process.

(Added by Stats. 1996, Ch. 915, Sec. 6. Effective January 1, 1997.)

STATE OF CALIFORNIA
AUTHENTICATED
ELECTRONIC LEGAL MATERIAL

State of California

EDUCATION CODE

Section 48918.6

48918.6. In addition to any other immunity that may exist, any testimony provided by a pupil witness in an expulsion hearing conducted pursuant to this article is expressly deemed to be a communication protected by subdivision (b) of Section 47 of the Civil Code.

(Added by Stats. 2002, Ch. 136, Sec. 1. Effective January 1, 2003.)

State of California

EDUCATION CODE

Section 48919

48919. If a pupil is expelled from school, the pupil or the pupil's parent or guardian may, within 30 days following the decision of the governing board to expel, file an appeal to the county board of education which shall hold a hearing thereon and render its decision.

The county board of education, or in a class 1 or class 2 county a hearing officer or impartial administrative panel, shall hold the hearing within 20 schooldays following the filing of a formal request under this section. If the county board of education hears the appeal without a hearing conducted pursuant to Section 48919.5, then the board shall render a decision within three schooldays of the hearing conducted pursuant to Section 48920, unless the pupil requests a postponement.

The period within which an appeal is to be filed shall be determined from the date a governing board votes to expel even if enforcement of the expulsion action is suspended and the pupil is placed on probation pursuant to Section 48917. A pupil who fails to appeal the original action of the board within the prescribed time may not subsequently appeal a decision of the board to revoke probation and impose the original order of expulsion.

The county board of education shall adopt rules and regulations establishing procedures for expulsion appeals conducted under this section. If the county board of education in a class 1 or class 2 county elects to use the procedures in Section 48919.5, then the board shall adopt rules and regulations establishing procedures for expulsion appeals conducted under Section 48919.5. The adopted rules and regulations shall include, but need not be limited to, the requirements for filing a notice of appeal, the setting of a hearing date, the furnishing of notice to the pupil and the governing board regarding the appeal, the furnishing of a copy of the expulsion hearing record to the county board of education, procedures for the conduct of the hearing, and the preservation of the record of the appeal.

The pupil shall submit a written request for a copy of the written transcripts and supporting documents from the school district simultaneously with the filing of the notice of appeal with the county board of education. The school district shall provide the pupil with the transcriptions, supporting documents, and records within 10 schooldays following the pupil's written request. Upon receipt of the records, the pupil shall immediately file suitable copies of these records with the county board of education.

(Amended by Stats. 2000, Ch. 147, Sec. 1. Effective January 1, 2001.)

State of California

EDUCATION CODE

Section 48925

48925. As used in this article:

(a) "Day" means a calendar day unless otherwise specifically provided.

(b) "Expulsion" means removal of a pupil from (1) the immediate supervision and control, or (2) the general supervision, of school personnel, as those terms are used in Section 46300.

(c) "Schoolday" means a day upon which the schools of the district are in session or weekdays during the summer recess.

(d) "Suspension" means removal of a pupil from ongoing instruction for adjustment purposes. However, "suspension" does not mean any of the following:

(1) Reassignment to another education program or class at the same school where the pupil will receive continuing instruction for the length of day prescribed by the governing board for pupils of the same grade level.

(2) Referral to a certificated employee designated by the principal to advise pupils.

(3) Removal from the class, but without reassignment to another class or program, for the remainder of the class period without sending the pupil to the principal or the principal's designee as provided in Section 48910. Removal from a particular class shall not occur more than once every five schooldays.

(e) "Pupil" includes a pupil's parent or guardian or legal counsel.

(Added by Stats. 1983, Ch. 498, Sec. 91. Effective July 28, 1983.)

Made in the USA
Las Vegas, NV
12 December 2024

13938665R00176